# You Could Argue But You'd Be Wrong

# You Could Argue But You'd Be Wrong

PETE FRANKLIN

WITH TERRY PLUTO

CB

CONTEMPORARY BOOKS

CHICAGO · NEW YORK

**Library of Congress Cataloging-in-Publication Data**

Franklin, Pete.
You could argue but you'd be wrong / Pete Franklin with Terry Pluto.
p. cm.
Includes index.
ISBN 0-8092-4674-0 : $17.95
1. Radio broadcasting of sports—United States 2. Sportsline.
I. Pluto, Terry, 1955- II. Title.
GV742.3.F73 1988
070.4'49796—dc 19 87-35218
CIP


Published by Contemporary Books, Inc.
180 North Michigan Avenue, Chicago, Illinois 60601
Manufactured in the United States of America
Library of Congress Catalog Card Number: 87-35218
International Standard Book Number: 0-8092-4674-0

Published simultaneously in Canada by Beaverbooks, Ltd.
195 Allstate Parkway, Valleywood Business Park
Markham, Ontario L3R 4T8 Canada

*To my wife, Pat, and my children, John and Susan*
*. . . these are my real fans.*

# CONTENTS

# ACKNOWLEDGMENTS

Thanks go to Roberta Pluto and Pat McCubbin, who spent countless hours transcribing the tapes and offering suggestions on the manuscript. Also, to Faith Hornby, who not only had the idea for the book but, more importantly, sold it.

# You Could Argue But You'd Be Wrong

# 1
# THE FANS

Nobody talks to more sports fans than I do. And because I spend so much time on the telephone talking to people like you, I know more about you than anyone else. That much is a fact. Just ask *Sports Illustrated, The New York Times,* the *Wall Street Journal,* or any other rag worth its ink. You can go into some beer and shot joint anywhere—Brooklyn, Chicago, Cleveland, even Chattanooga, Tennessee, for God's sake—and there will be two guys sipping some suds, staring at the television up above the bar, and arguing about sports. And when they want to know who was a better centerfielder, Mantle or Mays, they pick up a telephone and call me. They ask me, I tell them.

You want to know who was better?

Mays, no contest.

Willie could do everything—run, hit, throw, steal bases. Not only was he a better centerfielder than Mantle, he was better than anyone else who ever played the position.

Mantle?

Overrated. A New York creation. A good ball player, yes. A great one? Only at times. Mostly, what you've got with Mantle is the mystique. The questions about what he could have been if he didn't have bum knees or even if he didn't think he was gonna kick the bucket by the time he was 40 years old or if he could have passed on a free J&B once in a while.

I will say this, Mantle was a better ball player than he is an announcer. I mean, it was easier for him to get four straight hits than put four straight words together.

Okay. I say Mays, you say Mantle, and we got something going.

That's what my sports show is all about. Of course, my opinion counts and yours doesn't. Never forget that. When people hear me call some guy an idiot, they think I'm kidding. They think I do it just for ratings or to liven up the show. But I'll tell you this much: I know an idiot when I talk to one because in my line of work I end up talking to so many. And after a while I can tell when one is coming. All he has to say is, "Ah, duh, Pete?"

Anyway, you've got me and some bozo on the other end of the line screaming at each other about Mantle and Mays while 38 states and half of Canada listened every weeknight on radio station WWWE (1100 AM), 50,000 watts out of Cleveland. "Sportsline" was a monster, and I was its master. This show not only had the highest ratings of any sports talk show in the country, it was the longest-running show of its kind in the history of broadcasting. Now, I've taken my show to WFAN (1050 AM) in New York City.

Does it sound like I'm blowing my horn? Well, considering my credentials, I should.

You want to disagree. Fine. You'd be wrong, but you can still disagree. That's the beautiful thing about being a sports fan. You don't have to know anything, and you can change your mind every 10 seconds. We all can be experts in sports because what happens if we're wrong? Nothing. The world keeps spinning, you keep your job, and you can still blame the manager for everything from a crapola pitching staff to world hunger.

I go to a lot of basketball games, and it is amazing to listen to the folks in the stands. They paid their four bucks to park, and they put out ten more for a seat, and that means they can tell Magic Johnson how to shoot fouls.

"Hey, Magic, your left elbow is out too far," yells some schmuck.

Magic is knocking down two million a year, and there's schmucko yelling about his left elbow. And our friend schmucko looks more like a walrus than Magic Johnson. Schmucko was the kid who never got picked to play basketball on the playground, and for good reason.

It is absolutely absurd. For 25 bucks, he figures he can coach Magic Johnson. It would be the same as sitting in Carnegie Hall, and there's Arthur Rubinstein playing Chopin, and some guy in a tuxedo stands up and yells, "Hey, Arthur, watch the right arm, will ya? Too hard, Arthur. You're hitting the keys too hard."

Or yelling at Leonard Bernstein, "Put that stick down and get outta here—you don't have it today."

Yet a guy goes to a sports event, and he tells Gary Carter how to catch or Dominique Wilkins how to dunk, and then 10 other fans start yelling, agreeing with the first bozo.

The fan knows more than the manager, the owner, the players. Then the fan decides to go for the ultimate thrill, Valhalla at long last. He calls Pete Franklin.

BOZO: "Hey, Pete."

PETE: "Yes."

BOZO: "Ah, you Pete Franklin?"

PETE: "No, I'm Warren Harding—who do you think you're talking to?"

BOZO: "Well, ah, like are we on the air and everything?"

PETE: "Of course we're on the air. You think I'd talk to you on my own time? Why would I talk to you unless I was getting paid for it?"

BOZO: "Well . . . ah . . . I . . . I don't know."

PETE: "That ain't all you don't know."

BOZO: "Pete, what I was wondering was what you think about Eddie Murray."

PETE: "You were wondering about what?"

BOZO: "I'm worried about him. I've been up all night thinking about this."

PETE: "With your brain, I can believe it."

BOZO: "Come on, Pete, give me a break."

PETE: "Why?"

BOZO: "Duh, I dunno. I just figured . . . well . . . like . . . I think maybe the Indians ought to get Eddie Murray."

PETE: "You think the Indians should get Eddie Murray."

BOZO: "Uh . . . yeah."

PETE: "And how do you propose to do this?"

BOZO: "Like . . . I was thinking . . . there should be a trade."

PETE: " So you want to make a trade."

BOZO: "Yeah, like . . . um . . . maybe Pat Tabler and . . ."

PETE: "Pat Tabler for Eddie Murray."

BOZO: "Yeah, something like that."

PETE: "You ever hear of the Golden Gate Bridge?"

BOZO: "Yeah . . . why?"

PETE: "Maybe you ought to walk to the middle, look down, and jump off."

Then I cut the bozo off. He deserves to be cut off, and if I had my way, I'd follow him out on the Golden Gate and give him a push.

Most guys doing my job are nice to everyone. Bozo calls them up, and the host asks him:

NICE GUY HOST: "What's your name?"

BOZO: "It's Bozo."

NICE GUY HOST: "And where are you from, Bozo?"

BOZO: "Gary, Indiana."

NICE GUY HOST: "I hear it's nice in Gary this time of year."

That's what you get from most sports talk show hosts. What do I care about Bozo? It doesn't matter what his name is. Who cares? And then this crapola about Gary, Indiana. The only time it will be nice in Gary is when the last mill closes and everyone finally moves out of that burg.

Well, it's back to this scintillating conversation.

BOZO: "I was thinking about great fielding shortstops."

NICE GUY HOST: "That's interesting."

Well, to Nice Guy Host, staring at his own navel is interesting.

BOZO: "I think the best shortstop I ever saw was Jerry Dybzinski."

NICE GUY HOST: "That's something to think about."

BOZO: "He was really good."

NICE GUY HOST: "Well, Bozo, thanks for your opinion. You've given us all something to think about. And say hello to everyone in Gary for me."

Why thank a guy for his opinion when it's dumb? But most guys doing my job couldn't tell Jerry Dybzinski from General Pulaski. They're a bunch of ex-jocks who don't know a microphone from a cucumber.

## THE TRUTH

I've lasted longer doing what I do for one reason—The Truth.

I tell it.

When a guy stinks, I say he stinks. When Bozo calls up and says Jerry Dybzinski is the greatest thing since Marty Marion, I call Bozo a bozo, and I slam the phone in his ear.

And you know what?

The people out there, you who are listening, like it. You want me to give the bozos hell, because we all run into these kind of guys and we all want to tell them to stick the phone in their ears.

Sports is a harmless way for us to vent our frustrations, to get some release from having to cope with all the bozos at home, at the office, or driving 20 mph in front of you in a 55 mph zone. If we didn't have sports, we'd create them. Think back to the days of Nero. Now Nero was a very disturbed guy, burning down cities, crucifying people every day. So once a week, Nero would get the gladiators together and let them try to cut off each other's head. And when he got tired of that, he'd bring out the Christians and the lions, and you know what?

One bozo was in the Forum telling the bozo sitting next to

him, "I don't think that lion goes well to his left. It's his shoulder."

And the other bozo nodded.

Just like back to the cavemen. Alley-Oop would be pounding the beans out of some dinosaur, and there would be some bozo watching and yelling, "Give him another belt."

The thing to remember about sports is that it is a form of entertainment. The overwhelming majority of us lack the ability, the guts, and, yes, even the brains to play, but none of us is without the capability to second-guess. We don't have to make the General MacArthur kind of decision like, Should we storm the beaches? We don't have to figure out what the interest rate ought to be.

I call sports the great equalizer.

Say you're in the bleachers at Yankee Stadium or Wrigley Field. You don't know who is sitting next to you. A stockbroker, a bank president, or some crummy broom pusher. Sports is the one form of entertainment that crosses all cultural, racial, social, and economic lines. It brings us all together at least for a brief moment when we all agree that the manager is a moron.

People go to games for the same reason they listen to my show—it takes their minds off their jobs, their lives, even their wives. You can do things at a game or on my show that you can't do anywhere else in the world. Sports fans are the most opinionated people in the world. They know nothing about sports, but that doesn't stop them. Of course, they will also do things associated with sports that they'd never do in real life.

They will go to a game with their faces painted with all sorts of crap.

They will go to a game in their underwear.

They will go to a game in a tuxedo.

They will take off their shirts . . . when it's 10 below and snowing.

They will get bombed on awful, overpriced beer and not complain.

They will run on the field, knowing they'll get arrested,

but they don't care as long as they can step on home plate.

They will walk up to a 20-year-old pitcher from Nowhere, Lousyana, and they will ask this kid for his autograph. The kid has a single-digit IQ, and all he can do is make an X, but the PhD fan doesn't care because he has the Kid from Nowhere's autograph.

Why do it?

Because fans want to identify with something other than themselves. It is a vicarious experience. In life, we all want to win. But in a nine-to-five Go-to-the-office-get-your-head-beat-in job, a victory is getting through the day without the boss coming down on you for some stupid reason. At work, fans wear uniforms, say "Yes, sir," to a guy they hate, and think about the weekend. The oft-quoted line that "Most men lead lives of quiet desperation" is true. Most of us get up a little after the crack of dawn, go outside, spend a half-hour knocking the snow and ice off our cars, and then we drive to some godforsaken factory or we wear a silly hat and flip hamburgers for the minimum wage. Even if the guy has a great job, usually either he's worried about someone stabbing him in the back and taking it, or else he's thinking about how he can go from being the assistant managing director to full managing director.

Say you have a plumber and a stockbroker. Now what are these guys going to talk about? House Bill 835? Hell, most people don't even know the name of their lamebrained congressman. Are they going to talk about mutual funds or the latest model of plunger? Hell, they can't even talk about cars because the stockbroker is tooling around in a BMW and the plumber has a six-year-old Torino that needs a muffler. I mean, the stockbroker doesn't care why the crap goes down the toilet so long as it goes, and the plumber thinks an IRA is a bunch of guys running around planting bombs in Ireland.

But at a game, they will wear costumes. They'll cheer and rip up paper and throw it in the air and say any damn thing they please. And the guy next to you, he's got a different job, but it's the same crap, and he's happy just to be out of the office or the sewers and at the ballpark. They both want to know if the dummy at the plate can hit a curveball or if the guy warming up in the bullpen is ready. They both have this one thing in common: they think they know more than the manager.

Most fans remember playing as kids. Of course, that memory is very selective, because most guys who are fans really stunk as athletes. They may have gone to the plate 200 times in high school and hit one pop fly double. Ten years later, that pop fly has become a 400-foot homer in their minds. But that's all right. If Fred the Barber wants us to believe he hit the ball 400 feet, if that makes him happy, who cares?

And if Fred the Barber from South Bend walked out of his shop and started running down Main Street with only green four-leaf clovers painted on his cheeks and a pair of shorts with huge shamrocks, they'd haul out the big butterfly net and put Fred in a joint where they keep the scissors under lock and key. But if it's Saturday afternoon in October and Fred is watching Notre Dame butt heads with Michigan, he'll have 70,000 friends. And if their team wins, they all run out on the field, rip up the goalpost, and tear up the turf. It is even worse in Europe and South America, where they like to stomp each other to death while watching soccer games.

Sports fans are everyone from regular people to the little nebbish no one ever talks to. In real life, he is a nonentity, a social reject. He was rejected in the hospital by the nurses, rejected in the crib by Mama, rejected by Dad, rejected by his schoolteacher and then by society. He never made the team, and people were always yelling at him. But at games, he is a sports fan, a member of the club. This slug couldn't make it at Notre Dame because he spells *cat* with a K, but he can be a member of Notre Dame's subway alumni. It doesn't matter if the nebbish is Irish or Catholic, because he can root for Notre Dame and all of that school's other great Irish Catholic athletes such as Austin Carr, Joe Montana, and Orlando Woolridge.

## THE CASUAL FAN

The casual fan comprises 80 percent of all sports fans. He

is the average guy. You only see him at the ballpark a few times a year, at the most. He really doesn't love, much less follow, sports that strongly. He isn't the guy who watches a game just to see a game. He is not into the beauty of the sport and all that. He doesn't know a good play from a bad one, unless someone tells him.

But he knows one thing—win, win, win.

Suddenly the team is winning, and the guy says, "I always knew the players had it in them. From the start, I could see something special. I've been behind them all the way, backing them for the last 10 years."

Okay, it's a damn lie, but he's having a good time, so we let it go.

Most fans are terrible front-runners. When their team is winning, they wear their team's colors and tell the world that they're Chicago Bears fans. Some fans love to buy those shirts that say "Property of the Chicago Bears." They hope someone will see them and think, "Hey, maybe that guy in the T-shirt does something for the Bears. Maybe they let him pick up the dirty socks."

It is a fact that when your team is winning, the city does feel good about itself. The smoke from the mills may still be choking you to death, the rats may still be feasting on the kids, and Main Street is a ghost town, but the Browns or Bills are winning, so everything is great.

This is when the casual fan gets involved. Most of the time, he barely notices the local team, but all of a sudden every time he picks up a newspaper or turns on the boob tube, he sees something about the Browns. He walks into a bar, and he sees guys in Browns caps and shirts, and he feels like this might be fun and he'd like to be involved. So he buys a cap, a shirt, and puts up a pennant in his bathroom. He joins the crowd. He stamps himself with the emblem of the team. By association, he becomes a winner. See my Cleveland Browns underwear? I've got a big C right here on my can!

Now this is no longer a game; it's an event. Fans have painted their cars, their houses, their bodies the team colors. Politicians are showing up to have their pictures taken with the coach, as if this crummy mayor is somehow responsible for the team's winning. In the real world, the politicians can't get the garbage picked up or make the buses run on time, but they can tell the world, "Hey, we got a helluva football team."

Then you have the national media in town, and they pick up on this. You got a network guy from New York—actually, he was born in Dubuque. This guy is real excited because he got the hell out of New York for a few days, and he's even more excited because he knows if he can keep this television hustle going, he'll never have to go back to Dubuque. So he's in Cleveland, the Browns are winning, and so why not say this great team plays in a great city? The Browns' winning can't stop unemployment or get rid of the muggers, but it does make the fans feel better, and there is a lot to be said for that as long as we keep it in perspective.

## THE FLOATER

Some guys are pretty dedicated sports fans, but they have about as much loyalty as the politicians. They float from winner to winner. One year the Yankees are winning, so they wear Yankee caps. The next year it's Boston on top, and they've got a Red Sox cap on. As for the Yankees, they can go to hell, they're losers . . . until they win again, of course.

The floater is an obnoxious scum who walks up to you and says, "How did the Yanks do last night?"

He knows damn well that the Yankees won. What's more, he knows that you're a real sports fan, true to your team, and that the Yankees humiliated your team.

He is a real pain in the neck, a constant irritant, and he will be like this for the rest of his life. He is a menace. He rejects his own community, and he deserves to spend the next 20 years in a dentist chair having one root canal after another.

## THE LOSER

These guys are the most pathetic cases of all. They are

floaters in reverse. They follow a team as long as it stinks. The minute it starts to win, losers will find another club in the dumper and then revel in that team's inadequacy.

These guys are masochists. They've got no self-esteem. Any time their boss calls them into the office, they don't bother to go. They just write out their resignation and hand it in because they're sure they're going to get the sack. They think they're inferior and second-rate. Know what? They are.

I always thought that what should happen is that we ought to cut out a hunk of the Mojave Desert and set it aside for only the losers and the floaters. That way, they'd be happy and the rest of us would never have to see them again.

## THE HARD-CORE FAN

About 10 percent of the fans are your loyal, hard-core fans. These are stubborn people. Common sense means nothing to them. These were the folks who wanted to stay on the Titanic and sing "Nearer My God to Thee," while everyone else was running for the lifeboats. Their teams are usually someone like the Indians or the Cubs, and they've been going to the games for 30 years, taking the losses even harder than the players. But it doesn't faze them. They are loyal. They would make great beagles. They see their master, and they wag their tails, even if their master happens to be a chain-saw murderer.

For the most part, I like these people. They have substance and sincerity, and there certainly are worse things you can say about a person. One of the problems with these people is that they don't exactly have well-rounded personalities. They read the sports section; they listen to the games and the sports talk shows. If they heard that there was a Shaw play at the Palace Theatre, they'd think that the old pitcher Bob Shaw was coming to town to give a talk about his baseball career.

They know about every kid in Butte or Batavia, and they know all 99 guys who ever played third base for the Mets, and they have memorized all the statistics. A lot of them collect baseball cards and autographed pictures, which is all right when you're 13 but a little peculiar at 53. They're loyal and they're harmless, and they all listen to my show religiously, so they're not all bad.

## FANS YOU DON'T WANT TO MEET

There is a guy who calls my show all the time. His name is Steve, and he has a deep, dark obsession—the Milwaukee Bucks.

This guy lives in Brooklyn, New York, and he spends every waking hour thinking about the Milwaukee Bucks. What 's a guy from Brooklyn doing as a Bucks fan? What does that say about the guy?

I don't think I want to know.

All I know is that I can see Steve's room. He doesn't have walls, just pictures of the Bucks everywhere. You go into the bathroom, and he's got Don Nelson's face on his toilet paper.

So when my producer tells me that Steve is on the line, I know I've got more than just a nut here. He's a super banana split. But I also know that the audience likes to hear me talk to the nuts. For two years, Steve asked me if the Bucks were going to trade for Joe Barry Carroll.

Monday, the phone rings and the banana split says, "This is Steve from Brooklyn. Pete, be honest with me. You think da Bucks are gonna get Joe Barry Carroll?"

Tuesday, the phone rings. Same nut, same question.

I'm talking about two years of Joe Barry Carroll. No Christmas, no Easter, and the only birthday he celebrates is Don Nelson's. I made the mistake a couple of years ago of actually treating this guy like a normal person. He asked me if the Bucks were going to trade for Terry Cummings, and I happened to know that a trade for Cummings from the Clippers to the Bucks was in the works. So I said, yeah, the Bucks were going to get Cummings, and it would happen the next day. Well, I was right, and the nut has been worshiping me ever since.

Over the years, I've called him every name you can call a guy on the radio.

PETE: "You scumbag."

NUT: "About Joe Barry Carroll."

PETE: "Admit it, your parents didn't have any children who lived."

NUT: "Come on, Pete, give me a break."

PETE: "How did you get outta the home, and who let you use the phone?"

NUT: "Pete, you can trust me. Please, tell me about Joe Barry Carroll."

On and on it goes. It doesn't matter how many times I unload on the guy; he just takes it and comes back for more.

Will the Bucks get Joe Barry Carroll?

Will the Bucks re-sign Terry Cummings?

Will Don Nelson be lifted straight to heaven and given a box seat at the right hand of God?

A normal guy will be driving along, and he'll hear the nut on the radio, and the normal guy will think, There's a nut. I hope Pete dumps on him. When I do, the normal guy laughs.

## PEOPLE WANT TO BE ABUSED

Some guys just call my show because they know they're going to get it. This kind of guy wants to be punished. At tax time, he goes to an accountant, and the accountant tells him that he can take a deduction for his wife and kids. But this guy says, "No, I want to pay." The accountant isn't even done with the form, and this guy has his checkbook out, his pen in hand, and he wants to give away his life savings.

I suppose all of us have this desire to harm ourselves, but we understand this emotion, and we don't let it get out of hand.

Some guys just can't help it. They call me up and say, "Hey, Pete, don't ya think the Indians would be better if they had Babe Ruth in their lineup?"

What am I supposed to say? Nah, I don't think Babe wouldn't help them because he'd be 93 years old?

The guy wants me to tear him apart, so I tear him apart. I tell him that he's stupid, that he has no right to live on the Earth, he's mentally ill. If a guy calls me often enough with enough dumb questions, I honor him with a nickname. It's like being canonized. He gets a name and is officially recognized as a moron who gets trashed by Pete Franklin.

Basically, 25 percent of the callers are the same yahoos. They have nothing better to do than to call people who are on the radio. These are the kind of people who never get out of their bathrobes and eat cereal straight from a box of Fruit Loops all day, which tells you what you need to know about them. The nuts are sick, and they need me to do outpatient work. I give their lives some meaning. One guy says, "Hey, I'm the Slasher, and I call Pete Franklin every Tuesday night." Without that, he'd just be another yahoo who wears a ratty bathrobe and eats Fruit Loops from the box.

There was a guy we named the Fat Man from Akron. This was one of these bathrobe and Fruit Loops guys who never went outside. I mean, he never even left his room. Once a year, someone came in wearing a gas mask and cleaned the joint out around him. The man weighed about 900 pounds, and when he died, three guys carrying his coffin ended up with double hernias. But in his obituary in the *Akron Beacon Journal,* it said, "He was the Fat Man, a regular caller on the Pete Franklin show."

Now you know why, when I hear a voice on the phone, I try not to imagine what these people look like. Why would I want to meet these people? Why ruin my day, give myself ulcers?

## WHO KNOWS THE ANSWER?

I do.

At least people think I do, which is all that matters. And when I consider it, I suppose I do know the answer when it comes to sports. I've worked everywhere from New York to

Los Angeles and a lot of dumps in between that I'd like to forget. The point is that in my million years in this business I've interviewed everyone who is anyone in the world of sports. And when I talk to you, it's not for 10 seconds on the boob tube. I'm not the Plastic Man with the microphone. Turn on the news, the networks, and here's what you get:

PLASTIC MAN: "Gee, Reggie, that was some game you guys played."

REGGIE: "It sure was, Plastic Man."

PLASTIC MAN: "What were you thinking when you hit that grand slam?"

REGGIE: "I was thinking that we needed a homer to win and I'd sure like to hit one."

PLASTIC MAN: "And there you have it, the real story of Reggie's grand slam."

You get the idea. We've heard thousands of these inanities, and we all know they're nothing but garbage. But when Reggie and I sit down, we talk for at least an hour, sometimes hours. After a while, Reggie loosens up and tells me that he was shaking in his spikes and he could taste the beef Wellington he had last night because Reggie knew if he didn't come through the *New York Post* was going to run this headline: REGGIE CHOKES.

Then George Steinbrenner would be all over his butt, and Reggie didn't need any of that crap.

So why did Reggie hit the grand slam?

Because Roger Clemens screwed up and hung a curve, and Reggie guessed—and the key word is *guessed*—it was coming. That's what you get when a ball player is interviewed by someone he trusts, someone who has been around and knows that there actually were good pitchers before Roger Clemens.

On my show, I begin with three premises:

1. I know more than anyone else about sports.
2. You know nothing.
3. I say, "I told you so," whether I did or not.

Remember, if you tell people things often enough, they believe it.

Things Go Better with Coke.

Things Go Better with Coke.

Over and over, it's Things Go Better with Coke. People have spent billions of dollars—to discover that all we can remember something for is about 10 seconds.

So the New York media tell us that Lenny Dykstra is Pete Rose.

Over and over, Dykstra is Rose, Dykstra is Rose.

Of course, what would you expect from those guys in New York? Remember, everything about New York is great, even the muggers.

Well, I'll tell you this—New York is crap, and Lenny Dykstra would be just another guy if he played anywhere else.

Since no one really knows anything, maybe I do know more about sports than anyone else. Get the 10 smartest guys together, and they can't even agree that the world is round. There was that famous New York Giants scout who watched a young Sandy Koufax pitch in a sandlot game, and the scout said, "Sandy, you're a nice Jewish boy, and I think you should forget about baseball and take the basketball scholarship to the University of Cincinnati."

Scouts, sports fans, and everyone are searching for one thing—The Answer.

People look to religion, and maybe they don't find it. So they stuff their noses with dope, they rot their liver with scotch, they buy books that tell them how to stop smoking, how to get the girl, how to start smoking, how to get a divorce, how to make a million in real estate, how to lose a million in a day, how to be dumb, and how to be smart.

That guy who told Sandy Koufax to forget baseball isn't alone. There isn't one human being in any area who really knows anything to a great extent. I firmly believe that. Yet there's some guy on television saying, "Send me 50 bucks, and I'll show you how to get rich, and I'll throw in a vegetable slicer at the same time. Ask me—I have The Answer." The hucksters on the boob tube say it; the TV preachers say it because they want you to think that they can put their hands on your head and you're going to see Lana Turner or suddenly figure out how to balance your checkbook.

Here's the secret: I don't have the answer either, but I've got a great line of BS, especially when it comes to sports. As Benjamin Disraeli once said, "When a man recognizes his own ignorance, he has taken a step toward intelligence."

The fans don't know anything. The scouts don't know anything. The media sure as hell doesn't know anything. Even the people playing the games don't know much. And the guys running the teams? We all know they don't know the first thing about what they're doing.

So there's The Answer.

You don't get it?

The Answer is that there is no answer.

So why read this?

Because there is something called an honest opinion from a guy who has been around. That's what I'll give you. I suppose there are times when dealing in sensitive areas that it might be wise to show a little tact, but I can't think of any.

Sometimes I wish I was like my wife, Pat. She knows nothing about sports and cares even less. A couple of years ago, she sat with me in the press box during the Ohio State–Michigan game. It was a great game, one of those where you had no idea who'd win until the last play. My wife watched the first half because she wanted to see the bands. After the halftime show, she leaned back and went to sleep and didn't get up until it was over. That's why we have a great relationship. Home is the one place I can go when I want to hear about the drapes—what color they are, which way she wants to hang them, all of that. If I told her that I had Babe Ruth with me, she'd want to see the candy bar.

My wife did listen to me once, but she got so frightened by the things I said, she said she'd never listen again, and she hasn't. She lives in a world without sports, and my life is sports. For whatever bizarre reason, my wife is attracted to me, and for whatever crazy reason, I'm hooked on sports, all sports, and I plan to explain to you how simple these games are and what the people in them are really like.

Okay, this won't stop the world from spinning, but no matter what anyone will tell you, there is nothing more important than sports. Forget politics. Half of America doesn't even vote. Ronald Reagan got to be president, and he used to broadcast the Cubs games. As an actor, he portrayed that great pitcher, Grover Cleveland Alexander. It is mandatory that the president of the United States stop negotiating the arms deal with Russia long enough to place a call to the Super Bowl winner, the World Series winner, or whomever. If a guy is running for office, he has to loosen his tie and mingle with the bums in the bleachers.

For better or worse, sports are America and sports are us.

# 2
# FANS LIKE TO GAMBLE

A lot of people aren't going to like this, but what people like or don't like has absolutely nothing to do with the truth, and the truth about sports fans is that a lot of them—the majority—are gamblers.

I'm not saying that most of them bet their paychecks every week, but they like a little action. They say it keeps their interest in the game. When you hear a guy say that, you know that what he likes isn't the sport, but the action.

There's the case of Harry.

Harry has been working at the wing nut plant for 22 years. I mean, he has worked his butt off. The boss asks him to stay late, Harry stays late putting wing nuts into boxes. The boss asks Harry to come in on Saturday, there's Harry working Saturday, sticking the damn wing nuts in the damn boxes. Twenty-two years, and what does he have to show? That's not a question Harry wants to think about.

Anyway, Harry has been working his butt off at the wing nut plant, and he's got three kids, and one of them is taking piano lessons, which cost Harry a few coins. His wife, Mabel, isn't a bad woman, but like Harry she's just plain tired. I mean, about all they have to look forward to is two lousy weeks getting sunburned at the beach.

Sound bleak?

That's real life.

So Harry needs something, anything. He becomes a Packer fan, and every Sunday morning during football season Harry is putting down 25 bucks and going to games in 10 degrees below zero, getting his toes frostbitten and praying he doesn't get pneumonia. There is a guy at the plant named Sam, and he thinks Harry's elevator doesn't go all the way to the top. Why else would Harry freeze while watching a losing football team?

Suddenly, Harry has a problem. Either he can say "Yeah, it's stupid watching the Packers play on the North Pole," or he can come to the defense of his team.

HARRY: "The Packers ain't that bad."

SAM: "Oh, no."

HARRY: "They're pretty good."

SAM: "Who says?"

HARRY: "I says."

SAM: "Well, you're fulla crap."

HARRY: "I'm fulla crap?"

SAM: "Yeah."

As you can tell, our friends are having a real intellectual discourse on the merits of the Green Bay Packers. But wait, the climax is coming.

HARRY: "I still say the Packers is all right."

SAM: "Prove it."

HARRY: "Prove it?"

SAM: "Yeah, put some money where your mouth is."

Harry is now faced with a crisis. Sam is questioning his brains, his manhood, and trying to get into Harry's wallet at the same time. When a conversation reaches this point, a guy like Harry is finished.

HARRY: "Well, 10 bucks says the Packers beat the Steelers."

SAM: "Ten bucks says they don't."

HARRY: "That right?"

SAM: "Yeah, that's right."

HARRY: "Well, make it 20."

SAM: "What's 20 bucks?"

HARRY: "All right, 50. Yeah, 50 bucks says the Packers beat the Steelers."

SAM: "Okay, you're on."

Basically, what we now have is two guys trying to beat each other out of 50 bucks. Nonetheless, this is the most civilized form of gambling. There is no casino, no bookie, no house to beat. Sam's a slob and Harry's a slob, and they both don't have enough money to throw 50 bucks around on a football bet, but they both think the other guy is a pigeon.

And after a while, it isn't enough just to go to the games or bet with one guy. The boys at the wing nut plant got football pools going, and one of them is a real-life bookie, taking bets in the men's room during the morning break. Soon, Harry finds himself betting $25 to $50 a week, playing the pools and putting down a little extra each week on the Packers' game.

When the Packers win, and when they beat the spread—remember that the spread is the most important thing—Harry feels like he's done something. He's picked up another $25 to $50 that week. Of course, most weeks he drops $25 to $50, but he doesn't talk about that. All he knows is that suddenly watching the Packers isn't enough—he's got to have a bet down.

If Harry happens to get lucky—and that's all it is, luck, not skill—and he wins the plant football pool, he gets a little recognition. Somebody puts a note up on the bulletin board that Harry won last week's football pool. The foreman, even the president of the crummy wing-nut plant, sees the sign, and maybe one of these bigwigs asks Harry how he did it. And if the ultimate happens and Harry wins the pool for the year, then he gets to stand up at the company party, drink a few beers, and get slapped on the back. And then the situation gets worse.

"I need a rooting interest," he'll tell you.

Or he'll say, "I only bet what I can afford to lose."

That's when you know he's hooked.

This isn't to say that Harry is about to bet the wife, the kids, and the piano lessons on the Packers-Saints game. Most guys don't go that far, but it can happen. Besides, let me ask you what a guy like Harry at the wing-nut plant can afford to lose? He can barely make the mortgage payments.

But what Harry really is thinking is that he knows and understands gambling. He'll start mumbling something about having "a system."

Suddenly, Harry thinks he's ready to take on the pros. And oh baby, are the pros ready for Harry.

## HARRY AND JAKE

Years ago, when I was growing up and going to school in New York, we had a guy called Jake the Bookie. In the summer he would sit outside on the street corner in a lawn chair as if he were at the beach. Everyone knew he was Jake the Bookie; even the cops who used to walk by always made sure to wave at Jake. Jake was kind of like Jackie Gleason smoking a cigar. He wore one of those caps with green visors as if he were playing cards or trying to keep the sun out of his eyes. Jake also favored sunglasses, even at night when he went home. He wore things like a green sportcoat, red pants, and a carnation in his lapel. For two weeks every year, Jake went on a little vacation. Actually, he'd pack up his suitcase, stop at the bank, make a deposit, and then go to the slammer because that was part of his deal with the cops. Jake could operate for 50 weeks if he went in for two. So Jake was happy because the law didn't hassle him 90 percent of the time, and the cops were content because Jake would occasionally slip them a few bucks, and then, once a year, he was an easy bust.

As for Harry, he figures he has conquered the office. He decides it's time to find a guy like Jake. Someone at the wing-nut plant told Harry that Jake was a good guy, a guy with "inside information." So Harry tracks down Jake. It could be on a street corner, in a bar, or in the basement of a drugstore.

And what are the first words out of Harry's mouth?

"What looks good?"

Well, what looks good to Jake is Harry. In fact, Harry looks like green to Jake, just another sap ready to be squeezed.

But what Jake says is "I hear good things about the Browns."

Of course, Jake mumbles. Bookies always mumble in the movies. They talk out of the sides of their mouths like Bogart; they might even twitch a little, too. If they're not smoking a cigar, they're sucking on a cigarette, and they don't hold it between their fingers; they cup it in their hand.

Harry says, "Inside information?"

Jake nods.

Think about that. Inside information? How the hell would Jake the Bookie have inside information? The only thing he's trying to get inside is Harry's pocket.

But Harry knows that he doesn't know anything. He has very little self-esteem, or he wouldn't be talking to a guy like Jake in the first place. So for whatever insane reason, Harry thinks Jake knows something, that the game is fixed, and that someone told Jake about it.

Then there is the ultimate madness of the scenario—Harry cons himself into believing that Jake would tell him the secret, that Jake wants him to win.

There is one other thing about Jake. He usually is part of an organization. He is working on a bonus or commission plan, and he is tied to the mob. In the back of Harry's mind, he knows that Jake is just another hood, but Jake has this great dialogue going, and he listens to all of Harry's crap, really listens like what Harry has to say means something. No one else listens to Harry or asks Harry what he thinks, so this makes Harry feel good. And maybe on Christmas, Jake gives Harry a box of chocolates and one free bet on a college basketball pool.

Think I'm kidding? Think that people are on to guys like that, that Jake went the way of the silent movie?

If that's the case, what the hell is Jimmy the Greek doing on television?

The guy isn't just on television; he is on a national network. He's a real bad Edward G. Robinson. I don't even know if Jimmy is Greek, but there he is on television, making his picks, and there's Harry betting on what Jimmy the Greek says on the boob tube. That tells you all you need to know about Jake and Harry.

## "I CAN MAKE A LIVING GAMBLING?"

This brainstorm usually hits Harry after he's been hanging around with Jake for a while. For whatever reason, it seems that most novice gamblers hit a few early. It's just like the guy who gets drunk at the bar for the first time—he usually manages to drive home without wrapping himself around a light pole.

Then Harry says it: "I can make a living gambling."

This means he thinks he is better than the players, the managers, even the bookies. He can beat City Hall, beat the IRS, beat the system. Today Jake the Bookie, tomorrow the world.

But if you really could make a living gambling, who the hell would work? And why would guys like Jake the Bookie and Caesar's Palace stay in business?

The worst thing in the world is winning in the short run. It keeps you hyped up, almost manic. "Hey, I hit seven of ten college games today, and it would've been eight if that idiot barefoot Indian from Texas hadn't kicked his field goal attempt right into the crossbar."

But what Harry finds out is that it grinds you down if you stay with it long enough for the odds to take hold. Harry may bet 100 games and win a lot, maybe 49 times. But that means he's still lost 51, and Jake or the house has its teeth in him. Most bookies don't want to grind a guy down fast. They want to make it slow, to tease the guy and bleed him at the same time. Jake wants Harry to think that he's only one hot streak away from breaking even.

Harry starts saying things like, "I'm due." Or he says, "Notre Dame owes me—they've been taking my money for five weeks." Finally, Harry collects on Notre Dame, and suddenly he "feels it." He says, "I'm hot, don't touch me, I'm on fire." If Harry should happen to get on a roll and get out of hock, then he thinks he knows something, so he keeps betting until he's up to his butt in debt again. Harry forgot that gambling is a lot like life—at the end of the trail is a guy with a box, a shovel, and a freshly dug hole in the ground.

## BETTING BASEBALL

The touts and the sabermaticians and all the other numbers freaks love to make baseball a mystery. If you want to know who will win a baseball game, check one thing—the pitchers.

For years, I've been insisting that pitching is the most important, the most crucial, part of any baseball team. If you have it, you win. If you don't, you stink. I don't want to hear any more esoteric stats about what happens to a hitter on odd Tuesday of the month when he's playing on artificial turf in the rain. Sometimes certain pitchers do well or do poorly against certain teams, and if any of the mumbo-jumbo numbers mean anything, it would be this one statistic.

Even the worst baseball team in the world has a great chance if it has a great pitcher on the mound. There are two bottom lines to betting baseball:

1. If a great pitcher is on the mound—a Sandy Koufax in his prime or Dwight Gooden before he started sticking the funny stuff up his nose—and if that great pitcher has his stuff and there is nothing wrong with his arm or his confidence, you've got a terrific edge. Of course, the bookies know this. That's why the odds on any baseball game change from day to day according to who is pitching.
2. Even if you have the greatest of the great pitchers on the mound, you still could lose all your money if the centerfielder stayed out all night, got bombed, and then blew the game because he lost a fly ball in the lights. That's why you can make the absolutely correct bet in baseball and still be wrong.

## BETTING BASKETBALL

Gamblers like basketball because it's a city game, and most gamblers are city guys. You don't see a lot of people like Jake the Bookie hanging around at Ellis Coomb's Feed & Seed in Pooler, Georgia.

Basketball is compact, played indoors, quick, and only 10 guys are on the court at one time. Besides, it has a great history of point-shaving—those tremendous Kentucky teams after World War II and the Tulane team of 1984–85 just to name a few. A sport with that kind of illustrious history has to attract any sort of sicko who is on a self-destructive binge.

I mean, think about the college game. You've got Bobby Knight, who is a lot of fun if you're into throwing chairs. This is one of the more vile, obscene guys you'll ever meet. And he is supposed to be a shining example of what is right with the sport.

The rest of the coaches are buying players, buying players' mothers and fathers, and praying that their players don't buy dope. Most of the players are black, and the gamblers are generally racist whites. They figure the black kids must be on the take because the black kids are from the city, and everybody plays the numbers in the city. The games are on television, there are a lot of points, so that means the spread is important, and the average gambler thinks the game is fixed. Ninety-nine percent of the time it's not. But the hint of scandal is enough to make the pigeon bettors listen to guys like Jake the Bookie when they start mumbling that they have inside information.

Basketball is the ideal betting game if you're the guy taking the bet.

## BETTING FOOTBALL

If football didn't already exist, the bookies would have created it. This is the best screw job for the bettor, because the heart of football wagering is the pools. You know the kind since they probably have them at your office. You put down a buck, and you try to pick three, four, or five games right. The more you pick, the more you win. Of course, you not only have to pick the three winners; you have to make sure your winners beat the spot. And remember, these guys are cheating you on the odds. If the winner gets 8-to-1, it should be 10-to-1. If it's 12-to-1, it should be 14-to-1. The bookie always shaves a couple of points off the odds to cover his expenses. So even on those rare occasions when you win, you lose.

Betting football is for the guy who takes a flu shot hoping the dose is too strong and he'll get sick. Betting football is for those who love to suffer. It's better than going to a shrink every week, because it can cost you more. It's even better than dope, because you don't get the feeling of being high, and it usually takes longer to destroy you, meaning the suffering is not only severe, but protracted.

Football is only once a week, so you have six days between bets to agonize about how much you lost last week and think about how much you'll blow this week. This is another sport where a tout will tell you he has inside information. How the hell can that be? Football coaches run their teams and practices like the KGB. When they practice, they kick everyone out of the stadium, and they have armed guards patrolling the parking lots. You need a letter from the president to get into the dressing room after practice. Suppose you find a tall building a half-mile from the stadium, and you watch practice through field glasses? What do you see? Just a bunch of guys running around who look like ants.

Some tout will tell you he had a conversation with Tom Landry.

Well, you can win one by betting that this never happened. And suppose you do talk to Landry. I have, and all I can tell you is that his lips may move, but not much comes out of his mouth.

So you can watch all the television shows, check all the charts, and you still don't know anything. And if you did get to talk to the coach, the conversation would be like this:

GAMBLER: "What's your game plan?"

COACH: "Well, we're gonna go out there and play the game

that we have to play, and when the game starts, we're gonna stick to our game plan."

GAMBLER: "Which is what?"

COACH: "To kick the crap out of the other guy."

And that's exactly what the bookies will do to you.

## BETTING THE HORSES

Why they call horseracing a sport is beyond me. No one would go to watch 10 horses run in a circle unless you could bet on it or unless you have a thing for horse manure. Remember this Franklin Rule: The word *bet* means "give," and the fastest place to give away your money without getting a tax deduction is at the track.

## THE TOUTS ARE EVERYWHERE

They are.

Just pick up any of the preview sports magazines for just about any sport. Hell, pick up something as respectable as *USA Today.*

They call it "a professional sports service guide."

You gotta be kidding me. How about sharks swimming around, smelling blood? Your blood.

I have in front of me a copy of the March 27, 1987, *USA Today.*

In one advertisement, there is a picture of George Washington. I guess you're supposed to trust this guy because he has George Washington's picture in his ad. He says he has the NBA "Game of the Year," which happens to be any game. In this case, it is a Bulls game. If that's the best game of the year, we're all in trouble.

Another guy, a nice-looking fellow named Kevin Duffy, immodestly states in his ad, "I own the NBA."

Okay.

And if you doubt it, there's a number, and you can talk to Kevin personally.

Another advertisement asks if you bet $300 a day. Three

hundred a day? I wouldn't bet $300 a day with God, or even George Washington. All these guys talk about guaranteed winners, free bets, and no up-front costs. If that were the case, if you didn't have to pay to bet, why would there be a stock market, a bank, or even a mattress stuffed with dollar bills? Hell, the whole world would be living in the state of Nevada. All these guys own the NFL or NBA. They all have the bet of the year, and if you believe that, then you believe in losing money, because that's what will happen.

Over the years, I've had touts on my show, and I've torn them apart. One guy called me and said:

TOUT: "Pete, I've got the biggest lock in the history of sports."

PETE: "Really."

TOUT: "I've been doing this for 20 years, and believe me, Pete, LSU is gonna dump on Indiana."

PETE: "Last night in front of this very microphone I told 38 states and half of Canada that Indiana will have no trouble with LSU."

TOUT: "I've got inside information."

PETE: "You guys all have inside information."

TOUT: "My people tell me that LSU will take them apart."

PETE: "Tell me, are your people the sportswriters who cover the team?"

TOUT: "Ah . . . no."

PETE: "Well, they're the only ones who know what's going on. They're the guys at every practice and every game."

TOUT: "Sportswriters don't know anything."

PETE: "But you do."

TOUT: "Trust me, Pete."

PETE: "Why should I trust a schmuck like you? You don't know anything. No one should talk to a schmuck like you. Tell me, what kind of defense does LSU play when it gets in front by a few points late in the game?"

TOUT: "Well, I . . ."

PETE: "How about Indiana? What do they play in a close game?"

TOUT: "I'm not sure."

PETE: "You don't even know if these teams play man-to-man or zone, but you're telling me that you know who's going to win? How many plays does Bobby Knight have in his offense?"

TOUT: "I . . . duh . . . I . . ."

PETE: "I'm asking you the fundamental questions of basketball, something that any high school coach could tell you if he watched a game, and you don't know."

Then I hang up on the guy. He's a creep, a hustler, a scumbag. He's a flop in life who can make a living only by taking money from guys who are bigger flops. If these guys knew anything about sports, they'd be coaches, writers, or broadcasters.

These guys want you to think that the games are fixed. Everyone is always looking for something for nothing. Like the guy who buys swampland in Florida thinking that one day it will be worth a million. Or the poor guy who buys a lottery ticket actually thinking he might be the one guy in a billion who gets drawn out of the hopper. Gamblers are people who are never going to find what they are looking for, because they don't want to work for it. Instead, they've found the tout, who is a guy who used to be gambler and wised up, realizing that he can make it by taking money from his old gambling friends. That's the American way: screw your buddies, put on a pair of shades, and go to work for the Godfather. It's amazing. The average gambler knows he'll lose. He knows Jake the Bookie and the house have all the cards, but he wants in the game anyway. It's like being on a plane that's been shot down. There's one parachute, and everyone knows it doesn't open, but some guy will take it anyway and pray.

Remember, a gambler's prayers are never answered. When you walk off a plane in Vegas, you may as well walk right into the prop. When you go to see Jake the Bookie, just get the misery over with and hand him your wallet.

And by the way, Indiana blew out LSU by 20 in that game we talked about.

# 3
# COLLEGE FOOTBALL

The call caught me by surprise. I've been asked a million questions. No, make that I've been asked about 10 different questions a million times each. Anyway, one night, I'm doing the show, and I have this conversation:

CALLER: "Hey, Pete, I got an important question."

PETE: "You want to know how to tie your shoe."

CALLER: "I'm serious."

PETE: "So was the guy who thought he could put wings on a pickup truck and it would fly."

CALLER: "I want to know who are the dumbest sports fans."

PETE: "You got about a week to listen?"

CALLER: "I'm serious. What group of sports fans are the worst?"

You know what? It was a helluva question.

Just who were the dumbest, the worst sports fans? What guys are so bad that rather than listen to them you'd walk headfirst right into a trash compactor?

It hit me.

Boosters.

College boosters.

In California, they take you on a boat ride, start drinking all that California wine, and then they almost fall over the side. After 15 minutes with them, you want to push them.

In Arizona, these wonderful folks take you into the desert in a jeep and fire shotguns at a cactus for kicks. A big thrill is running down a baby jackrabbit.

In Nebraska, they take you to a Grange meeting where they kick out all the women, lock the doors, pull down the shades, and show dirty movies on a home projector against a sheet hung up on the wall.

In Texas, they hire broads for the recruits.

In Arkansas, they roll on the floor, sweat a good deal more than they should, and yell "Ooo, eee, pig, souee."

You get the idea. These generally are guys who made a few more bucks than they thought they would, and now they don't know what to do with it. Lord knows, they don't want to give it to charity or even the local arts council. I mean, why do something worthwhile when you can buy a football player for good old State U?

When most of us were very young we had a sandbox, and we'd sit out there playing in the dirt. In our sandbox we could be anything we wanted. We made the buildings, and we were the king. But eventually we grew up. These boosters don't want to get out of the sandbox, even though they have made some coin selling inflated real estate, bogus stocks, and so on. Now what these guys do is spend five grand for a gaudy, ill-fitting sport jacket. They think if they wear the red of Nebraska, the blue of North Carolina, or the kelly green of Notre Dame, people will go "Oooh, aaah, old Sam there is a real booster." It's a natural progression from the guy who buys the "Property of the New York Giants" T-shirt so someone might think he sweeps out the dressing room to Sam and his friend. Buying the jacket is like joining the best country club in town. It's almost like wrapping yourself in the American flag, and when you stand up at halftime and sing the school's alma mater, it's a moving moment. So moving, in fact, that it doesn't matter that the only college Sam went to was Grease Monkey U or that Sam doesn't even know all the words to the alma mater. He's got a jacket, he's got thousands of other friends in jackets, and they all can go to the games, get soused, and second-guess the coach. In between, they may be able to cut a few real estate or investment deals.

This, friends, is really what college football is all about—a place for the boosters to get bombed and make deals.

Naturally, the faculty and anyone else who has even a remote interest in higher education detest these people. The professors know that boosters are the enemies of education.

And remember this—even the college coaches hate boosters. They are PIPs, Pains in the Posterior. In most cases, these clods didn't go to the school they support. They never went to any university, because they were too busy stealing tires and stereos and learning how to be pawn shop owners. No one likes these guys. Not the players, not the coaches, not even the other boosters. Unfortunately, some of these oafs actually are powerful. They know nothing about a BA, but they've got plenty of BS. And most of all, they donate money. Lots of money. Suddenly, they feel like they are helping to select the talent. After the team loses a few games, they want to fire the coach and personally hire a new one.

That's why the coach smiles at them, and the coach makes a point of knowing just who are the key boosters, and then he goes up to these yo-yos in their gaudy jackets, slaps them on the back, and says, "You know, Sam, we realee wanna win this here game. We wanna play good, solid, hard-nosed football. We wanna get us into a real good bowl on New Year's Day."

And Sam nods and stares vacantly as if Moses had just explained the Ten Commandments to him.

The ideal booster . . . drum roll please . . . is a car dealer. Our guy's name is Sleazy Sam. He probably started as the guy at the used-car joint who turned the odometers back. Once he mastered that skill, he bought a pair of white shoes, a white belt, and a lot of polyester. He went from sleazy salesman to sleazy sales manager to sleazy owner. Then he also bought a new-car lot and started making his own television commercials.

Sleazy Sam is very dangerous to the coach, but a smart

coach can use this guy. First, the smart coach will know that the guy would score in single digits on the SAT test. The smart coach also will know that Sleazy Sam isn't just low-class, but no-class, and that being associated with a university in any manner means more than setting a new sales record for the month of January.

So the smart coach goes down to the lot once a year and has his picture taken with Sleazy Sam, who hangs it on his office wall, and the coach gets to drive a new Buick for a year. The next year, it's another new picture in exchange for another new Buick. That way, when some slob walks into the showroom and is wondering if he should buy a used car from Sleazy Sam, Sleazy Sam can show him the picture of Coach Dull shaking hands with the fine proprietor of this upstanding business.

But this guy can do a lot for "his" school. Somebody has to give the star linebacker a summer job. And that summer job is to make sure that none of the cars drive away without someone behind the wheel. For this, the star linebacker is paid 15 bucks an hour. And someone has to give Slick Jones a new Buick, and the coach sure as hell doesn't want to do it. That way, when the NCAA comes around asking questions, Coach Dull can say he doesn't know where tailback Slick Jones got that new Buick. The coach can say " Sure, it's true that Slick grew up right poor. Didn't have nothin' but an outhouse and a Sears catalog to take care of his needs, but maybe he had an estranged rich uncle who died and left him about 50 grand. Hey, it happens all the time."

Sure it does.

And if you believe that, then you should be a football fan in Texas.

## FOOTBALL IS RELIGION IN TEXAS

It is.

But first, you need to understand a little about Texas, which will tell you how a guy like Sleazy Sam became a big man in the biggest state. Sure, Alaska is bigger, but they don't play football on the tundra, so it doesn't count.

But in Texas:

They have barbecue parties that often end up with folks taking off their clothes and jumping into the swimming pool.

They wear boots that cost as much as a small car.

They have the best snakes in America.

They have big hats that they wear while eating.

They've some of the best and worst Mexican food you'll ever eat.

They have a lot of dust.

Lyndon Johnson was the consummate Texan. He'd throw a barbecue party, wear a big hat, talk about killing snakes, and then grab a poor little beagle by the ears and wave the dog around. When things got really boring, he'd whip off his shirt and show everyone his gallbladder scar. Now you know why Lyndon Johnson was a great American.

For the most part, Texans are very outgoing and happy, as long as they beat Oklahoma. Now Oklahoma has been stealing some of their best football players for years, going right down into Wichita Falls and snapping those kids up. If that ain't a federal offense, what is?

Let's face it, you can get uptight living in a place like Dallas or Houston. The weather there is probably the most horrendous of anywhere in the country. It's either too damn hot or just a little too cold. The humidity is so smothering that people just wake up, step out of their air-conditioned houses, and end up in a bad mood.

Dallas is probably the richest city in the country, and it's got the First Baptist Church. Remember that the Baptists are against drinking, dancing, sex, swimming pools, barbecue parties, and breathing. So if you grew up in Dallas, you're probably repressed and have been thinking about getting laid from the time you could walk. So you go out and you buy a big car, a big house, a big cowboy hat, and even a big dog. At Neiman-Marcus in downtown Dallas, they'll sell you an elephant. Of course, you also run up big debts, but that's part of the deal.

In Dallas, ostentation and grotesque are in. Intelligence and common sense are foul, unspoken words.

Of course, Dallas and Houston have been engaging in this ageless battle to determine which is the greatest, most sophisticated city. But I will tell you this—any place where the biggest event of the year is a rodeo, where they let horses walk down the middle of Main Street and crap all over, has a stench I don't want to get near.

The problem with Texas actually is its inferiority complex.

QUESTION: What is the most famous battle in the history of the state?

ANSWER: The Alamo.

QUESTION: Who won?

ANSWER: Texans don't want to discuss it.

That is why Texans really want to forget Davy Crockett and the boys. Hell, the Mexicans wiped them out.

So they are still trying to deal with the Alamo.

The University of Texas has the world's biggest drum. They wheel this monstrous, hideous drum out, and everyone gets his jollies when some mental midget whacks it. But that is nothing compared to when they play "The Eyes of Texas" at a football game. Eyes water; the world falls off its axis. There is more reverence for "The Eyes of Texas" than you'll ever find in any Baptist church.

Of course, Texans also can get fanatical about religion. SMU is the Methodists; TCU is the regular, normal, upright Christians; Baylor is the Baptists; and A&M is the heathens. Every Saturday they fight these religious wars on the field. It's better than the Crusades.

You've got things like Aggie jokes. They are like Polish jokes in the East. It's heady stuff like "Hey, did you hear about the Aggie who stayed up all night studying because he had a blood test in the morning?"

The Texas A&M Aggies have a huge military band that looks like the Wehrmacht. They wear black boots and play the "Aggie War Hymn" about a million times a game. The 12,000 students at the game stand . . . for the entire game.

And if they have a girl with them, she stands for the whole game, too. If someone sits down, a couple of guys in black boots come by, grab the guilty party, and take him behind the stadium where he must write "Aggies are No. 1" on a blackboard for the next six years. Of course, there is seldom a need to do this. Most of the Aggie jokes are right. I mean, who of sound mind would want to go to a school in College Station, a place where the friendliest creature is a mosquito?

Baylor plays in Waco, where everyone is getting dunked in a pool of water so he can be saved every 10 minutes. You can't buy a drink in Waco, so everyone takes to the highway to buy booze out of town, and they drink while driving around, which makes for some impressive DWI statistics.

I could go on and on, but you get the point. Nonetheless, there is one thing that brings these schools together. They really love it when one of them plays Notre Dame, because none of them like the Catholics.

Keep in mind that football is a god in Texas. If you have any doubts, just check with the NCAA. They'll tell you that the most penalized league in the history of mankind is the Southwest Conference, which happens to feature a lot of schools in the great state of Texas.

Really, the whole state should have "Oh My Cheatin' Heart" for an anthem. There are all these millionaires with plenty of juice and their own private jets. They fly these kids in for a campus "visit." So what if the kid is so dumb he can't even recite "Mary Had a Little Lamb"? They'll falsify a few documents, set him up with a female tutor, preferably one who is stacked, and get the job done.

At SMU, the governor of the state of Texas was caught because he knew that football players were being paid and he didn't blow the whistle. We're not talking about Sleazy Sam here; we're talking about the governor of the whole damn state, who was on the board of regents. He said he wanted to phase out the payments gradually.

This made the Texans mad.

Not because he knew the players were getting paid. Not

because he didn't immediately end the payments. Not because he didn't decide to give the kids a raise. *But Texans didn't like it because he got caught.*

This means that the carpetbaggers from the NCAA descended upon Dallas like the dirty Yankees that they are, and they went and canceled the whole damn football schedule.

For SMU, there will be no games with Texas Tech, with TCU, or with A&M. This was a terrible blow to the cultural life of Dallas.

It's time for a little lesson in reality. Paying football players isn't an exception in Dallas; it's a way of life. That's because it's such a disgrace if your team has a losing record. The recognition that comes when Texas, Texas A&M, or SMU gets to be number one is the ultimate narcotic to these people. They'd be willing to live without air conditioning for a week if they knew their team would end up at the top of the polls and wind up in the Cotton Bowl. It's a way of putting down those New England snobs, those queers in San Francisco, and those intellectuals in New York. When a Texas team is number one, the state can say "We're better than anyone else."

## FOOTBALL IN OKLAHOMA

In Oklahoma, what have you got?

A bunch of Indians driving around in Eldorados because they struck it rich when someone found oil on the reservation. Now there's nothing that makes an Okie madder than a rich Indian, but we'll leave that topic for some other time.

Half of Oklahoma followed Henry Fonda to California in the 1930s in *The Grapes of Wrath*. The rest are sitting around waiting for Oral Roberts to raise another $10 million. The coach in Oklahoma is Barry Switzer, who lost a couple games one season, and they threatened to take away all his perks. So now you know why Switzer has been arrested for driving while impaired. If you lived in Oklahoma, you'd be impaired, too. Things are so bad in Oklahoma that these people actually think Houston and Dallas have something to offer.

## FOOTBALL IN NEBRASKA

I always wondered what it was like to be a black football player in Nebraska. Can you imagine some kid from Watts or the south side of Chicago out there among all the corn stalks and farmers? It would be like going to bed in New York on Monday night and waking up Tuesday in Afghanistan.

One thing I will say for Nebraska and Kansas is that this region has produced some great gangsters. Of course, the first thing Dillinger, Bonnie and Clyde, and all the rest did after they knocked over a few banks was get the hell out of Nebraska. There weren't enough banks worth robbing.

But they do play football in Nebraska, and they play it pretty well. Football is all that these people live for. If it weren't for Big Red football, all the farmers would be blowing their brains out because they know the bank is about to foreclose on them.

What do you have in Nebraska?

The county fair where they pick the fattest pig.

The 4-H club where kids try to grow the biggest rhubarb.

Four old geezers on a porch watching a pickup rust.

There is an unwritten law: unless the subject is football, if it happens in Nebraska, it doesn't count.

## WEST COAST FOOTBALL

Really, we're talking about UCLA and USC, and what we're really talking about is Hollywood. Californians don't take their college football seriously. It's something to do on a Saturday afternoon instead of going to the beach and playing Frisbee. In California, they go to the game to look at the girls, not watch some 270-pounder knock the quarterback's block off.

What can you say for California? They grow good raisins? It's the state that gave us Herbert Hoover, morons on roller skates, and Charles Manson.

But it's all very mellow, you know. USC has a guy on a white horse, and the guy rides around during the games, but no one much cares. UCLA has a very small band in blue suits, and they're lousy. You've got the music industry right there in Los Angeles, but UCLA has a crappy band. Don't ask me why. I mean, Texas has big, great bands. In the Midwest and South, the bands are good. So the next time some guy from California starts telling you how great the West Coast is, you tell him that the bands out there just plain stink.

## EAST COAST FOOTBALL

I ask you, who gets excited about the Yale Bowl? Who wants to see a bunch of kids who actually go to class play football? Yale vs. Harvard? Dartmouth vs. Princeton? At Dartmouth, they fired the coach because he was a loser, and the coach sued to keep his job. Well, the school felt so sorry for the guy, they let him coach for another year. In Texas, it would have been no problem. Sleazy Sam would have taken the guy out and shot him, and the judge would have given Sleazy Sam probation and then shaken his hand, telling Sleazy Sam that he did what had to be done.

I know all about the Ivy League because I went to Columbia. Lou Little coached there, and for 32 years he got his ass kicked every Saturday. But no one ever said to Lou, "Hey, pardner, you better get some big strong hosses in here, or we got a bullet with your name on it."

I am proud to say that in my four years at Columbia I went to one football game. I don't remember whom Columbia played, but I do know Columbia lost.

The Ivy League actually believes that the purpose of going to college is to get some type of an education, and I'm not talking about learning how to drink beer through your nose.

There are 25 high school football teams in the state of Texas alone that could beat any Ivy League school by four touchdowns.

Here's the bottom line on the Ivy League—a bunch of wimps.

## BIG TEN FOOTBALL

It really should be the Big Two, since only Ohio State and Michigan really count. Sure, Iowa or Michigan State or Purdue thinks it has a decent team once in a while, but once in a while doesn't cut it with me.

Between Ohio State and Michigan, you have some real hatred, and that's what college football is all about.

At Ohio State, they had Woody Hayes, who coached the team for 28 years while doing a great imitation of a maniac at the same time. He attacked everything—cameramen, yard markers, even a player from Clemson. He was a man who idolized General Patton, which wasn't so bad. But then he acted like Patton, and that *was* bad. Woody believed in running the ball into the line 50 straight times, and the only pass he allowed his quarterback to make was at a cheerleader.

Nonetheless, Woody Hayes was the most respected man in the state of Ohio, which also happens to be the birthplace of presidents. I'm not sure what that means, but I figured I'd throw it in.

At Michigan they have Bob Schembechler, a disciple of Woody Hayes. When those teams play, it is like two guys meeting in an alley and beating each other over the head with blackjacks. It is Neanderthal football. Instead of wearing shoulder pads and helmets, these guys should put on lion skins and carry clubs.

In Ohio and Michigan they think they are as crazy about football as Texans, but they're just kidding themselves. The Midwest still doesn't have any big-time cheaters. I'm talking about schools that year after year blatantly buy players and get thrown on probation and couldn't care less.

Midwesterners do take their football seriously, but they have a lot of other things to think about—the failing corn crop, Japanese cars, steel mill strikes, and everyone moving to the Sunbelt.

## ALABAMA FOOTBALL

To understand southern college football, you start with Alabama, and that means you really start with Bear Bryant.

There are only two people who have ever counted in Alabama—George Wallace and The Bean. Wallace was the ultimate redneck, keeping black kids out of white schools and all that until he figured out that black votes (when they finally let blacks vote) would help him win elections. Then Wallace became an enlightened southerner.

Now that I'm thinking about Wallace, it's easy to see why he wanted to keep blacks out of Alabama. It was good politics. But what I can't figure out is why anyone, black or white, would want to go to school there.

Bryant also saw the light in racial issues when he got a good look at how some of the blacks could run. Bryant symbolizes southern college football. In Alabama he was Christ walking the streets of Tuscaloosa. Schools are named for him. He has his own street. At prayer meetings they invoked his name. And all this was in spite of the fact that the Bear had terrible taste in clothes. He wore a hat worthy of Jake the Bookie. You kept looking for the tout's ticket sticking out of the headband. He looked like he was saying "I'm here in Alabama, but I'd rather be at Santa Anita betting the daily double."

You couldn't hear Bear much, because he raised mumbling to an art form. People couldn't understand him, and when southerners can't understand you, they think you're either a Yankee or a genius. In Bryant's case, it was the latter since he was born somewhere in Arkansas where they have a lot of snakes and opossums, and he then went to school (and I use the term in the loosest sense) at Alabama. Bear really started his coaching career in—where else?—Texas, at A&M to be exact. He almost killed his kids, but he won there, and then the Tide brought the Bear home, where he won some more without any fatalities.

We all know that the national anthem in the South is "Dixie" and that *Damnyankees* is all one word, but Bear Bryant and football did more for integration in the South than any piece of legislation or any civil rights march.

What happened was that Bear got tired of having his white southern boys get whomped by a bunch of black kids when they played Yankee schools in bowl games. Then Bear found out that these black kids were from places like Phoenix City, Alabama. So what the hell was all that talent doing at Michigan? It was a tough question for Bear to answer. Then Bear also realized that integration was coming, and if they had to have blacks at Alabama, they may as well carry the ball for the Crimson Tide.

So Bear started to recruit the black kids, and he won even more. Soon, Georgia, Auburn, LSU, and everyone else in the Southeastern Conference was doing the same thing, but Bear had gotten a jump on them.

Now the South became a liberal place. Of course, rednecks always liked the blacks because they made good biscuits and knew how to shine shoes. As long as they lived in the swamps and didn't expect to have a house with running water, everything was fine.

But after the Bear integrated Alabama, the rednecks came to appreciate blacks for another reason—black kids could help Alabama beat all them awful Yankee schools.

## LSU FOOTBALL

I once worked in Lousyana. It was at a station near the bayou. I was the morning man, and when I got there at six my job was to kill the snakes. They would always crawl out of the swamp and curl up by the station's warm generator. I was both a morning man and a snake bopper. I once got bit by a mosquito that was the size of a 747, so I know all about Lousyana.

Really, there are only two things about the state.

The first is New Orleans, where they have the Mardi Gras. It's a pseudo-sophisticated place where you can listen to jazz that's 100 years old. I like that part. But they spend far too much time trying to ruin what is a perfectly good piece of fish. One-hundred-year-old jazz is great; 100-year-old fish in some crummy sauce is not.

The other thing they do in Lousyana is drink. The Cajuns make the worst whiskey in America. It gets you drunker and sicker than if you drank a gallon of Valvoline. Drinking is very important, because there is no more insane place than Baton Rouge, Louisiana, when all the Cajuns get hopped up on moonshine and go watch an LSU football game on a Saturday night. The Cajuns have been drunk since Wednesday, just to get in the proper frame of mind for the game. That's why they can sing "Hold That Tiger" about 3,000 times every hour and not get bored. But what can you expect from a bunch of folks who live in the swamps and eat fish a cat won't touch?

## GEORGIA FOOTBALL

Let's start with UGA.

Say you don't know UGA? How about UGA III or even his son, UGA IV? In the Ivy League, when a guy has an initial after his name, it's a good bet that his old man probably owns Standard Oil. In Georgia, it means you're a bulldog.

That's right, some fleabag dog.

UGA, which stands for the University of Georgia—those folks in Athens are so clever—is the Georgia bulldog. He not only is on the field for all the games, but when he dies, they bury him in the end zone. In Texas they do the same thing—only it's the losing coach who has been shot who gets buried.

Anyway, there supposedly are four generations of this repulsive bulldog that have served as Georgia's mascot. The Friday before the Dawgs play in Athens, UGA spends the night in a Holiday Inn. In a bed at the Holiday Inn.

But in 1985 the Dawgs had a real crisis. You have to understand something about bulldogs. They are not great athletes. Their faces look like they've been stepped on by some linebacker. They don't have legs; they have stumps. And all in all, they seem about as bright as the Cajuns who keep screwing up their fish.

Well, one Friday night in 1985, UGA rolled out of bed at the Holiday Inn and—plunk—he hit the floor. And the mutt blew out his knee. He couldn't make it on game day.

This was cause for a day of mourning in Georgia. Flags were flown at half-mast. There was a moment of silence before the game. Women cried.

Well, the Dawgs went out and won one for UGA. And a week later UGA made a triumphant return after extensive and expensive knee surgery. This may have been the most inspirational sports story since Dave Winfield threw a baseball and killed a seagull.

## MISSISSIPPI FOOTBALL

I have one thing to say about Mississippi: this is a state that says it wants to leave the union, and I think we ought to let it go, because who cares if Mississippi is there or not?

## BANDS

Any good college football program has a big, loud band. Notice that I didn't say a good band or a band with a sense of melody and a feel for music. In fact, that might be considered a detriment.

What you want is a big, loud band. In Alabama, they have the Million Dollar Band. I don't know who got the million bucks, but if it was the musicians, someone got cheated because these people should be paying you to listen to them. Louisiana State has the Tiger Band, which knows how to play "Hold That Tiger," a million times in three hours. Texas A&M has a 350-piece band that wears black boots and marches around like the Nazis going through Paris during World War II.

Bands have a great legacy. There was a rich kid from Indiana who went to Yale a long time ago. He would later become one of America's greatest composers, but his first song was not a love ballad or an intricate symphony. Rather, it was a song worthy of any college football band.

The song was "Boola, Boola." The composer was Cole Porter, who also wrote the immortal "Bow-Wow" song at

Yale. With a guy such as Cole Porter writing football fight songs, you know that you are on to something important.

As I said, the key thing to remember about bands is that they have to be big and loud. And obnoxious. All they need to know is one or two songs, and they can play those songs badly as long as they don't get bored playing those songs. Football fans want to hear the same songs over and over. In fact, they often hear just a few bars of the same songs over and over. But what the hell does the average football fan care? He's so bombed that he can barely remember the seven words from the fight song. Just remember that fight songs are important. Michigan has "Hail to the Victors." Wisconsin has "On Wisconsin." High schools like to steal college fight songs, keeping the melody and changing the words so that "On Wisconsin" becomes "On Westwood High." Ohio State is different from most colleges because it has two fight songs. The first is "Buckeye Battle Cry," and the other is "Across the Field," which is played incessantly—and terribly—when the Buckeyes are in a tough spot. Having two fight songs makes the Ohio State band think it is twice as good as the other bands, and that is why Ohio State's band calls itself "The Best Damn Band in the Land."

Then comes the halftime show. Someone grabs the microphone from the regular public address announcer and says, "Now, presenting the Ohio State Marching Band." He makes it sound as if the Ohio State band came to Columbus direct from heaven, where it just finished a gig playing at the right hand of the throne.

Bands always have "tributes," at halftime, when they slaughter the works of some great American composer. If you notice, the guy who is being honored by having his music massacred is never there. They like to do Duke Ellington. Now Duke Ellington has written 5 or 10 songs that will just tear your heart out, but if you hear those songs performed by a marching band, you want to puke. Poor Duke, he's rolling over in his grave and looking for the guy who gave his music to the Alabama Million Dollar Band.

I like the bands for their uniforms and for their marching.

In addition to destroying Ellington, they will try to walk around the field and spell out something like *OSU.* This is why the band members go to class—to learn how to spell out the words on the field. Suppose the LSU Tiger Band was having a tribute to the musical *Cats,* and the band started marching, and the first letter it formed was a K. This would be very embarrassing, because even in Louisiana you are supposed to know how to spell *Cats.* But it isn't as easy as it seems. Take the tuba player. This is a person who has gotten very little out of life, and he knows that he will continue to be a nonentity. He has a big belly. He has asthma. No matter what kind of deodorant he uses, he still sweats like a pig and grosses everyone out whenever he raises his arms. He wanted to be a football player, but he was too slow and too soft. Then he wanted to be a cheerleader, but he was too fat and too sweaty. The girl cheerleaders wouldn't get near him. So he settled for the band, where he is big enough to stuff into the largest uniform and lug around a tuba. He doesn't even have to play it. I mean, who really hears the tubas in a marching band? But it looks nice when a guy is carrying around a tuba.

However, in addition to not dropping the tuba, he must remember where to walk and how to spell *Cats.* This isn't easy, but usually they put someone in the middle of the tubas who can spell, and everyone just follows that guy.

In case you haven't guessed, I don't think much of the boys (or the girls, for that matter) in the band. If they were real musicians, they would be attending a school such as Juilliard. If they wanted to be pop musicians, they'd be playing dives in Vegas or Atlantic City. So the band is a bunch of rank amateurs usually directed by a guy with a baton who couldn't get me from my bedroom to the bathroom. The band director is lucky to have a job, and his main concern is not the music, but making sure the tuba players remember where to walk.

Bands like gimmicks—nice-looking girls twirling flags or perhaps a girl throwing a baton up near the lights and then catching it. Every few years they change one set of awful uniforms for another set of awful uniforms. College bands even put out albums, and sports fans spend millions each year to hear the Ohio State band commit atrocities on Mozart's music. But what the hell? Also on the album will be "Buckeye Battle Cry" and "Hang On Sloopy." This makes the fans happy because they like the fight songs, the bands are happy because they are getting the money and music has been set back another 100 years, but who really cares? Certainly not the people making or buying the records.

# 4
# COLLEGE FOOTBALL COACHES

There is only one person who deserves to have to listen to a college football coach.

You got it—the boosters.

Why would anyone of sound mind want to spend 15 minutes listening to a college football coach? Take Michigan's Bo Schembechler. Talk about a bad Henny Youngman joke, that's Bo. This is a guy whose team won the Big Ten and was ready to go to the Rose Bowl, and he still had a heart attack. I don't mean to make fun of Bo's coronary, but if the guy has an attack after he wins, imagine what he's like when he gets beat. Of course, he may have buckled under because he knew he was going to lose the Rose Bowl. Bo always loses in the Rose Bowl, and no matter how many temper tantrums he has, nothing will change that fact.

But when I think of the two Ss—stress and screaming—I think of Bo, and who wants to hear that?

Then there's Georgia's Vince Dooley, who is boring enough to put Bo to sleep. Vince Dooley is a walking definition of the word *boring*. Here is a guy with some of the best talent in the nation, and what does he tell you?

DOOLEY: "Well, we got a real tough game this Saturday. We know that Sacred Heart has been in a slump lately, but I personally have been watching the films, and believe me, Sacred Heart can be a very explosive football team. I consider them highly underrated and capable of rising up to meet the challenge on any given Saturday."

PETE: "But Coach, Sacred Heart is a rest home. You're talking about 11 guys who are 95 years old, and 4 of them have had leg amputations."

DOOLEY: "That's just the point—they've been hurt, but they're healing."

You get the point.

Then there's Tom Osborne of Nebraska. I always thought that there's only one person Osborne should talk to, and that's Tom Landry of Dallas.

OSBORNE: "So Tom, you had a nice season."

LANDRY: "We did all right."

OSBORNE: "Won the Super Bowl."

Landry nods.

Osborne nods.

LANDRY: "Did all right yourselves, I see."

Osborne nods.

LANDRY: "Ranked number one."

OSBORNE: "Our execution could have been better."

LANDRY: "I know what you mean."

Osborne nods.

Landry nods.

The audience snores.

Now there's a couple of guys who could put the Sominex people out of business. Who needs pills? Put Landry and Osborne on the tube every night and make the insomniacs watch.

Speaking of coaches on television, there is only one thing worse than the test pattern, and that's the college football coach's show. These things are so bad, so boring, that they have to work to make them that way. The host is usually a guy like Jovial Joe, who is a hack radio announcer in town, and his ultimate thrill is to broadcast State's football games every autumn Saturday. One day Jovial Joe attains this lofty ambition, then he also is put in charge of the coach's show, featuring Coach Dull and films from last week's 75–6 win over Sacred Heart.

JOVIAL JOE: "Well, Coach Dull, that was some game we had against Sacred Heart."

COACH DULL: "It certainly was, Jovial Joe."

Remember, you get a lot of *we*s and *us* on this show, because Jovial Joe not only is a part of the system, he relishes it. In terms of getting out the party line, *Pravda* could learn something from the coach's show.

JOVIAL JOE: "Now we go to the key play. There are seven minutes gone in the third quarter, and we have a 49–0 lead."

COACH DULL: "I have to agree with you there. The interception made by John Boy Todd stopped Sacred Heart and set up our seventh touchdown."

JOVIAL JOE: "No, coach, I think it was the eighth."

COACH DULL (raising his voice for the first time): "You sure?"

JOVIAL JOE (suddenly getting worried about his job. He knows he's right. After all, he can count. But . . . ): "Well, Coach Dull, you just might have been right. But it was a key play, and John Boy did come through."

They go to the film. The legless 95-year-old quarterback from Sacred Heart Rest Home is surrounded by nine 300-pound psychopaths screaming for blood. The quarterback heaves the ball straight up into the air, and it comes down into John Boy's arms.

COACH DULL: "That was fine position defense by John Boy."

JOVIAL JOE: "And he is also a fine student-athlete."

COACH DULL: "John Boy's parents got every right to be proud of their son. He is serving the program and the university well."

Actually, John Boy has no parents. He was recruited out of the Green Acres Home for deranged and dangerous youths, and the only reason he is a fine student-athlete is that he hasn't been arrested . . . yet.

JOVIAL JOE: "We'll be talking to John Boy a little later on in the show. He is one of this university's fine student-athletes."

COACH DULL: "Ah, Jovial Joe, I'm afraid John Boy couldn't make it. He has to study for a big exam tomorrow. I'm sure the folks at home will understand."

Actually, Coach Dull is thinking, What the hell are you saying, Joe? You think we're going to bring that hood on the show? The last thing we want is for anyone to hear John Boy start to talk. A student-athlete? All we're trying to teach this turnip is how to stay one step ahead of the cops.

JOVIAL JOE: "It's nice to know that John Boy takes being a student-athlete very seriously."

COACH DULL: "We will have Lawrence Fields on the show."

JOVIAL JOE: "It's always a pleasure to have Lawrence on the show."

Lawrence Fields is the son of a doctor, and he's the kicker. He also is the only member of the team who can put five words together without an obscenity or saying "you know." Lawrence also has a streak worthy of Lou Gehrig as he is making his 52nd consecutive appearance on the Coach Dull Show.

JOVIAL JOE: "Now we go to the chalkboard part of our show. Coach Dull, tell us about that X-3 play that led to that big fourth-quarter touchdown for Roy Jones, making the score 64–0."

They walk to the blackboard. Coach Dull has told Jovial Joe to ask about this play, and now Coach Dull is prepared to totally dazzle the boosters watching. Actually, the X-3 play meant that the guard and the tackle knock Sacred Heart linemen into the Arctic Ocean. Then Roy Jones, who can outrun a coyote, bolts through the opening and dares the 95-year-old legless women to catch him.

But Coach Dull doesn't tell you that. He goes on and on, drawing Xs and Os and arrows and dark lines and light lines. Coach Dull doesn't know what the hell he's talking about, but he knows it sounds good. Jovial Joe is nodding, the camera is following every mark on the board. Coach Dull starts thinking that if he can keep this up he'll be another John Madden when he retires.

As for the booster sitting at home and watching all this

garbage, he's pointing at the screen and telling his wife that old Coach Dull really knows what he's doing.

His wife says, "But honey, what is he talking about?"

The booster says, "It's a trick play. You're not supposed to understand it."

Then we get the commercial. There's Coach Dull at some car lot with his arm around Sleazy Sam. Coach Dull is telling you that he always gets his cars from Sleazy Sam. Of course he does. Sleazy Sam gives Coach Dull a new car every year in exchange for doing this crummy commercial. So when Coach Dull says that Sleazy Sam can give you a great deal, he's right. Of course, you have to be Coach Dull to get one.

They come back to the Coach Dull Show, and Lawrence Field has joined Coach Dull and Jovial Joe.

JOVIAL JOE: "Tell us, Lawrence, that was a crucial extra point you made with two minutes left in the game."

LAWRENCE: "I just wanted to make a contribution to the program."

Coaches love it when someone mentions their program. It makes it sound professional, like they're trying to go to the moon instead of the Cotton Bowl. But come to think of it, more people in Texas care about the Longhorns' football program than the space program. And Lawrence knows that if he keeps making contributions to the program the boosters will continue to make contributions to him. Life is a lot easier after getting a hundred-dollar handshake from Sleazy Sam.

JOVIAL JOE: "It was a real team effort out there."

LAWRENCE: "Coach Dull said he really wouldn't feel safe until we got to 75 points."

COACH DULL: "I impressed upon the boys that Sacred Heart was capable of coming back at any time."

LAWRENCE: "The coach said exactly that."

What Coach Dull really said was that they were going to practice six hours a day in the Everglades if they didn't run up 75 points against Sacred Heart, so Lawrence Field's extra point was bigger than anyone knew.

JOVIAL JOE: "So tell us, Lawrence, what is your major and your grade-point average?"

And for the 52nd consecutive show, Lawrence Field tells the world that he has a 3.8 grade-point average in political science and he plans to go to law school.

JOVIAL JOE: "Lawrence is a real example of the kind of student-athletes Coach Dull's program is producing. We all can be proud of the job Coach Dull is doing for us at State U."

THE END.

Thank God, right?

## COACH DULL IN ACTION

The point is that if he wins, Coach Dull isn't dull. Bear Bryant mumbled so badly that no one could understand him, but he beat Georgia, Mississippi, and those scumbags at Auburn, so the Bear was a great man, a colorful character. So what if you couldn't hear him.

The typical college football coach ends up talking a lot. The boosters want to talk to him, the writers want to talk to him, sometimes even his wife talks to him. But he never says much.

"We gotta win."

"We gotta play hard."

"We can't let down."

"We gotta win, play hard, and not let down."

You get the idea.

To his players, there is one message—"You've got to pay the price."

Notice the switch to the word *you*. That's because the kids are the ones who have to "stick their nose in there." And when the kid sticks his nose in there, he gets it broken. But if enough kids pay the price and get their noses broken, then the team wins. And when the team wins, the coach wins.

At big-time programs, winning means a lot. It can be worth millions. Forget the base salary, although most of these guys are pulling down between $150,000 and

$250,000. I'm talking about the free cars from Sleazy Sam, the free house from another booster, the clothing store that supplies him with the best suits, the restaurants that give him the free meals and won't take his cash. Then there are things like the Coach Dull Show. Some of these guys even have their own newspaper columns and they are paid like Norman Mailer. Of course, Coach Dull doesn't write his column; someone in the college's sports information department takes care of that.

Now you know why the coach keeps telling the kids to pay the price.

If he could get away with it, the coach would go out on the field during practice with a whip and chair. But that would be brutalizing his players. If the NCAA ever got wind of such activity, Coach Dull could be in big trouble.

In and of itself, an NCAA investigation is not the worst of things. But if you get caught, you had better have won a lot of games, or the administration will dump your butt and find another crook to run its program. For Coach Dull, it's best to keep the NCAA boys away from old State U.

If the coach is a legend, a Bear Bryant, then he watches practice from a tower as if he were Moses on the Mount. Up there, he can take a nap and no one will notice. There aren't too many things more boring than football practice, unless it's hearing a coach talk about football practice. Anyway, Coach Dull has seen about a million of them. So that's why he has a hard time staying awake. But during those rare moments when he is conscious and he does see something on the field he doesn't like, he can cause a coronary arrest in half the players simply by leaving the tower and walking down to the practice field.

You know what the kids are thinking: Here comes Coach Dull. He's gonna take away my Buick for a week.

When Coach Dull finally gets to the field, he spots a 275-pound offensive tackle named Brick. If Brick felt like it, he could take one hand and turn Coach Dull into a potted plant. But here comes Coach Dull out of the tower, and he's coming toward Brick.

"Son," says Coach Dull, putting his arm around Brick. "You missed a block."

God almighty, the Brick missed a block. The Republic is about to fall because Brick missed a block.

Brick is shaking. He tastes his breakfast coming up. He whispers, "Please God, don't let me lose my breakfast while Coach Dull has his arm around me."

"Brick, you're not quitting, are you?" asks Coach Dull.

Coaches love the guilt trip. When all else fails, accuse the kids of quitting. Make them feel like third-rate citizens. Brick doesn't even have to be told that the worst sin is quitting. No one needs to remind him that quitters never win. People have been doing the Vince Lombardi act on him since he was five years old. Besides, quitting is a great rationalization for a coach. It's the I-did-my-job-but-those-dogs-quit-on-me mentality.

"Now Brick, we can't have that happening anymore," says Coach Dull.

"It won't, sir," says Brick. "Never again."

"Good boy," says Coach Dull, who then gives Brick a whack on the butt.

On the next play from scrimmage, they line up Brick against some walk-on defensive tackle. Brick would rather eat a railroad spike than have Coach Dull talk to him again. The ball is snapped, Brick breaks the walk-on's spine, and Coach Dull watches from the tower, smiling. Meanwhile, they carry the walk-on out on the Meat Wagon.

Hey, they really do call it the Meat Wagon. That's too good for even me to make up. But it also is symbolic of what they really think of the players. To me, the Meat Wagon says it all.

Usually, Coach Dull will have a young, ambitious assistant, someone like Coach Loon. It is Coach Loon's job to be the hatchet man, to terrorize the players.

Coach Loon is the guy who kicks the locker, who punches the wall, who empties the garbage all over the room.

When he was an assistant coach at the University of Georgia, Erk Russell shaved his head and then would butt heads with his defensive unit. This was an interesting event, since Russell wasn't even wearing hair but his players had on helmets. Erk and the players would butt away, and eventually Erk's head would start to bleed, and then the Bulldogs knew they were ready to go out there and kill Florida.

It's sort of like the cops when they arrest you. One guy is the good cop, the other is the tough guy. Coach Dull is the father figure, ever patient, willing to listen. Coach Dull can be like that because he knows that if some freshman drops a pass in the first half Coach Loon will get in the kid's face and not get out of it until the kid cries. Then Coach Dull comes over, puts his arm around the kid, and says, "Shake it off, son, we're not quitting on you." There's that word again. I'm not quitting on you, so you better not quit on me. Not unless you want to listen to Coach Loon for the rest of your life.

Never forget that most football players aren't Dr. Schweitzer—that's why Coach Dull has to keep using Lawrence Field week after week on his television show. There are no Fulbrights in the dressing room—just a lot of half-brights—so butting heads and punching walls go a long way with these guys. They are physical people. They crave contact, and that makes orthopedic surgeons everywhere happy.

## COACH DULL RECRUITS

Coach Dull had better recruit, or Sleazy Sam will take away the Buick and Coach Dull will end up driving a '79 Chevy and working at Mars Hill College.

In recruiting, it helps if Coach Dull has a nickname. Paul Bryant made a career out of being the Bear. Woody Hayes, that's a good name. Red, now that's pretty good, too. So what if Red lost all his hair 20 years ago? Fans like coaches named Red. How about Tark the Shark? That's outstanding. The Little General, the Old Professor—all those will work.

Let's say we have Coach Dull recruiting Bobby Ben, aka

Bonecrusher. The scene opens at Bonecrusher's home in Lyons, Georgia. Coach Dull comes in, takes off his hat, and extends his hand to Bobby Ben's mother.

"I'm Red Dull from State U," says Coach Dull. "I really like your living room carpet."

Right away, Coach Dull has established himself as a regular guy. He's Red Dull. He also has shown the mother that he has taste. He likes the carpet. Who cares if Coach Dull wouldn't put that rag in his garage under Sleazy Sam's Buick? You have to compliment the mother and do it right away.

The carpet touch is a good one. Mrs. Bonecrusher is used to coaches saying nice things about her son or talking about the weather or even complimenting her dress. But to mention the carpet, that indicates that Coach Dull is a man who notices the little things.

Next is the apple pie. Mothers always give coaches apple pie. Sometimes the pie is fine; other times the coach takes a bite into a piece and immediately needs about $700 worth of bridgework. But no matter how rancid it is, he must say, as Coach Dull does to Mrs. Bonecrusher: "This is mighty fine pie. Think you could spare another piece?"

As Mrs. Bonecrusher is serving a second helping of her jawbreaker apple pie, Coach Dull excuses himself and heads for the bathroom. There he emits a silent belch, then he reaches into his coat pocket and pulls out not a flask, although he'd like to, but a bottle of Kaopectate. Coach Dull knows that once again, he is trading his digestive tract for a 17-year-old semiliterate.

Back at the dining room table, Coach Dull forces down the second piece of pie.

"Would you like some more?" asks Mrs. Bonecrusher.

"Ma'am, I'd be fatter than a slaughterhouse pig if I lived here," said Coach Dull. "I'd surely love to go for another piece, but my waistline just couldn't stand it."

Speaking for the first time, Bonecrusher says, "I'll take that piece." Mrs. Bonecrusher cuts her son a slice, he takes it off the plate, and he eats it with his bare hands. Coach Dull smiles. He likes players who eat with their hands. That's a sign of character in football.

Then Coach Dull launches into his speech about education.

"What would you like to do after college?" asks Coach Dull.

"Bonecrusher is interested in physics," said Mrs. Bonecrusher.

Physical education is more like it, thinks Coach Dull.

Coach Dull says, "Why isn't that something, Mrs. Bonecrusher? State U has the best physics department in the state and one of the three best in the country, and the other two schools don't even have football teams. At State U, we have a tremendous academic support system, tutors on call day and night. You want Bonecrusher to go someplace where he could get his degree, don't you?"

Actually, Coach Dull is telling Mrs. Bonecrusher this: Both you and I know that our boy here is an escapee from a special education class. The only way he'll ever get a degree is if there are three people doing the work for him, and we at State U can get it done. We've got a dozen professors in the booster club, and they are driving cars from Sleazy Sam, too. These profs know that football means money and that no one ever paid 20 bucks to go sit in a library, so they take care of kids like Bonecrusher.

"I'm glad you are interested in my son as more than a football player," says Mrs. Bonecrusher.

"When he comes to State U, he isn't just your son, but he's mine, too," says Coach Dull, meaning "The minute Bonecrusher puts on a State U uniform, his butt belongs to me."

They make some more small talk, then Coach Dull asks when Mr. Bonecrusher will be home from his job of loading sacks at Hick's Feed & Seed. Mrs. Bonecrusher says six o'clock, and Coach Dull says that a "friend of the program" will stop buy to visit later that evening.

And that is the end of Coach Dull's recruiting. He walks

out that door scrubbed so clean that you'd think he was Robert Redford. The NCAA will never be able to lay a finger on him.

But this is only the start of the recruiting process for Bonecrusher.

The infamous "friend of the program" is a guy like Sleazy Sam. He talks to Bonecrusher's old man, and they cut the deal. It could be a car, it could be a large amount of money in small bills, or it could be a job for Mr. Bonecrusher at Sleazy Sam's lot.

Coach Dull knows that the key to any program is to be surrounded by alumni and boosters who are tremendous salesmen. The boosters love this work. They feel like they are both talent scouts and spies. They like to look at the field and know that they bought Bonecrusher for State U.

In fact, Sleazy Sam thinks he discovered Bonecrusher. One day Sam called Coach Dull, and they had this conversation:

SAM: "Coach, I think I found us a big one."

COACH DULL: "Who's that?"

SAM: "Boy's name is Bonecrusher."

COACH DULL: "Really."

SAM: "I hear he eats with his hands."

COACH DULL: "Is that right?"

SAM: "I saw him out in a field near Lyons. He was riding a tractor, then something went wrong. He got off the tractor, tried to look under one of the tires. He couldn't see, so he lifted up the whole damn tractor and pointed to something on the ground."

COACH DULL: "I'm sure you know the family."

That means Sleazy Sam ought to get to know the family. Of course, Coach Dull has been aware of Bonecrusher's activities with a tractor for years, but he was just waiting for a booster to come forth and offer to "be a friend of the program."

In college the key to winning is recruiting, and recruiting is selling and con job. The deals are cut. When Bonecrusher signs with Coach Dull, Bonecrusher's old man finally gets the hell out of Hick's Feed & Seed and gets a real job at Sleazy Sam's used-car lot. And when Bonecrusher is at State U, he comes to the realization that Coach Dull is exploiting and taking care of him at the same time. Coach Dull is asking Bonecrusher to risk his body, but at the same time he is making sure that after Bonecrusher's four years are up he gets a job hawking cars for Sleazy Sam. All of this is predicated upon Bonecrusher's keeping his mouth shut and doing what Coach Dull tells him, no matter how stupid or dangerous. And that is how college football really works.

# 5
# TRASH SPORTS

I want you to know that I like sports. Hey, I love sports. No one has spent more hours of his life talking about sports than Pete Franklin. I just had some fun with college football and those wonderful folks, the boosters. But I can honestly say that one of the great pleasures in life is to go to a place like Columbus, Ohio, on an autumn Saturday afternoon. The grass is a brilliant green, the leaves are brown, and the weather is just right. Sweater weather. I don't care how modern and sophisticated we're supposed to be—nothing looks better than a college football cheerleader in a short skirt and a letter sweater. There is something about the fall. I like walking down a street and seeing little kids jumping into piles of leaves in the front yard. I like talking about Ohio State's prospects of beating Michigan (they're usually not very good) or debating the merits of Joe Paterno. Even my wife likes college football. Not the game, the bands, but that counts for something.

What I'm trying to tell you is that I really love sports. I want you to remember that as you read this chapter.

Why?

Hang on the line with me for a minute.

There are three cardinal rules if you call my show:

1. Don't be boring. If you're boring, you're gonna get a phone slammed in your ear.
2. Don't act like an idiot with me unless you expect to be called an idiot. Dumb is dumb, a moron is a moron, and we'd all be better off if those unsavory characters had to go through life with a sign on their backs saying "Don't talk to me—I'm a bozo."
3. Don't mention indoor soccer.

If you're a sports fan, you are not an indoor soccer fan. If you're a sports fan, you know that indoor soccer just may be the ultimate obscenity. If you're a sports fan, you think the MISL is the name of the latest nuclear defense system, not a professional soccer league.

Indoor soccer is the latest pseudo-sport, a con job designed by some egomaniacal millionaires trying to get inside your wallet. Indoor soccer ranks right up there with bowling, auto racing, horseracing, and all the other trash sports.

Take baseball. Now that's a real sport. I'll talk about baseball.

Football? Great.

Basketball? Wonderful.

Hockey? They've got too many guys named Jacques and Pierre, but I like it anyway.

Boxing is brutal but legitimate. And remember this: we Americans like our sports sort of brutal. Blood and guts rank right up there in our hearts with the red, white, and blue.

Track and swimming on the Olympic level require great skill and a tremendous amount of training. They're real sports even if no one wants to talk about them. Come to think of it, don't ask me about swimming. You spend too much time in the water, and you come out looking like a prune.

With the exception of this chapter, this book is about sports. Real sports. The sports I love.

But now what I plan to do is to tell you what is a sport and what isn't, especially what isn't. Let's start with what may be the worst nonsport:

## INDOOR SOCCER

This is a bastardization of a great game, and a real sport, by the way. I'm talking about soccer. Outdoor soccer. Soccer under the sun, even under the lights, but not under a roof and played on the kind of surface best used for a game of eight-ball.

Anyone who really likes and understands real soccer hates indoor soccer. When a real soccer fan sees an indoor game on television, he can watch it only with a barf bag by his side.

The people (notice I'm not using the word *athletes*) who play indoor soccer are guys who aren't good enough to play outside. They'll deny it. Of course, they also tell you that there's no real difference between the indoor and the outdoor game. Well, if indoor is the same as outdoor soccer, then there's no difference between Raquel Welch and Phyllis Diller. And if that's the case, I want to know who stepped on your glasses.

What they've got playing indoor soccer is a bunch of has-beens and never-weres, guys who couldn't cut it in Europe.

Outside, soccer is a man's game. You gotta run until you drop because there are no substitutions unless a guy has been axe-murdered. Look at it like this:

Outdoor soccer: no wimps need apply.

Indoor soccer: a game for the lame.

The indoor game has this Ping-Pong mentality (and speaking of Ping-Pong, that's another trash sport). In the indoor game they score goals by bouncing the ball off walls. That's right. They bounce the ball off the wall as if it were Larry Bird sinking a 15-footer from the wing. They bank it, for God's sake. This would be like playing baseball with a ray gun instead of a pitcher.

Someone who understands soccer can appreciate the fact that it's hard to score. A goal is a significant and rare event.

The real soccer fan doesn't have to see the ball go into the net every 10 seconds. He likes the ball-handling and the passing, the play in the midfield. He realizes the skill and endurance the game demands.

Real soccer fans take their game seriously. They like to riot and aren't totally against killing each other. Their players are protected by moats. Okay, maybe they're a little too serious, but when they get together for the World Cup, everyone keeps trying to replay World War I. Instead of soldiers, they have their warriors in short pants. Countries in Europe and South America just hate each other, but that's not soccer's fault.

People who watch the indoor game are dumbbells of the first magnitude. They go to the games because they're inside, so the weather won't be too hot or too cold. And there is lots of scoring, so they don't have to bother to learn anything about how the game is supposed to be played.

Indoor fans are the same kind of folks who go for Wrestlemania.

A lot of these indoor soccer players have one name.

Scarface. Headcase. Bellybutton.

They score a goal, then they rip off their shirts, run around the arena, and finally throw the jersey to the fans. If the fans had any sense, they'd throw the shirt right back at the jerk who scored the goal. Can you imagine how those jerseys must stink? Remember, I said indoor soccer players weren't athletes, but I didn't say they don't sweat.

I ask you, what is the difference between Bellybutton throwing his shirt around and Hulk Hogan throwing his opponent around?

What we've done in America with soccer is take the world's most popular sport and totally ruin it. Hooray for Hollywood.

## PING-PONG

I was in China for two years after World War II, and I can attest to the fact that the Chinese are very good at won ton soup and Ping-Pong. I also found out that they don't have any chow mein over there, or even chop suey, which did surprise me a bit. It was sort of like being a person from China and making your first trip to America and discovering there was no such thing as a Big Mac in the States. Well, I'll let someone else ponder those mysteries.

I was stationed in North China, and it was like the North Pole up there. Talk about nothing to do—everyone stays inside and plays Ping-Pong, even the GIs. Once in a while, you might wander outside and look for a panda, but you never find one. You just end up coming back inside and playing more Ping-Pong.

I will say this for Ping-Pong: it's fun. The ball is real small, and it's hollow, so even if you get hit in the noggin with it, it won't hurt. The paddle is light and easy to handle. There's strategy. You can stand near the table or away from the table. You can hit the ball hard or soft. You can play it with a woman or a man, and either way it's socially acceptable. You can set up a table in your basement, and it won't cost you a lot of bread. It's a good game for everyone, but so is checkers, and that doesn't make either activity a sport.

There are three things I remember about my stay in China:

1. I never saw a panda.
2. Chinese really like to eat steak with a fried egg on it. They eat the egg like we eat french fries.
3. The Chinese know how to kick butt around a Ping-Pong table.

## WATER POLO

If water polo is such a terrific game, I want you to name the 10 best water polo players ever. All right, how about the five best? Okay, I'll let you off the hook if you can name just one.

All I hear is silence.

The defense rests.

## BOWLING

Bowling is great because everyone can do it. Uncle Louie bowls. Aunt Millie bowls. They have their own leagues, and they have dime jackpots, and they all get to go out and buy those team shirts with a little bowling pin dressed up like a penguin on the front pocket and an inspirational message such as "Eat at Joe's" in big letters on the back. It's sort of like an extension of Little League. But instead of the parents watching their kids mess up, the kids come along and make fun of the old man when he rolls a 123.

I have nothing against bowling because it serves a purpose and preserves marriages. If you like your wife, you can bowl with her. If you don't like your wife, you can go out bowling with the boys and let her stay home, put curlers in her hair, and watch "Dynasty." And what makes it even better is that if the wife is sick of your face she can let you sit at home and watch ESPN while she goes bowling with the girls.

They even have bowling on television. Professional bowling—the PBA, which I always thought stood for Potbellied Bowlers Association until Chris Shenkel set me straight. Actually, the best thing about professional bowling on television is that it gives Chris Shenkel a place to work, and Lord knows he needs one.

No one would call bowlers athletes. I mean no one of sound mind and body. How can you call Uncle Louie an athlete? He's 62, wears bifocals, and has a 56-inch waist. He's the typical guy in a bowling league, where they all think they're getting great exercise because they lift the ball.

Another thing about bowling—the sponsors are always beer companies. That's what makes bowling a great game. You can get smashed and still do it. As long as someone points you and the ball in the right direction, you won't cause any harm.

Did you ever see a guy pour a can of beer down his throat and then walk up the plate against Goose Gossage?

But that's bowling, which is another name for a gin mill.

People all over the world go to bars. In Ireland they go to the pubs in the morning and they're drunk by noon, but they're still drinking at sunset. No one says anything. It's acceptable behavior. Bowling is sort of the son of the pubs, where folks went to get smashed and play darts. The Dutch came to Manhattan, and they brought this great game of bowling with them. Then the American entrepreneurs took over and thought, Why don't we put together the idea of bowling and drinking? We'll put it indoors so you can do it all year, all day and night, which is very good for business.

Bowling is three things:

1. A place to get away from the wife.
2. An excuse to buy a silly shirt with a penguin on the pocket.
3. A place to get bombed and tell everyone you're getting your exercise.

## BULLFIGHTING

I'll say one thing for bullfighting: Uncle Louie and Aunt Millie don't do it. And I ask you this: Did you ever see a bullfighter who wasn't sweating?

If you had to wear one of those costumes, you'd sweat, too. I mean, the poor guy's crotch is wrapped so tight in there that it's surprising his voice doesn't rise about 47 octaves.

A lot of people like bullfighting. Some of these people are even somewhat sane, such as Ernest Hemingway. But it comes down to the fact that people are fascinated with death, and when you mess around with a bull, you can wind up waving around his ears to the cheering crowd, or you can end up with a couple of horns where your digestive track used to be. What really captures people's imagination is how the guy uses the cape. A really good bullfighter gets the bull to charge very close to his body, and everyone in the stands is wondering if the guy is going to get gored between the legs. Now that's real drama.

The one I feel for is the bull. That's because no matter what happens, the bull always loses.

The bull is never allowed to fight twice, because the bull supposedly remembers all the tricks the bullfighter played on him, and he's not about to fall for the same schlock act again. So they take this poor animal that they haven't fed all week, and they let him loose and tell him to get the guy in the tight pants.

If the bull gets the guy, they kill the bull.

If the guy gets the bull, the bull is dead, too.

No matter what happens, the bull dies. Somehow, this doesn't strike me as sporting. I mean, if you beat the guy, you ought to be able to live. And when the bull is down, they whale away on him, sticking spears into him and whatnot, then the guy cuts off the bull's ears and tail, and he gives them to his girlfriend, which is reason enough not to date a bullfighter.

I really don't have a lot of respect for a bullfighter. Who can respect a nut?

In the movies, it's always Anthony Quinn playing the bullfighter. He wears one of those hats that look like a leftover from the Mickey Mouse Club. He does a lot of staring, as if he's pondering life and death, violence, and truth. But in reality, bullfighters are nothing but pock-faced kids from the barrios who want to make some coin so they can get the good-looking broads and never have to go home to their shacks again.

For the most part, being a bullfighter is a good gig so long as you don't have to fight a bull. You're pretty well paid. They throw roses at you. Good-looking ladies like you. Rich guys buy you drinks, and you get to wear a lot of silk.

I guess that's why they have all these lamebrains in Pamplona. These kids all want to be bullfighters, and about 10,000 of them take to the streets every year so they can fool around with the bulls. Instead, you get a lot of teenagers running from these 3,000-pound monsters while "Wide World of Sports" films the whole thing. Getting it from a bull really is the agony of defeat, wouldn't you say?

## AUTO RACING

This is another place people go hoping to see someone die.

I keep trying to figure out the appeal of racing, other than the obvious specter of death. I don't underestimate that aspect, either. Why else would people stand in the street for hours waiting to see if some confused psycho will or won't jump off the roof of a skyscraper?

Okay, so people like the fact that an auto race is an event where a driver could turn into a french fry with one bad turn.

But what about the rest of it? What about the gasoline?

Go to any track and the joint stinks. It's like these guys all work at a filling station, and they kept missing the tank and ended up pouring ethyl all over their pants.

After the race, the poor slob driver is a stinking mess. He has been in the car for 12 hours, and in one of those cars the temperature is about 190. He's worried about running into a wall. He's worried about the clown in front of him, the clown behind him, and the clowns in his own pit. Will they remember all the lug nuts when they change the tires? If not, he's going to end up looking like a cheeseburger. He can't help thinking of all the times he has seen some Chevy go up in flames. All the guys run out of the pits with fire extinguishers and pull the driver out of the car, and he looks like a flaming shish kebab.

So what have we got? Drama? Tension? Death? Grease? STP stickers?

To the winner goes the bimbo. Think I'm kidding? Remember that our hero smells bad enough to make a railroad spike wilt. You like the scent of Valvoline? Well, the bimbos must because they run to our hero, throw their arms around him, give him a big kiss, and end up with grease all over their pretty little faces. They have official titles like Winston Cup Girls. That's good. Everyone should have an official title.

For the most part, racing is boring. It's hours and hours of around and around and around. Walk into the middle of a race and you have no idea who's ahead or behind. It's just a bunch of cars going in a circle, making so much noise it's as if you have an exhaust pipe directly attached to your ear. People go to sleep, telling the guy next to them to wake them up when there's a "real good wreck."

In the pits, they time the guys changing the tires and putting in more gasoline. What would you rather watch? Four rednecks change a tire or Sandy Koufax throw a no-hitter?

Races are nothing more than a redneck version of Woodstock. Our dear friends from Alabama, Georgia, and Mississippi get together, eat fried chicken, drink domestic beer, sweat, swear, try to pick up each other's girlfriend, and start fights. These people have the kind of mentality where they think it really means something if you drive a Dodge rather than a Ford.

Burt Reynolds and Elvis Presley made movies about stock-car racing, and that tells you all you really need to know about the subject.

There *is* one amazing aspect of auto racing. I mean, people go to places like Talladega, Alabama, and Indianapolis to watch it. I can understand people *leaving* those places, but to actually go there for a weekend? It must be something in the gas fumes.

Now that I think of it, auto racing and bullfighting have more in common than death. I mentioned all those kids in Pamplona who run through the streets while the bulls chase them. I've got a better idea. Let's put all those kids on the Hollywood Freeway and give them capes. And let's take all the racing fans and put them in cars and let them drive at the kids. This way, everyone (at least those who live) will be happy.

## DOG RACING

If dog racing is such a great sport, name the greatest dog trainer of all time.

## GOLF

Any sport where you ride around in a cart isn't a sport. And any sport where you can walk around and look at the leaves and listen to the birds isn't a sport—it's a walk in the park. Finally, any sport where you wear a little gator on your socks sure as hell isn't a sport.

The main thing about golf is that it's accepted. The country club is where business often is done, contacts are made. It's part of the American ideology: the better country club you belong to, the better person you are. The closer you live to a golf course, the more your house is worth. So what if golf balls keep coming through your windows?

Golf used to be a sport where you had to be at least an executive vice president of something to play. Country clubs have always been some of the most understanding and compassionate organizations. They never met a millionaire they didn't like, so long as the money was made before 1925.

Golfers are very boring people. They like to replay their rounds. "On 17, I drove into the rough, then I took out a 5-iron, and I got back to the middle of the fairway, but I had a bad lie. Then I went in to the sand trap on the left, chipped onto the green, and six-putted."

Who wants to hear that crap? I sure as hell don't want to put it on the radio.

When he first started playing big-time golf, we used to call Jack Nicklaus "Fat Jack." Then he lost some weight, won some tournaments, and got to be the "Golden Bear." Today we have Jack Nicklaus golf balls, Jack Nicklaus golf clubs, Jack Nicklaus golf shirts and sweaters, and even Jack Nicklaus golf courses. Jack gets a buck out of the golfers at every turn.

What really galls me about golf is that they expect the audience to be quiet. You are supposed to watch in rapture as the golfer addresses the ball. After about 15 minutes of staring and aiming, he looks like he might actually hit it. You'd think this guy was about to explain the Theory of Relativity or some other mystery that would change the world. Hey, there is nothing wrong with being quiet in school or when attending a lecture by a Harvard professor. But shutting up for some guy who drives a golf ball?

To think that people actually pay to watch a spoiled country club brat address the ball is mind boggling. Even more so is the fact that they put this junk on television. Sponsors are paying big bucks so that we can hear Pat Summerall whisper that Greg Norman is addressing the ball. This guy is getting some heavy bread to say "Greg Norman can't seem to decide if he wants to use a 5- or a 6-iron."

Basically, golfers have been ripping off the world for a long time, starting back when their rich daddies paid for their lessons at the country club. They have sponsors who pay for their own expenses and in the process give them a free ride. The sponsor is supposed to "clear the golfer's head," so he can just concentrate on playing golf. First of all, there isn't much of anything in these guys' heads. Secondly, why don't minor league baseball players have sponsors so they don't have to worry about trying to live on seven grand a year? But who wants to sponsor some kid playing in Butte, Montana? What glamor is there in that? The sponsor wants his kid to be playing somewhere nice like Pebble Beach; then the sponsor can get a nice vacation and a tax write-off at the same time when he goes to watch his golfer play. No one wants to go to Butte, no matter how great the write-off.

Most of the golf tournaments are played in the Sunbelt, and these cities get the Chamber of Commerce and all the local hotels and restaurants to kick in with freebies, or at least cheapo rates. They get all kinds of "community-minded individuals" to volunteer and do the dirty work of the tournament for free.

I suppose golf on a certain level can be a lot of fun. You get outside and smell the fresh air. It's better than going to a bowling alley, because the lounge is much classier even if you have to pay more to get bombed.

Women play golf, so this is something they can do with their husbands. Or it's something the husbands and wives can do with anyone but the people they are married to. It gives you a lot of options. You get to drive a cart, you hit a ball into a sand trap, you throw a club into the air, and it makes you think you are venting your frustrations in a healthy manner. It also is a game of gentlemen. You keep your own score, which means you can cheat like hell before anyone calls you on it.

I will say this for golfers: they always set the fashion trends. In the old days, they wore the knickers and cabby hats. Now guys in Harlem wear the same kind of hats and it's cool.

When I think about golf, I can't help remembering what that great philosopher Groucho Marx once said: "Any country club that would have me as a member is a country club I'd never join."

## TENNIS

Tennis is one step beyond golf. Uncle Louie and Aunt Millie can also play tennis, but they probably will look very foolish doing so. Ever see a 50-year-old fat guy on the court? It's pretty embarrassing for all concerned. So let's forget Uncle Louie and Aunt Millie.

Tennis is played outside, but they don't let you ride around in a cart, so the game does have that much going for it.

Golf is a game for the rich, but most of the golf fans are pretty boring despite their wealth. Tennis also is for the rich—the obnoxious rich, to be exact. We're talking about the jet-setters. "Oh darling, I just lunched in Paris, then Holden and I took our Cessna, and it was a beastly flight, I'll tell you, and we had to settle for dinner in Madrid. Can you imagine the indignity of that?"

Nobody said being a tennis fan was easy.

And no matter what Blinky and the rest of his lovable crowd tell you, tennis is one giant snoozer. You have two guys hitting a ball back and forth forever and they don't even keep score properly.

What is all this love crap?

You have 15–love, 30–love. Then comes 40–love. Shouldn't it be 45–love? Don't they keep increasing the points by 15? So why go from 15 to 30 to 40? Probably because guys like Blinky can't count.

And what does love have to do with tennis? No one has an answer for that.

Like golf, you have to be quiet if you're watching tennis. Is this DaVinci painting or Mozart unveiling his newest symphony? No, it's Chrissie Evert's ex-husband serving the ball into the net. Or it's McEnroe or Jimmy Connors calling a line judge everything but a human being.

Women are a big deal in tennis. Of course, some of them, such as Dr. Renee Richards, used to be guys, but I'll leave that subject to Gore Vidal. But if you notice, a lot of the women playing professional tennis are . . . how shall we put it . . . well put together. In the sense that Mean Joe Greene is well put together. What the hell, we're talking about big broads, women you wouldn't want to arm wrestle with.

But what about the male tennis players?

Let me ask you this: If you have to spend an hour in a room with John McEnroe or Ollie the Orangutan, whom would you pick? I say give me a bunch of bananas and Ollie and we'll pass the time eating. That way we wouldn't have to hear each other talk. Give McEnroe a banana, and he'd complain that it was too green or not green enough or that he doesn't like bananas. McEnroe is the typical tennis player—an odious, whining wimp. He has shamed America in all parts of the globe. Why send McEnroe to Wimbledon unless you want to film *The Ugly American* in England?

In case you didn't notice, all American tennis players are white, except poor Arthur Ashe, who had a heart attack in his early thirties. If you were Arthur Ashe and you had to spend all this time around guys like McEnroe, you would have had a coronary, too.

And the parties you have to attend. What do you say to a numbskull named Blinky, whose biggest setback in life was that he broke a shoelace five years ago? Since then, Mummy solved that problem by making sure he always wears loafers.

In all my years in sports, the most disgusting people I've had to interview have been the tennis players. They are the most arrogant because they have been petted and coddled and wined and dined since they have been in diapers. Remember, even Blinky no longer has to worry about tying his shoes. These people didn't have mothers; they were born in a bowl of caviar. They don't have fathers; they have butlers.

Tennis players are so spoiled that when they hit the ball into the net they don't have to go get it. Some little kid does it for them.

At least in the old days, tennis players used to jump over the net, and that was sort of athletic. But now, they walk around. Next thing you know, they'll be taking a cart from one side of the court to the other. Then it would be the perfect game for Aunt Millie and Uncle Louie.

## VOLLEYBALL

If volleyball is such a great sport, name the 10 best volleyball players ever. How about naming one?

## BILLIARDS

First of all, the real name of the game is *pool.* Second, when I think of pool, I think of Jackie Gleason. Right there, you know it can't be a sport. You think of baseball, and you say Babe Ruth or Sandy Koufax. Basketball, Bill Russell or Magic Johnson. Football, Jim Brown or Walter Payton. You think of real athletes. But when you think of pool, it's an actor, not an athlete, that comes to mind.

Most of the guys playing sports are not exactly wonderful people. They tend to come from the wrong side of the tracks, and they usually spent most of their time in school asleep. But they at least went to school . . . sort of—enough to stay eligible so they could play ball.

But pool is a game for dropouts and social outcasts. Walk into any pool hall, and the teenagers you see there are members of the Future Felons of America Club. These guys want to grow up to be Al Capone.

Before they even let you pick up a stick, they check you for a tattoo. One that says "Mom" may be old-fashioned, but it's still acceptable. A Marine Corps insignia is good, even if you were never in the Marines or you were such a degenerate that the Marines threw you out. And as a former Marine, I can tell you that you've got to be really a walking definition of sleaze to get the boot from those guys.

My favorite tattoo for a pool player is a girl on the guy's arm. Then the guy makes a muscle and the girl dances. It's very clever.

So once you've got a tattoo you're on your way. You aren't supposed to wear a tie in the pool hall, but if you must, it isn't supposed to be knotted. It should just sort of hang around your neck. You also have to smoke, and you should watch some Humphrey Bogart movies for background. Bogie really knew how to dangle a cigarette from the corner of his mouth. He also was an expert at putting the cigarette right at the corner of the table so that it looked like it would roll off, but it never did. I mean, you can't have your cigarette fall on the floor, because then you go from being Bogie to being Woody Allen.

The guys running pool halls are always fat, and they usually have a midget helper. Then there's a bookie hanging around, answering the phone and writing down numbers on the back of an envelope. In the movies they make about pool, the girls sitting by the table always look great. In real life, their faces are enough to cause the Great Wall of China to crumble. I mean these are tough broads, broads who haven't just been around the block, but have been around the block with the Fifth Infantry. That's why gangsters always start out in pool halls, but then they graduate to more tolerable forms of behavior such as manslaughter and armed robbery. If pool halls are so great, why do the thugs always grow up and leave?

There is such a thing as billiards, and James Bond is the guy who plays it. Billiards is played in English Men's Clubs. But in our country, we don't have James Bond, and we don't have billiards, we just have pool halls.

One last thing about this great American game.

It's the smoke in the pool halls.

That's what makes this game an art—the ability to see through all that smoke. Firemen make great pool players. So do guys who work near a blast furnace. A pool hall would be a great place to do a public service commercial for emphysema. Some guy walks out of the smoke, gagging, and says, "If I spent five more minutes in there, I would have lost my left lung."

Some people call pool a sport. I call it a waste of time.

## WRESTLING

The only kind of wrestling any self-respecting guy should want to do is with his girlfriend. That makes sense, and it's kind of fun, too.

The real wrestling is done in some small, stinky gym before about 50 relatives and friends. It's played in high school and college, and nobody but the guys on the mats and their girlfriends and parents cares about it.

Go ahead, name the greatest amateur wrestler of all time.

But the wrestling we all know and hate is really the rasslin' we see on television. It comes on after roller derby and before the "PTL Club," which tells you a lot about it.

Rasslin' is the perfect outlet for all the Bubbas and Bubbettes of the World. You've got to believe that the people who like rasslin' never miss an issue of the *National Enquirer.* I can see them now, reading a story under the headline "SIX-YEAR-OLD MOTHER HAS HEADLESS TWINS." Of course, their lips are moving as they read the story, and when they're done they're mad because the story didn't tell them the names of the headless twins.

Basically, Bubba and Bubbette ask for very little out of life, and they get exactly what they ask for. They are content to see a couple of fat broads rolling around in the mud or to see 10 midgets racing around a ring, biting each other. They are life forms of the lowest common denominator, and believe me, there are a lot of Bubbas and Bubbettes out there.

I know it's a frightening prospect, but spend a moment thinking about what these rasslers look like, which is more than Bubba and Bubbette have done. These are guys who flopped on the amateur hour. They have taken bad acting to new and more appalling depths. The key to being a good rassler is to look grotesque. Fat is great, but deformed is better. If your face looks like an unsuccessful experimental skin graft, you've got the look of a star. You've got 500-pound blobs and midgets in black capes who got kicked out of the pool room. To be a great rassler, you've got to wear tight pants so that your stomach hangs over your waistline, all the way down to your knees if possible.

Bubba and Bubbette love rasslin' because Bubba and Bubbette should really walk around wearing a sandwich board that reads "QUICK, SOMEONE GIVE ME A LOBOTOMY." Bubba and Bubbette love the lurid, the social rejects of the world. In rasslers, they finally have found someone more obscene than they are.

In the old days, rasslers would have been the freaks working for Barnum and Bailey, lifting up cars and then, for an encore, eating the hubcaps. When rasslers were young, they were fat kids with pimples, and all the girls hated them, for good reason. They always had chocolate stains on their clothes, and they smelled a bit like cooked cabbage. Since they had nothing better to do, they started lifting weights in between banana splits. So then they got not only fat but also big and ugly.

A number of years ago I spent a week one afternoon in Bakersfield, California. They filmed *The Onion Field* in Bakersfield, and for good reason. If you were there a few hours, you'd want to start shooting people, too. Anyway, I had to meet someone at a gym in Bakersfield, and I went into the wrong one. What I walked into was a rasslin' rehearsal. I refused to call it practice, because these lugs were getting ready for a show, not a game. For 15 minutes I watched, and one fat guy would tell the other, "Now make sure that when you get hit you duck your head down to the left, or else they'll make lasagna outta your nose."

They practiced their grunting, their moaning, and their yelping. They practiced jumping up and down so that the ring made a lot of noise. I understand they have a school for rasslers—Grunting 101, Hand Slamming 102, and Graduate Hair Pulling 403. When you're really good, you learn how to eye-gouge and head-bash.

Did you ever notice how every wrestling show has a champion? They all have one belt, but they want another one. I mean, this sport has more champions than Bubba has broken refrigerators on his front porch. And everyone is undefeated. Finally, the bout always ends on time, right before the commercial. Funny how that happens.

The scary thing is that Bubba and his buddies actually bet on who's going to win. It's like watching the movie *Hoosiers* and betting against Gene Hackman's team.

The other scary aspect is that women really go for rasslin'. I guess that means that for a certain segment of the female population the ideal man is a fat slob. I guess that means there is hope for us all. As for the guys who go for women rasslers, forget it. Why would you want to date a broad who can snap your spine in a dozen pieces?

**How to Tell When Something Isn't a Sport**

1. If you can play it in your basement.
2. If one of the biggest fans is named Blinky.
3. If you have to go to an onion field in Bakersfield to learn how to play.
4. If "love" is part of the score.
5. If you ride in a cart from one place to the next.
6. If you play it at a country club.

# 6
# BOXING

Before I say anything else, I'm telling you that boxing is a sport. Brutal? Yes. Dangerous? Of course it is, knucklehead. (Don't take it personally. *Knucklehead* is just a part of the boxing lexicon that has slipped into our language, which has to do with why boxing is a sport.)

So what's the difference between a boxer and an alligator wrestler or a boxer and a guy who eats a flaming blowtorch?

How about this: boxing is a sport because I say it is.

Not good enough? Well, it ought to be. But I'll be the kind, warm, and understanding person that I usually am and give you another reason—boxing requires great skill, courage, and *athletic ability.* Think about how people describe a boxer:

He's strong.

He has quick hands.

He has great reflexes.

Forget that this chapter is about boxing and suppose that you heard that an athlete is strong, has quick hands and great reflexes. You tell me what sport this guy is playing. Basketball, football, baseball, about anything. I never heard anyone say that a bowler had quick hands, unless he was talking about how the bowler reached for a beer.

I'm not about to tell you that there are great guys in boxing. I mean, some of these people are so X-rated they were kicked out of pool halls for breaking billiard cues over their friend's head. Boxers often come from the dregs of society. They eat raw meat with their bare hands. They spend an inordinate amount of time talking about broken noses and possible brain damage. One of the premier boxing promoters is Don King, who did some time in the can for manslaughter. Only in boxing can Leon Spinks, a guy with more eyes than teeth and more teeth than brains, become a champion. Yet another boxing promoter is Bob Arum, and *Bob Arum went to Harvard.*

So what does that tell you about Bob Arum? Or about Harvard?

Well, it does say that Bob Arum knows where to find the big bucks, so that tells me that he learned something at Harvard.

Boxing cuts through all the class lines. The sport has crept into our language. I remember telling people when I was in the hospital with a heart attack that "I was on the ropes." Two guys in an office argue about something, then they go out and look for a third guy to be the referee. When something unexpected happens, a guy might say that he got caught with his gloves down. Salesmen talk about getting a customer in a room, sticking a pen in his hand, a contract in front of him, and going for the knockout punch. And if the deal is getting dirty, the salesman says he's going in there with his gloves off.

Then there's the classic line from *On the Waterfront.*

"I coulda been a contender," says Marlon Brando.

How many times have we heard people say that? How many times have we thought it? At some point in our lives, we all think we coulda been a contender for something, if only . . .

For better or worse, boxing is a part of us.

Norman Mailer, who has won a Pulitzer Prize for literature, has written a book about boxing.

Joyce Carol Oates, who won a national book award, also has written a book about boxing. Yes, Joyce Carol Oates, for God's sake. I mean, Mailer is a Jewish guy from New York who thinks he can box and has gotten into a few fights, including one with his ex-wife. But Joyce Carol Oates is a middle-aged woman who lives in Windsor, Ontario, and likes to write novels about the angst suffered by teenage girls. Yet, she knocks out 250 pages on boxing.

Then there are the songs from such folks as Paul Simon. I'm not about to make a value judgment about his song, "The Boxer," but they study Paul Simon's lyrics in school as examples of modern poetry, so somebody thinks Paul Simon knows something, and Paul Simon thinks he knows enough about boxing to write a song about it.

I could go on and on, but there's the bell. Besides, I don't want to hit you over the head with it. By now, you should be getting the message.

Boxing is popular because it's legitimate. I'm not talking about the fight game so much as I'm speaking about the boxers. There is no pretense. Two guys get into the ring, and they want to kill each other. People relate to that; they really do. From the beginning of history, we've had two guys in the ring who want to kill each other. In Rome, they called them *gladiators.* Later, they were knights. One guy went into the ring with a sword and a shield; the other guy had a ball and chain or whatever. Skulls were bashed, blood flowed, and the crowd cheered. The emperor watched, and at the end he always gave the thumbs-down signal to the loser. The crowd carried off the poor bastard's body, and everyone went home happy.

Then came progress.

Someone invented the Marquis of Queensberry rules, which simply meant you had to put on a pair of gloves before you punched a guy in the face and made his nose look like lasagna. Now they also have a limit on the number of rounds. In the old days, when men were men and boxers were boxers, and they made no gestures toward being civil, guys like John L. Sullivan fought 99 rounds, and a round didn't end until you knocked a guy down.

So we have reached a point where the gloves are on and the brain deaths not out, but down. In the world of boxing, that is as much progress as you're going to get. But we really don't want to look at our boxers too closely. I mean, why spoil the fun and risk perhaps asking ourselves some tough moral questions? If Sugar Ray Leonard wants to come back and fight with a detached retina and maybe go blind, that's fine as long as there's $50 million in the pot.

Let's face it: we like boxing. We watch it in the arenas, on "Wide World of Sports," on closed-circuit television, even in the movies. Some of us even pay $25 to see a couple of guys who are so old that their punches couldn't dent a piece of cardboard, but once they were somebody. And by God, one thing the American sports fan loves is an athlete who was once somebody. He still is an autograph worth having, a hand worth shaking, even if we don't exactly know what we are supposed to do with him after he has been punched so silly that he doesn't know a right cross from a left jab. But I guess that's okay, since there's always some casino ready to hire him, and considering all the money boxers have been worth to casinos, the boys from Caesar's and the Sands and everywhere else almost have an obligation to give these poor old pugs a check.

And yes, part of the reason we so love boxing is because we can bet on it. In ancient Rome they wagered horses, chariots, and their wives on either the Christians or the lions. Now it's a couple of hundred at the sports book joint, but what really is the difference?

We like boxing not so much for what it is but for the myth.

The idea of fighting your way out of the ghetto remains as alive now as it ever was. All minorities box. At the turn of the century it was the Irish. They ate potatoes, drank Irish whiskey, and beat each other to a pulp. It was great entertainment. Now it's the blacks and the Latins. But what we're really talking about is the dream—the low man on society's totem pole literally fighting to get to the top.

It's the underdog, and Lord knows that America loves the underdog. Just ask Sylvester Stallone.

More movies have been made about boxing than any other sport. Any American actor who has ever been worth a damn has been in a boxing movie. There's *The Golden Boy,* with William Holden, Barbara Stanwyck, Edward G. Robinson, and Humphrey Bogart. How's that for a heavyweight cast? And how's *heavyweight* for another example of boxing being woven into our language?

We've seen these boxing movies a million times. There's some poor, exploited son of a bitch who came up from the wrong side of the tracks. His old man is dead or in a wheelchair. His old lady has 42 kids and 46 part-time jobs. He's a crummy pool player, and the sharks are always getting into his wallet, so he ends up in fights. Then he either joins the army, where he gets discovered by a crooked manager, or goes to the YMCA and starts knocking the hell out of everyone, whereupon he is discovered by a crooked manager. He slugs his way to the top, then loses and finds out he has nothing. The crooked manager has ripped him off, his wife has split, and his hands are so busted up that he can't even start a second career as a concert violinist. By the end of the movie, he spends far too much time talking to himself, and everyone assumes he has brain damage.

In boxing, all the clichés of great literature are there—victory, defeat, love, betrayal, suspense.

That brings me back to Sylvester Stallone, and in case you didn't know it, Sylvester Stallone would not be SYLVESTER STALLONE if it weren't for Chuck Wepner, who was a nice liquor salesman from Bayonne, New Jersey. I have nothing against liquor salesmen, and I have nothing against Bayonne, New Jersey, so long as I never have to go there. I mean, it's just another Jersey dump near the refineries, and it literally stinks. But I won't hold that against Bayonne. After all, at least it has the distinction of being one of America's armpits. In case you are wondering, Gary, Indiana, is the other. And that happens to explain why a lot of boxers also come from Gary. They are willing to kill people to get out of Gary.

But back to Chuck Wepner and Sylvester Stallone.

Chuck had the marvelous nickname of the "Bayonne Bleeder."

Let us pause for a moment here.

Now I really shouldn't have to tell you why they call him the Bayonne Bleeder, should I?

Some boxers hire a cut man to stand in their corner. So suppose Rocky gets busted in the eye, it swells, and he can't see. Here comes the cut man with his trusty razor. He cuts the bruise, the swelling goes down, and Rocky can see. He's bleeding, but he can see, and the fight goes on, which, after all, is the most important thing.

Well, the Bayonne Bleeder doesn't need a cut man in his corner. Instead, he has a doctor on duty whose specialty is tourniquets.

So the Bayonne Bleeder gets a gig with Muhammad Ali, and they stage the thing at the Richfield Coliseum, which is outside of Cleveland. Ali knows this is an easy paycheck, and he knows the Bayonne Bleeder is one helluva fighter for a liquor salesman. So Ali danced a lot, and once in a while he gave the Bleeder an occasion to do his stuff by jabbing Wepner in the eye. It wasn't much of a fight, and the crowd booed, and a few folks even wanted a refund. I suppose some people may have enjoyed watching Ali make this New Jersey salesman stumble around and embarrass himself. A few guys even wrote that it was a racial statement, the oppressed black man getting revenge on the white middle class, and they wasted a lot of ink on how Ali taunted Wepner and made some very nasty faces.

Which brings us to something you also should be aware of—just because someone writes about boxing doesn't mean he knows a damn thing.

But I guess you could say that Ali was telling the white media and white America to go to hell. Why not? It was good for his image.

Well, Stallone knew about Ali and the Bayonne Bleeder, and he saw that this was a good boxing story, as long as you don't let the facts get in the way of the plot.

Instead of the Bayonne Bleeder, we have the Italian Stallion. Instead of New Jersey, we have Philadelphia. Instead of a liquor salesman, our hero is a thumb breaker for the mob, but he is endearing because he's not very good at it. Instead of Ali, we have Carl Weathers, who does a third-rate Ali imitation. Instead of a movie about black pride, it's about white pride because Rocky goes the distance. Say this much for Stallone—he knows more whites buy movie tickets than blacks, and white pride makes for better box office than black pride.

Given all that, admit it—you loved the first Rocky movie. Remember Rocky in the warehouse, punching that slab of meat? Where else but in a boxing movie would you buy a scene like that? Or Burgess Meredith showing Rocky his old, yellow newspaper clipping from when he was fighter back in 1901. Is that great or what? Burt Young as the brother-in-law. Rocky running up and down all those steps, doing one-handed push-ups and running through the garbage in Philadelphia and then capping off the morning of hard training by drinking three raw eggs.

I'm very serious when I say those were terrific scenes, and any sports fan who saw that movie and couldn't get into it is a guy with a tin can for a heart. It's a wonderful, time-tested theme: "I'm really gonna show someone. I got something. I ain't no bum. All I need is a shot, one shot . . . duh, duh, duh."

But that's the thing—most of us want to show someone something. We don't want people to think we're bums. And all we really want is a shot. "Put him in charge of the dairy department and just watch what happens to this story." How many times have we heard someone say that?

For this reason, I like most boxers. Outside the ring, most are gentle people. Simple, but gentle. They can't talk very well, they're on the edge of going broke, and the sharks have been gnawing away at them since they first put on a pair of trunks. But they still have the dream. They still want to buy their mothers a nice house or their fathers a new wheelchair. And guess what? They're still looking for one more shot.

The problem happens when the promoters and other leeches step in. Suddenly, the most important thing isn't what happens in the ring, but what takes place in a lawyer's office.

I'll tell you something about the people who run boxing: they are so sleazy that most of the fights are in Las Vegas, which just so happens to be the gambling and prostitution capital of this country. And get this, they don't even let the fights take place in the actual casinos. Instead, they throw up a tent in the parking lot. You see the parking lot, and you see the tent, and you're not sure if it's a fight or Tammy and Jim Bakker making a comeback.

But we drop a lot of bread to watch these fights from the Caesar's Palace parking lot or wherever, because boxing gives us what we expect. First, there is the element of two guys trying to turn each other's brains into Jell-O. We can identify with that. Next there is the ringside chatter:

"Who do you think is gonna win?"

"The guy's gotta get in there and cream 'im fast, or he's gonna be tap city."

"The guy, he ain't got no right hand. I'm tellin' you, he ain't got no right."

"The guy, all he's got is a right, and it ain't much. But watch 'im. It's right after right after right, and you tell me, what's he really got, you know?"

"The guy that bleeds first is in trouble."

"The guy that bleeds last is in trouble."

"I ain't ever seen a bleeder yet worth a damn."

"Hit 'im once, and he's finished."

"I'll say this much for the guy, he can really take a punch."

That last line is my favorite one—the guy can really take a punch. That's sort of like saying that George Custer could really take a scalping.

Ah, what the hell? It's all hype. There was Muhammad Ali telling us that he was the greatest. Well, he was right—he had the greatest mouth, and good old Muhammad, he too could really take a punch. But when he tried to punch his way out of a paper bag, Ali ended up with broken knuckles. But, hey, he had a good hustle working, so good for him.

Sugar Ray Leonard not only boxes, but he hot-dogs, makes faces, and on the side he even makes television commercials. He is a nice, good-looking kid who can put four words together without saying "you know." Kids and mothers see Leonard on the tube, and they like him because he's so clean-cut. Then comes his fight with Marvin Hagler, and Leonard is calling Marvin all kinds of names. After the fight, Hagler and Leonard embrace as if they had just climbed Mt. Everest together. It's all hype, and it's all show. Muhammad Ali started it, and others have wisely (for their bank account) followed. No one wants to see a fight where the boxers like each other, even if the facts are that boxers generally do like and respect each other.

There is another side of boxing, the racial hatred.

One night I had Larry Holmes and Don King on my show. Holmes was searching around for another guy to knock out for about $5 million. The same night Gerry Cooney was fighting in Alaska, and Cooney knocked out some no-name Eskimo. Holmes and King went crazy as if they had just hit the lottery. That's because they had. Cooney is white, he clubbed an Eskimo, and there is nothing better than to have a black champion defending his title against the Great White Hope. King knew that Cooney was a stiff. Holmes knew that Cooney was a stiff, and if you asked Cooney he'd probably tell you that he's a stiff, but it was a matter of black and white, which equals lots of green in the fight game.

As it turned out, Cooney was a stiff. But the fight made millions, and Cooney didn't die, so everyone was happy.

What bothers me about boxing is that every day it seems to be getting closer and closer to wrestling. Try to name all the boxing champions. Okay, try to name all the classifications. What ever happened to heavyweight, middleweight, lightweight, and so forth? Now we have super-duper cruiser light-middle-kind of heavyweights. We have WBC and all these other alphabet organizations, and all that means is there are more and more thieves, and the criminal element is more entrenched in the game than ever before. Every week we have a new "Ultimate Confrontation." We have another "Fight of the Decade," even "Fight of the Century," or "The Fight to End All Fights."

Boxers retire, they unretire, they announce that they might retire, and then they announce that they're still not sure if they should retire.

It's all nonsense.

Which leads us to the last question about boxing: should it be outlawed?

Of course it should.

Remember, Howard Cosell told us it should be outlawed, so why even bother to ask? After all, Howard watched it for 20 years from ringside. He made his $88 million. He has seen the inhumanity and the corruption up close, and he knows it when he sees it. Then one night he sees the beleaguered Tex Cobb getting his brains turned to Wheat Chex, and Howard screams, "I've had enough. This can't go on any longer."

Actually, what Howard meant was that he had enough in the bank and he didn't need this gig, so now that he's loaded he can make moral statements.

Well, I'll make a moral statement, too. Only I'll speak from the perspective of a guy who lives in the real world.

Boxing should be banned. Guys fight for a few years and end up with mashed potatoes for brains. Once in a while someone dies. But you know what? No one cares. The fighters still want to fight because the bread is good. The fans still want to buy the tickets because we like to see one guy belt another. Hollywood is now making *Rocky 54*, and who knows? Maybe Jackie Collins will be the next broad to try to write about boxing. After all, the fight game always was and always will be pretty good business.

# 7 COLLEGE BASKETBALL

Lester didn't have much going for him. Here's a quick bio:

He lived in Harlem, in the projects near 125th Street. Father? You gotta be kidding. Brothers and sisters? He had lots. Mother? A nice woman from Mississippi who took in ironing and walked around the apartment talking to Jesus as if He were in the next room. She kept the place clean, she fought off the rats with a baseball bat, and she prayed every day that none of her children would be knifed by an addict or end up on drugs. Money? You gotta be kidding. School? Lester's mother knew it was important, and she made sure her children at least went in the direction of the building every morning, but the bottom line was that Lester's mother could barely read and write and feared that her children would end up the same way. Future? In Lester's neighborhood, the future was five minutes from now. After that, no one speculated.

But Lester did have one thing going for him. When he was 11 years old, he was 5′. When he was 12, he was 5′6″. But a year later he was 6′1″, and Lester's mother was praying for more laundry to take in because she needed more money to keep Lester in pants. The Goodwill store didn't charge much, but it didn't give its clothes away for free, either.

By the time Lester was a sophomore in high school, he was 6'7".

In school, he was embarrassed by his height. His clothes never fit and his pants legs ended about in the middle of his calves. His shoes were so tight that he took to cutting open the toes. He hated to talk, because he was afraid he would say something stupid. He went to class, but he didn't pay much attention and always sat in the back, nearest the door. A good day was one where no one shook him down to see if he had a couple of coins in his pocket. The street guys called him Goofy, because that's how he looked and walked. He'd walk down the hall and trip, and the girls laughed at him.

Then Lester found ball.

In his neighborhood, that's all basketball was called. It's just ball. You go out, you play ball, you go to bed, you get up and do it all over again the next day. He spent 10 million hours on the playground practicing his jumper, practicing his hooks, and most of all, practicing his slams. At first he was awkward, but then the game started to come easily. And two other things began to happen to Lester, things that had never happened to him before:

1. He started to win.
2. People started paying attention to him, telling him that he was a great kid because he could take the ball to the rack.

He went out for the high school team and made it. There aren't too many 6'7" sophomores, not even in New York City. The girls stopped laughing. His mother was proud because she went to the games and saw everyone cheering for her son.

He went from being a physical freak, almost a social reject, to a kid who was a candidate to attend virtually any university in the country.

What Lester had become was a big-time college basketball prospect, and no sport nurtures The Dream more than college basketball. Lester's friends started asking him what he would do with the first million he made as a pro. His teachers started giving him better grades, not because Lester was studying more, but because he'd need the grades to go to college, and everyone knew that Lester had a legitimate shot at college.

Lester's mother still talked to Jesus, but she thanked Him for sending her a son who might be 6'10" by his senior year in high school. Lester loved his mother and kept telling her that one day he was going to make enough money to move her the hell out of Harlem and buy her a nice house somewhere safe. Lester's mother talked to her son about the house, about how she always wanted one of those white picket fences like she saw on television. She talked about dishwashers, garbage disposals, and a dryer so she no longer would have to hang the wash on the line that went from one rat-infested building to the next.

Other people also talked to Lester. These were guys who really were too sleazy to be used-car salesmen. They looked like Danny DeVito, and they wanted Lester to play for their AAU summer teams. They talked about getting the best young high school players in New York and taking them to New Orleans, to Vegas, even to the Bahamas for tournaments. They gave Lester tennis shoes, sweat suits, T-shirts, and sometimes they slipped him a few bucks and said, "Go buy yourself an ice cream."

Lester had made his first step into pro ball, and he was only 16. He learned that folks would offer him things because he was 6'7" and he could jam, and Lester also figured out that only a fool didn't take what was there to be taken.

What I'm saying is that all the clichés about the kid trying to run-and-gun until he's out of the ghetto are true. You can tell Lester and his friends how the odds are against them, how even if they go to a big-name college they won't be pros. You can talk about knee injuries and other acts of God. You can talk forever, but all Lester knew was that he loved his mother, and now his mother was talking to Jesus about the new house Lester would buy her and that the only way Lester could make that happen for her was through ball. Once in a while a kid does get out of Harlem and makes a name (and a few million) for himself. He ends up on television, and everyone on the playground knows the story. It's the same attitude that causes people in Lester's neighborhood to play the numbers or buy a lottery ticket every day. They are convinced that their ship will come in. They each believe that they are the one person in that hellhole who will make it over the wall.

Lester thought that he might be the one-in-a-million shot. And basketball had done a few good things for Lester:

1. It kept him from getting hit on the head. For the most part, the thugs go easy on the players.
2. It kept him out of heavy dope. He may have blown some weed with a few guys after a game on the playground, but he stayed away from the hard stuff.
3. It got him free meals, clothes, and shoes from the so-called coaches, recruiters, and high school talent scouts.

By his junior year everyone knew about Lester. Guys were coming out of every sewer and subway station you could imagine. The guy might have been an assistant coach at Lester's high school. Or maybe he was a coach on one of Lester's summer teams, or he could just be a leech from the neighborhood. But this guy started telling Lester and his mother that Lester needed a father figure. He said he could supply Lester with a positive male role model and that he could "take care of the boy and protect him from those recruiting sharks."

What this guy really wanted to do was take a cut of Lester's talent. He wanted to be an auctioneer, to sell the kid to the college that made the best offer, and all the while he wanted to "make sure that Lester does what is in his best interest."

At this point, the crapola was really starting to stink.

We're going to give Lester and his mother a little credit. Let's just say that Lester's mother consulted with Jesus, and Jesus told her that she should give this leech the boot and forget all the garbage about male role models. So the leech was gone, but this was the first of many guys who would try to get their claws into Lester's back and ride with him wherever he was going.

Think I'm pushing it?

Then you don't know the real world of college basketball. These kids are recruited just about from the crib. Hell, Bobby Knight went to scout a 13-year-old kid named Damon Bailey, and Knight drove back to Bloomington saying that Bailey was better than any of the guards he had. And by the way, one of Knight's guards at Indiana that season was Steve Alford.

There are parasites who run these basketball camps and recruiting services. They supposedly are the connections between the players and the college coaches, and they also have their hands out.

By now the pressure was getting pretty heavy on Lester. He was only a junior, and everyone was either asking where he was going to school or telling him where he should go to school.

Lester's high school coach was a civics teacher who had been in Harlem for seven years. He never made more than 18 grand, and all of a sudden, there was Lester, his glands running wild and standing taller than any player this civics teacher ever had. And the civics teacher's phone was ringing. One day it was Jerry Tarkanian. The next it was Bobby Knight, and after that it was Dean Smith. Of course, all these college coaches were praising the civics teacher, telling him what a great job he had done with Lester and how he was a great teacher and a wonderful handler of youth. Reporters were calling about Lester, and the civics teacher was getting quoted in *The New York Times,* telling the world how he was bringing Lester along. College recruiters started taking this guy to dinner so they could get better access to Lester.

In most cases, the kid and the coach have a decent relationship. The coach often volunteers to "screen" the recruiters and set up Lester's appointments. Of course, the civics teacher then gets a lot of free meals and gets to talk to a lot of other big-shot coaches who wouldn't even know he was alive if it weren't for Lester.

Unfortunately, most high school coaches are good people, but not very good coaches. Their idea of handling a Lester is to tell the other four guys on the court to throw Lester the ball. To their credit, most high school coaches do recognize overwhelming talent when they see it. The question is, how far do they go? How much do they try to cash in?

Because if Lester were a high school All-American, more than a few schools would hire the civics teacher as an assistant coach if he would deliver Lester to that college. And remember, this was a guy who had been teaching in the ghetto for seven years, making 18 grand and praying that no one would slit his tires, or even his throat. It takes a strong person not to take one of these offers and try to ride out of Harlem with Lester.

You don't think this happens?

Kansas hired Ed Manning as an assistant coach because Ed's son was 6'11" Danny Manning. Before he was an assistant coach, Ed Manning was a truck driver.

But in the case of Lester, there were no high-level hijinks such as fathers or high school coaches becoming assistants. In other words, the civics teacher was going to have to wait for his next McDonald's All-American to get the hell out of Harlem.

So that meant Lester would be recruited by "legitimate means."

Now there's a laugh.

Most of the big-time schools have "the black recruiter" or the "black coach." I'm not being racist; I'm just telling you that is exactly what this person is called. He usually is a former player for the coach he now works for. His job is to move through the ghetto, to make the initial contact, and to win over the mother. He also is supposed to dress well and is yet another guy who is supposed to convince the mother that he could be a positive male role in Lester's life. It's the same hustle, only the faces have changed. And what is happening to Lester is that there are about 25 of these positive male role model types parading to his door, representing colleges on both coasts and practically everywhere in between.

The main job of the recruiter is to find out who will make the decision.

Is it Lester?

Is it the mother?

Is it the civics teacher?

Is it some junkie uncle who crawled out of a manhole and now claims to be very close to Lester?

Once that person is identified, the assistant goes to work in that area. You'll hear recruiters say, "I'm into the mother, but I don't know about the kid." All that means is that the recruiter figures he has the mother in his pocket. Or, the opposite is, "I've got the kid wrapped up, but I'm worried about the mother."

After the recruiter does the legwork, the head coach shows up. Remember, you wouldn't go into Lester's neighborhood without a submachine gun. That's because most of the guys in Lester's neighborhood are walking around with submachine guns. When the head coach arrives, and 95 percent of the time he is white, the guys in Lester's neighborhood think one of two things:

1. The stranger is a cop.
2. The stranger is a coach.

Those are the only white guys who go into Lester's part of town. If he is a cop, he better have a lot of friends carrying big guns. If he's a coach that the guys have seen on television, the guys will come up and shake his hand. Remember, the coach is a hero, a savior. Of course, the coach also will hear from all the playground guys about how he ought to forget about Lester and sign them. These kids all think they can play in the NBA and make millions, even if they were cut from their high school team or dropped out of school in the ninth grade.

Even a raving maniac like Bobby Knight is revered by the street players. He is established, he wins, and he's a big name. That's all that counts. Remember, if you win, you're not crazy, and it doesn't matter how many books are written about you or how many hatchet jobs you suffer at the hands of writers and television people. Like a lot of coaches, Knight is paranoid. Everyone is second-guessing guys like Knight, and everyone says he knows more than the coach does. The coach may be paranoid, but he's not deaf. He hears what people are saying about him. When he gets beat, some jerk dumps garbage on his lawn or kills his dog. He knows not to turn his back on too many people for too long. He also knows it doesn't matter if he cracks the whip with his players, if he calls them names they never even heard in their scummy neighborhood, if he makes them work 24 hours a day and run around with bank vaults on their backs, so long as the team wins. Because in college basketball, coaches who win are great educators and humanitarians. So what if Isiah Thomas hated Knight most of the time, and it got so bad that Isiah hit the road for the pros after only two years of college? Knight can use Thomas as an example of The Dream. Isiah came from a terrible neighborhood in Chicago. He signed with Indiana, and the Hoosiers won a national title. Isiah went pro, got his millions, and bought his mother a new house.

That's The Dream, baby, not a degree in sociology.

Recruiting also has become a passion for the fans. They want the best kids to go to their schools. High schools are like farm systems. Fans in Chapel Hill can tell you the name of the best high school players in New York and Chicago. *Sports Illustrated* even prints lists of the top high school players and where they will attend college.

There were coaches showing up at Lester's door and going down on their knees, begging Lester to attend their schools, pleading with Lester that if he didn't sign, the coaches would lose their jobs. Know what? That sometimes happens. How would you like your career hanging on the whim of a 17-year-old kid?

But a smart coach doesn't prostitute himself. Nor does he come in wearing a thousand-dollar silk suit and talking fast. The smart coach dresses nicely, but nothing too expensive. He is polite, but after a few visits he calls the mother "Ma." He talks a lot to the kid, but he makes a point of listening to the mother. If he has kids, he tells the mother about his family. If he doesn't have kids, he should make up some to talk about. The coach has to act like he really cares about the kid and the mother.

And you know what?

Lester's college coach probably will care about him. Because the coach knows what Lester can do for him. It's like buying a good car—you look after it, you make sure it's clean, and you change the oil and always check the motor.

Most kids can tell the real hucksters from the legitimate coaches. Most kids won't be bought outright. If some coach walked into Lester's house with about $15,000 in a suitcase, Lester's mother would probably get frightened and throw the guy out the door. All that cash in one place looks as if the coach robbed a bank.

Factors in why Lester picks a college are as follows:

1. The mother likes the coach and thinks he will keep Lester out of trouble and maybe even teach him something.
2. The school has a lot of games on television, so the mother can watch them. Never underestimate the power of being a regular on ESPN. That's why kids from Los Angeles go to Syracuse. Chalk it up to the Big East Game of the Week and seeing all those people in the Carrier Dome.
3. The school is away from New York. Just about every mother wants her son to go to school away from the city so he can stay out of trouble.

4. The school's basketball reputation. "Man, I want to go to North Carolina because that's where Michael Jordan went."
5. The school can set Lester up with a nice summer job.

The summer job is how the money moves around at most established programs. Lester gets $15 an hour to make sure none of the cars drive away by themselves at Sleazy Sam's Used Cars. Lester also gets to tool around town in the biggest and best car on the lot. And if he doesn't feel like working, he can stay on the payroll as long as he spends that time in the gym working on his jumper or in the weight room bulking up.

Lester's mother naturally was suspicious of all the coaches hanging out at her door, but she also knew that these men were her only hope. She believed that "anywhere is better than here" for Lester. And as messed up as kids often become in college, the mother's instincts are still right. For Lester, anywhere was better than Harlem. So in the end it didn't matter if he picked Indiana, North Carolina, or Louisville, as long as he got out and got one more chance to chase The Dream.

You may have wondered why I picked Lester, a black kid from Harlem, as the prototype high school basketball recruit. If you do, then you're the kind of person who stares at the television set during the Final Four and asks, "Why are all those kids black?"

Okay, why are all the basketball players black? Or at least 90 percent of the basketball players who are worth a damn?

And what ever happened to the white kid from the Midwest? When is there going to be another Larry Bird from French Lick, Indiana? And wasn't *Hoosiers* such a nice movie? There was Gene Hackman as the old, washed-up basketball coach, and he took all those white farm kids and beat that all-black team for the Indiana state championship. There were all those nice panoramic shots of corn fields and Mail Pouch barns and dusty roads. There was that scene where Hackman sits in the kitchen staring out the window at his future star, who is drilling one 20-footer after another, and the kid is playing on a dirt court.

Made for a great movie. So did *Rocky I.* But in real life, and I mean life as we are looking at 1990, five white kids from Hicksville are not going to beat five black kids from Gary for the Indiana state basketball championship, just as a little white guy like Sylvester Stallone is not going to go the distance with a big black guy like Carl Weathers.

In basketball terms, the white kid from the farm is disappearing because the farms are disappearing. The Steve Alfords are going the way of the family farm. This part of America is being foreclosed upon. Every year there are fewer places like Hicksville where high school basketball is a religion. Instead, *The Last Picture Show* becomes just another building waiting for the wrecking ball. Stores shut down, Main Street crumbles, and Hicksville becomes a ghost town.

So there are fewer white basketball players because basketball is no longer entrenched in the white culture. Now it's all Little League baseball because the fathers get to wear uniforms like the kids, and these old men also get to chew tobacco and make fools of themselves screaming at the umpire, who is really just another father who happens to be wearing another uniform. Little League baseball is actually for the parents, and they force their kids to play. Everyone keeps score, and in a town like Hicksville they even put the scores in the paper. Little League coaches get interviewed, and they even have a Little League World Series that is broadcast on national television. We're talking about 10-year-olds on television. What kind of crap is that? I ask you, when was the last time you went by a diamond and saw maybe 15 kids who had gotten together on their own to play baseball? I'm talking about hardball, not softball. Usually, the only time you see a baseball game is when adults are running it.

Basketball is different. It always was and always will be a kid's game, and I don't care how many 40-year-olds you find shooting hook shots at the playground. On the playground, there are no coaches, no officials. If there are any adults, they are still playing. It is a place where the kids make up their own rules and start and end their own fights.

In fact, *playground* is the key word. Because the players go there and just show up. They wear anything they want, play how they want, and make up their own rules. There's winner's out, loser's out, 33, 21, and a million other playground games that have different names and different nuances, depending upon the neighborhood. Basketball is a playground game, and most playgrounds are found in the city.

And who, dear Watson, lives in the city?

Black kids.

At last, we are getting somewhere, making some progress in an attempt to supply an answer for our beleaguered friend who wonders why most big-time basketball players are black.

The first thing you hear is that blacks are stronger, they can jump higher, and they are genetically superior to whites. For the sake of argument, give the white bigot his say. Because the flipside of blacks being these superior physical machines is that they are intellectually inferior to whites . . . sort of God's way of evening out the game, you see. Basketball players are black, but coaches and professors are white. You've heard this drivel for years, so there is no reason to dwell on it.

Why really are most good basketball players black?

It's very simple.

Blacks own basketball because they have made it their game. They spend 10 billion hours on the playground running and sweating their asses off. They are superior because they spend more time at basketball than any other group. They are superior in basketball because they have a fanatical devotion to and love for the game.

Blacks remain subjugated, persecuted, and dumped on because of the color of their skins, and there are no ifs, ands, or buts about it. That's also a part of life as we look at 1990, just as it was a part of life in 1890.

Orientals don't like blacks. Whites don't like blacks. Even Latins don't like blacks. The color of their skin makes it so difficult for them to assimilate into society's mainstream. If you're black and you're living most anywhere from America to New Zealand, you have to be a bit neurotic because you are viewed as a bit of an outcast.

But basketball remains the way out and, for many kids, the only way out. I'm not saying this is good, I'm just saying that this is life in the ghetto. You walk through Lester's neighborhood at 125th Street and you're not going to find many golfers, tennis players, and swimmers, but there are going to be some guys who are hell on the court.

Blacks are better basketball players because of environmental factors, nothing else.

And in no other sport does a coach have such a hammer on his players. If Lester goes to State U and screws up, all the coach has to do is threaten to send Lester home to Harlem, back to the rats, the dopers, and his mother, who will be heartbroken because Lester's getting kicked out of school means there will be no new house. At best, Lester might find a job in a stockroom.

None of this is right or fair. Even if Lester is getting paid by the boosters and has a cushy summer job with Sleazy Sam, he still is a victim. Constantly, he is being told that he has to sacrifice part of his game for the good of the team. Think pass first, shoot second. Think defense, defense, defense. Teamwork. Win, win, win. Sometimes it works for kids like Lester; it makes them better players, rounds out their games. But sometimes they end up giving too much, not shooting enough, and are passed over by the pros.

Then the game and The Dream end for Lester.

That's why the most important decision Lester will make is where he will go to college. That's because the coach can make or break his career.

With that in mind, here's a quick guide to the major college programs:

## MEMPHIS STATE

I would not put this real high on Lester's list unless he had some severe, and I mean very severe, personality and intellectual problems. The former coach, Dana Kirk, got caught paying kids and taking part in high-stakes card games, so they gave him the boot. But believe me, Dana Kirk wasn't the only problem in Memphis. This is a town where they worship Elvis Presley. People flock to his Graceland mansion and his grave as if it were the Holy Land during Easter. As for Elvis, we are talking about some ex–truck driver who made millions by shaking his fanny and wearing pants that must have given him kidney problems. He was the King, but he also was a junkie and a junk-food addict. Remember that Elvis has a shrine because he is the most significant intellectual influence ever to grace Memphis. What else can you expect? The town has a real inferiority complex. Nashville has the Grand Ole Opry, Chattanooga has the Smokey Mountains and Rock City, but all Memphis has is the polluted Mississippi River and 140 percent humidity.

## NORTH CAROLINA

If Lester is one helluva player and the kind of student who never took a knife to a teacher's throat, North Carolina is a good place for him. But Lester had better be a great player, because Dean Smith recruits more high school All-Americans than anyone else. He usually has 8–10 on the team in any given season, which is why a strong case can be made that the Tar Heels usually have more talent than anyone.

As for Dean Smith, this is a guy who has become such a legend that he has a building named after him, and he's still coaching! Smith is an interesting character. A guy from Kansas, a Yankee with a very annoying whiny voice. This man is a superb coach, but he is dull. I mean *DULL.* He is like some poor soul who wanders endlessly through the reference room of the New York Public library looking for a book he knows he'll never find. In between, he thought up the four corners and other stalling tactics, which were some of the more demented things thrust upon the unsuspecting sports fan. But for all his faults, Smith isn't a big-time crook, and his kids do graduate. Besides, who would want to investigate a man who is so boring? Certainly not the NCAA. That's why the rednecks love Dean Smith. Or at least they love him so long as he doesn't lose two in a row or ever lose to North Carolina State.

North Carolina has a strange psychology. Several of the counties are still "dry," yet they have more drunks on the road than anywhere else. The rest of the South likes football, but North Carolina likes basketball. Part of that may stem from the fact that the schools in the deep South—Georgia, Alabama, and the rest—just beat the crap out of North Carolina and the other ACC schools in football. So North Carolina has decided to go the elitist, intellectual route. They do something daring—they ask their athletes to go to class, at least a couple of times a week. They also know that if you want basketball players you had better be prepared to go into Lester's neighborhood. North Carolina has been recruiting heavily in New York since Frank McGuire coached there in the 1950s. Of course, McGuire was an Irishman from New York. The influx of kids like Lester also changed a few attitudes in North Carolina. Until they decided they wanted to win on the court, blacks were needed in North Carolina only to clean up the cafeteria. It was basketball, not the civil rights movement, that changed all that.

As for the boosters, they don't care who is on the floor as long as they win. Of course, many of these people earn their living in the tobacco industry, and they have some real conflict. North Carolina may be the buckle of the Bible Belt on one hand, but its economy is based on poisoning the population. At least basketball takes their minds off such moral questions.

Down the road from Chapel Hill in Raleigh (which is named after a cigarette) is NC State. This is a school that does not feel very good about itself. Everyone says that the other members of the Big Four in the state—Wake Forest, Duke, and North Carolina—are pretty classy. NC State's the Billy Carter of the ACC. It's a good place to throw beer cans, throw parties, and throw up. NC State even won a national championship with Norm Sloan, David Thompson, and

Monte Towe, but then the Wolfpack got thrown on NCAA probation, which told us how they got the players who composed the best team in the country. Sloan is gone, and NC State got smart and hired a New Yorker, Jimmy Valvano, as its coach. But that won't change the fact that Dean is king in North Carolina. Valvano will always be a second-banana to Dean Smith and the Tar Heels.

## KENTUCKY

When I hear Kentucky mentioned, I think of the following:

1. horses
2. bourbon
3. basketball

So what can I tell Lester about Kentucky?

Maybe, if you go there, you'll be a drunk basketball player who likes to gamble?

All right, perhaps that is a bit harsh. But have you ever been to Kentucky? Abe Lincoln was from Kentucky, but he hated to admit it. He'd rather have said he was from Illinois.

What about that great song "My Old Kentucky Home?"

Well, there certainly is an Old Kentucky Home. It's called an outhouse.

In Kentucky the highlight of the year is when everyone goes to Churchill Downs in Louisville for one Saturday afternoon and drinks every drop of bourbon they can find. Over and over again, they sing "My Old Kentucky Home." Then they have the Kentucky Derby, the race is over in two minutes, and that's it. Talk about a lot of singing and drinking over nothing. All I know is that the whole joint smells like booze and horse manure.

They do play basketball in Kentucky, and they have been doing it pretty well for a long time. And they do take it seriously. The late Bear Bryant would have been an expert witness because he had the unfortunate job as the head football coach at Kentucky. That means he got as much respect as the weekend french fry bagger at McDonald's. Nobody in Kentucky cared that Bear was going to be a legend, that his football teams weren't half-bad, or that he had a good nickname. After a few years of being totally ignored and having a budget that was worth about as much as the french fry bagger's salary, Bear hit the road and left Kentucky to the Baron, another guy with a good nickname. And even better for the Baron, he was the basketball coach. Of course, the Baron was Adolph Rupp, who was always old and bald. I'm convinced he was born at the age of 70 and stayed that way.

Too bad that one of the Baron's greatest teams also happened to be guilty of shaving points. But the team was so good that it was not only able to win, but always beat the spot to keep the gamblers happy. Obviously, someone was doing some great coaching, even if the Baron had no idea what was going on.

Joe B. Hall took over for the Baron, and he had the honor of coaching in Adolph Rupp Arena. Joe B. Hall wore glasses, he was overweight, and no matter what he wore he looked like an unmade bed. I suppose Joe B. Hall was a decent guy, a competent coach and all of that, but the Kentucky fans wanted more. Joe B. Hall was too boring, and no one could figure out why he was always called Joe B. Hall. Why not Joseph or just plain Joe? But it was JoeBHall as if it were only one word. And when Joe B. Hall finally quit coaching, no one much cared. He won a national title, but so what? Kentucky fans just didn't like him. Ask the new coach, Eddie Sutton, about working at Kentucky.

I'll say this much for Sutton: he did one thing right. The first time he played Louisville, he beat the corn liquor out of those hicks. If Sutton had not won another game all year, his job would have been safe because he took Denny Crum to the woodshed.

Louisville is the other school in the state of Kentucky that really plays basketball. In fact, Louisville went from being the ugly stepsister to the queen since Denny Crum has won not one national title but two. It wasn't easy for Denny, because he had to win one national title before Kentucky would schedule him.

Crum is building his own legacy at Louisville. He used to be an assistant at UCLA, and he always sat next to John Wooden. Wooden spent a lot more time rolling up his program than he did talking with Denny. But Denny did learn a few things, and he saved up a lot of pep talks and recruiting pitches, and he has put them to good use. He has a pipeline into Camden, New Jersey, which doesn't sound like much to the outside world. But Camden is one of those hotbeds of high school basketball players, and the best always go to Louisville.

Why Louisville?

To get out of Camden, of course.

Camden is right over the Walt Whitman Bridge, across from Philadelphia. Well, Philly ain't much, but Camden is a lot worse. It is like a garbage can that catches all the crap out of Philly. Camden can't help itself. The town just has an odor that causes bumpers to drop off cars. It also has the RCA headquarters, and if you'd grown up all your life in Camden smelling that stink and looking at pictures of that dumb little RCA dog with its head in the Victrola, you'd jump at the chance to go to Louisville or about anywhere else that would have you.

## LOUISIANA STATE

When he applied, the PTL club already had Jim and Tammy Bakker running the show, so Dale Brown wandered down to LSU and became the basketball coach. Louisiana is a bizarre state with all those Cajuns running around. One of the state's biggest heroes, Billy Cannon, went from being a football star to a guy arrested for printing his own money.

Louisiana is filled with bugs and snakes. Even when something good happens there, something bad will come along very soon and make it worse. Louisiana starts with the letter L, and L stands for losers. It doesn't need a government; it needs a warden. In the middle of all these Cajuns and swamps are Jimmy Swaggart and Dale Brown babbling away. Brown once talked about Donner Pass at a Final Four press conference. He once tried to recruit a Russian. He is a nice diversion in a state that really needs something to laugh at. And if you ask me, Lester doesn't need LSU unless no one else will have him.

## UCLA

I don't care what the folks in Westwood try to tell us, basketball at UCLA really started and ended with John Wooden. Sure, Westwood is a nice place, an island of tranquility in that cesspool of smog that is L.A. The kids all have nice suntans, and they drive BMWs or Audis that Daddy bought for them.

John Wooden stayed away from all that just as he steered clear of Sam Gilbert, who may be the most famous (or infamous) booster in college basketball history. Wooden cared about only one thing—basketball. He was a great player and a coach. He had a very simplistic approach to the game. He watched his players and learned. The guys who could shoot he let shoot. The guys who could jump were told to rebound, and the dribblers were told to dribble and pass.

Sounds elementary, but Wooden understood talent, and he kept it under control. His players always played to their strengths. If they didn't, they didn't play at all, because Wooden had another high school All-American sitting on the bench who could take their place. Of course, Wooden had the best talent in the nation, but he probably used that talent as well as anyone could. He wasn't a celebrity or a flimflam man. He didn't care about making commercials or writing a book that hit the best-seller list. All he wanted to do was teach and coach. He believed in getting the biggest and fastest players and letting them play. He didn't need to show off his ego by coming up with junk defenses or telling his players to stall.

Once Wooden retired, the mystique retired with him. It's now a Mickey Mouse program because it is like all the other programs in the country. When UCLA went in to see Lester, they got in line with Vegas, LSU, and Louisville. In the past, Wooden didn't recruit; he drafted. The best players wanted to go to UCLA because they knew that even a backup center like Swen Nater ended up being a first-round NBA draft pick.

As for the coaches who have come after Wooden, those poor bastards don't have much of a chance. Wooden still sits in the stands, watching the game. He may be retired, but he's still Coach. He even has an office in the gym, and he travels all over the country for basketball clinics. Making matters even worse is that Wooden is so classy that he won't second-guess the current UCLA coach, and he has no desire to stab the guy in the back or play power broker to get his own favorite son the coaching job. The guy spends his whole life taking the high road, which makes it impossible not to respect him. You know that whoever is coaching UCLA has nights when he wishes Wooden would just go ahead and die so they could have the funeral and get it over with. As long as he's alive, UCLA will be a graveyard for coaches.

## GEORGETOWN

Georgetown is located in Washington, D.C. which has the highest density of blacks of any city in the country. A strong case also can be made that the Baltimore-Washington area may be the hottest of all the high school basketball hotbeds. Everywhere you go, you see a playground with about eight million kids working on their jumpers.

To me, it's no surprise that so many blacks have migrated to Washington. It's right in the shadow of the White House, and the government offers a lot of civil service jobs and affirmative action programs. In other words, blacks have some sort of a chance of finding work here.

But Washington remains one of the poorer cities. It's an interesting collection of crooked politicians, millionaire bankers, and welfare mothers. But it also is like any other city: it likes to win.

Enter John Thompson.

He was a backup center for the Boston Celtics, who liked to pound people until they quit or were carried off the court. He played under Red Auerbach, and he took a lot of notes. In fact, Thompson should have received a PhD from Red's school of basketball.

When Georgetown was shopping around for a coach, it found Thompson. He is big, black, and tough. He talks about winning and going to class, and his players get the feeling that if they don't do both he'll box their heads until their brains are rhubarb.

Because of his sheer size, the strength of his will and personality, and the proximity to all this high school talent, Thompson single-handedly has built Georgetown into a power and made it a very attractive place for a kid like Lester to go.

## MARYLAND

No one is going to like to hear this, but the only bad thing that happened to Lefty Driesell was that Lenny Bias died.

You hear what I'm saying?

If Bias hadn't overdosed, or at least waited until he got to the Celtics to kill himself, then Lefty would have been off the hook. Hell, everybody would have figured that Lefty did a great job of "handling" Bias at Maryland, and then he got out of line once he went to the pros.

There is something else you should notice. There wasn't exactly a herd of coaches rising up to condemn Lefty about Bias.

Want to know why?

Because they know it could have happened to them.

Drugs are so insidious and so prevalent that the Bias death scares every coach in America. Lefty had very few clues that Bias was snorting up. The kid didn't miss practice, the kid played hard all the time, and he was a star. Everyone heard his name and cheered. On the playgrounds in Washington and Baltimore, little kids pretended they were Lenny Bias and imitated his moves. They dreamed of going to Maryland and playing for Lefty like Bias did.

Hell, everybody was happy with Lefty, Bias, and Maryland. The Terps were selling out at home, selling out on the road, and everyone in the ACC was making big bucks. The NCAA wasn't on Lefty's back, so it seemed that he was running a good program.

Then one night after being drafted by Boston, Bias decided to put about 200 tons of crap up his nose, and he died. Lefty was at the funeral, crying. Everyone was crying and saying what a waste and so on.

Next, Lefty got canned. He was the scapegoat for a system that is predicated on one thing—getting the best players and winning.

Well, Lefty did that.

But Bias died, and Lefty got the sack. Maryland then borrowed a page from Georgetown and hired Ben Wade, a black high school coach from Baltimore Dunbar. To me, it seemed obvious that Maryland hired Wade not because he was the best man available, but because Maryland wanted to placate the black community and defuse the Bias situation.

Of course, Wade deserves a college job. He has had great teams at Dunbar and probably would have been hired for a college job earlier if he had not been black. So this really isn't tokenism. It's just an example of the right move being made for the wrong reasons.

As for Lefty, he will always be tormented by Bias. He will look back at that tragedy and wonder what else he could have done. But the thing to remember is that Lefty was not coaching any differently that year. He treated his players as he always did. Until Bias died, no one talked about Maryland's players not going to class during spring quarter. No one said Lefty wasn't good for his players.

But Lenny Bias died, and someone had to explain the body. Maybe Lefty knew about Bias and dope. Maybe he knew that his players were skipping class. Maybe he knew other things that would clear up this mystery. But we'll never find out, and if Bias had lived for just a few more months and died anywhere but on the Maryland campus, no one would have even cared enough to ask the questions.

## NOTRE DAME

Notre Dame is one of several Catholic schools that would love to have Lester. Priests and coaches at Catholic schools often view themselves as social workers. They'll take the kid from Harlem and work with him, and usually the kid is better off for the attention. Either that or he quits and goes back to the ghetto.

Digger Phelps is the coach at Notre Dame, and he has a great nickname. Only two guys named Digger have ever amounted to anything. The first was a character on the old "Fibber McGee and Molly" radio show, an undertaker named Digger. The second famous Digger is Phelps.

For my taste, Digger is too self-righteous. He goes to all the conventions and tells about all the NCAA rules that are being broken. He can be very sanctimonious. But what the hell? Digger doesn't have to buy kids. He has the entire Catholic Church recruiting for him. There are coaches all over America praying that one day Digger will get caught doing anything. Then those coaches will get together and have a very long and drunken celebration because they know Digger will finally have to can that sanctimonious garbage.

As a coach, all I can say is that most of Digger's players are better in the pros than they were at Notre Dame. That's because Digger has the genius complex. It isn't enough for him to have more talent than the other guy and just let his kids play. He has to go out there and outsmart the other coach, too. So that means stalling, junk defenses, and all the other signs of coaching egotism.

There are worse places for Lester than Notre Dame, but there are better ones, too. At least as long as Digger is there, handcuffing his players.

## KNIGHT vs. TARK THE SHARK

When many people talk about college basketball, they expose themselves for what they are—dumb sports fans. Well-meaning sports fans, but still dumb. And one of Pete

Franklin's credos is that dumb is dumb, and when something or someone is dumb, I say so.

Which brings me to the people who think that Bobby Knight is the white knight of college basketball, just because he has never been investigated by the NCAA. And it also brings me to Jerry Tarkanian, who is supposed to be college basketball's Darth Vader just because he can't write a recruiting letter without the NCAA looking over his shoulder.

This debate came to a head during the 1987 Final Four, when Indiana faced Nevada–Las Vegas in the semifinals.

For Knight, it was a religious crusade.

Knight did compliment Tarkanian as a coach. Of course, he thanked Tarkanian for telling him to sign a junior college kid named Dean Garrett, who became Indiana's starting center. And yes, Knight went on and on about all the respect he had for the Las Vegas program and how Tarkanian's kids played so hard.

But he still loathed the idea that Tarkanian's team was in the Final Four. And down deep, Knight had to believe that Tarkanian cheats. What the hell? Knight believes that just about everyone cheats but him and his university. And making it worse for Knight was the fact that Las Vegas played as hard on defense as Indiana did.

This game was a wonderful microcosm of the college game.

There was Tarkanian, whose act is to win in a town where losing is what it is all about. Vegas sells losing because it wants everyone on the street to walk into a casino and get cleaned out.

Tarkanian started his college coaching career in junior colleges, where he dragged kids off the streets of Los Angeles, got them to play a little ball and stay out of trouble. Then he went to Long Beach State, which never had won a damn thing until Tark got there. Then Long Beach is in the Top 20 and even starting to make John Wooden and UCLA a little nervous. Tarkanian takes the Vegas job, the NCAA slaps Long Beach on probation, and suddenly Vegas comes out of nowhere to become a national power. That brought the

NCAA to Tarkanian's door and another probation. Only this time, Tarkanian took the NCAA to court and won, showing that the NCAA was harassing him.

There are several problems with Tarkanian.

First, it is where he has coached. He is a man who has been under constant investigation in a city that's always under investigation.

Second, Tark looks like he should be a pit boss at the Dunes. His hair is gone, his face is sadder than a basset hound's, and he's sucking on a towel. This is the picture of a guy who lost his last nickel in a slot machine by the door of the Quickie Food Mart on Freemont Street.

Third, Tarkanian takes kids no one else will touch, and he basically keeps them straight. He's sort of like Al Davis with the Los Angeles Raiders. He takes transfers, junior college kids, you name it. He relishes the Father Flanagan role.

Tarkanian was born in Euclid, Ohio, which is a suburb of Cleveland, but he really grew up on the West Coast.

Knight is from Orrville, Ohio, about 40 miles from Cleveland. Rural Ohio and rural Indiana are about the same, which is why Knight is so comfortable in Bloomington.

While Las Vegas has casinos and 100-foot neon signs, Bloomington has silos and barns that say "See Rock City" on the roof. While Vegas is a town of endless entertainment, in Bloomington basketball is first, second, and third on everyone's list in conversation. High school teams sell out, and why not? What else is there to do down in Indiana? People slop hogs and pray the bankruptcy court doesn't take their farms.

Las Vegas loves Tarkanian because he looks the way the people feel—so sad, as if they were broke.

Indiana loves Knight because he acts the way they feel—angry, kicking up a fuss, wanting to grab the world by the collar and try to shake some sense into its head.

Indiana remains an idealistic state. It's the white kid shooting his jumper at a basket nailed up on the barn. The kid can't run, but he knows how to set a pick, and baby, he can really bury the shot.

Las Vegas is jaded. It knows the evils of the real world because so many of those sins are found right on the strip. The Vegas players are like Lester. They have had a knife at their throats from the moment they were born. They are trying to avoid the last cut, trying to hustle out an existence when the odds are stacked against them. For these players, basketball was asphalt and a bent rim at the playground. The Indiana kids played H-O-R-S-E and all these other solitary shooting games. The Vegas kids came from playgrounds where it was winner's out and 50 other kids were waiting on the side to get into the game. The Indiana kids smelled manure; the Vegas kids sniffed the fumes from passing buses and cabs.

So there are the contrasts.

Ironically, Tarkanian and Knight both understand basketball. The way to win is to get your kids to play defense. I don't care if Vegas scores 100 points a night; it wins because Tark's kids keep their butts low to the ground and their arms out wide and stick their noses right in the face of the guy with the ball. They know the meaning of man-to-man defense.

In basketball, the way you control the game is by defense. A good coach has to sell that to his kids. And you play better defense by getting kids who not only are bigger, stronger, and faster than their opponents but who are more maniacal. Knight loves to get a kid who has been a star since he was 10, a kid like Steve Alford, who was worshiped by the entire state of Indiana before he even got to college. Knight looks at Alford and thinks, "If I can get this snot-nosed prima donna to scrub the floor and play defense, then everybody else will do it. And the kid will still score his 20 points for me." Knight can get away with dumping on Alford because Knight is a legend, and part of that legend is that Knight dumps on everyone. Knight's relationship with Alford was like Vince Lombardi and Bart Starr with the old Green Bay Packers. Lombardi screamed and yelled and did his lunatic bit while Starr was cool, collected, and intelligent. He took Lombardi's crap, and his hair never even got out of place. Alford and

Knight got along the same way. No matter how much crap or how often Knight threw Alford out of practice because the kid wouldn't play defense, Alford never cracked, and he always came back for more. Like Starr, he knew that the coach is the general and he's the soldier.

Knight and Tarkanian never worry about scoring enough points. They know that their kids have been trained to score; all they ever thought about doing was scoring, and they will always score. For these kids, putting the ball in the basket is the same as breathing. Both of these coaches know that defense is effort and determination. Assuming you have the same natural talent as the other kids playing big-time basketball, a player can be a good defender if he simply wants to. But playing defense is no fun. You don't get to see the ball go into the basket and the points go up on the scoreboard. The team rewards are great, but the individual rewards are few.

Tarkanian does this through love. He puts his arms around the kids. He cons them into thinking that defense is fun, that defense is almost, and I say *almost,* as good as putting the ball in the basket. And the bottom line is that if Tark can't get his kids to play defense, they don't play at all. But his style is the gentle hand and the kind word.

Knight prefers the sledgehammer to the side of the head. He made his reputation as a task master, a dictator, a whip-cracker. But as a player Knight was a shooting guard who was terrible on defense. He couldn't guard a fire hydrant. So when he yells at his players for not playing defense, it is like the father who jumps on his kids for having a sloppy room and then sits down, takes off his socks, and throws them in the middle of the floor.

As a player Knight was fortunate to be coached by Fred Taylor, who was fortunate to have stars such as Jerry Lucas and John Havlicek. Knight didn't start, but he supposedly learned the game from sitting on the bench next to Fred Taylor. When Knight graduated, Taylor set him up with a job coaching at Army. This was a perfect meeting of the minds. Knight's players were as batty and as single-minded as their coach.

At Army, Knight was able to perfect his vision of the game. Remember, to Knight, basketball is war. It's shoot first and ask questions later. Everything is winning and finishing first. There is no such thing as a nice try or a moral victory. There is only total victory. In fact, many victories aren't good enough for Knight, who often equates them with losses. Knight loves to talk military history. He worships Patton. The fact that Knight has never been in the service does not alter his self-image as a general, a leader in war, and each basketball game is a battle.

So Knight throws chairs. He swears, he grabs kids, and shakes them. He is obscene, vile, and odious. He pouts, he throws tantrums and fits. He is like a little kid who always wants attention. But he also knows that as long as he wins he can be as vile as he wants, and they'll never throw him off center stage.

Knight's entire identity is tied up in his teams. He seems to measure his self-worth by how his team played in its last game. He has nothing but basketball going for him, and he thinks about nothing but winning. He may even say that there is more to life than being a coach, but he doesn't believe it. If he had some other interest, another passion, he would not throw himself so completely into basketball. I believe that Knight knows he has little else going for him but basketball. If he loses, there goes his name, his reputation, and everything. There would be no turning back.

A shrink would have a field day with Knight's wardrobe. He walks around in those awful red sweaters, and he folds them up so that his belly sticks out. He is an exhibitionist, a professional rebel. If Knight were in Hollywood, where everyone wears loud, casual clothes, Knight would walk around in gray, three-piece suits and never even loosen his collar. His clothes are Knight's way of spitting in the face of society, of telling us all to go to hell. For Bobby Knight, basketball has become a means for him to act like a disturbed, bratty child. As long as he wins, he'll have his players, the state of Indiana, and everyone else conned. And it doesn't matter how many players he insults or how many chairs he throws. He just has to keep his players thinking as he does—that basketball is everything. That you have to think about it and practice it a million hours a day. That losing is worse than death. When you lose, a part of you has died, a part you'll never get back. People ask if Knight is heading to the edge. Heading to it? This guy is so far over, he'll never see it again.

*Season on the Brink* was a great title for John Feinstein's fine book about Knight. On the brink of what I'm not sure. Like many great coaches, he's already bananas.

And in his own way, Tarkanian's tunnel vision equals Knight's. At Long Beach, Tark was introduced at a Booster Club meeting as a man who "didn't know there was a war in Vietnam but a man who can find the best forwards in the country."

The fact is that most coaches and sports executives are limited people. They like to talk about sports and that's it.

But we don't care. The American sports fan is fascinated with guys like Bobby Knight. Knight is the Vince Lombardi of our age. When Lombardi died, flags were flown at half-mast. The first best-selling sports book was about Lombardi, Jerry Kramer's *Instant Replay.* The biggest-selling sports book of all time, the only sports book to stay at the top of *The New York Times* best-seller list for months at a time, was Feinstein's account of a season with Bobby Knight. I do not find this coincidental. Americans do not want to be wimps. Americans want to win; they want to kick ass and take names. They like to bully and push. Those are the values Knight represents. He called his 1987 team "the worst I've ever had." This team was something like 18–1 at the time, and it went on to win the national title.

So Knight is like everyone else—he's full of crap.

He used to say that he wouldn't recruit junior college guys or guys who wear gold chains around their necks. But he needed players, so he signed Keith Smart, a junior college kid who liked gold chains. Smart made the basket that won the national title for Knight, so everyone is happy.

Okay, I'll say that by NCAA standards Knight does not

cheat. And by NCAA standards Tarkanian has cheated. So does that mean there was some kind of moral righteousness when Knight beat Tarkanian and went on to win the NCAA title? Hell, Knight even said, "The good guys won," in his press conference after the Indiana–UNLV game in 1987.

Well, believe me, there are no coaches wearing white or black hats in the world of college basketball. Knight was stung by a John Wayne movie in early life, and Tarkanian looks like he was born to suffer. But the point is that they both win, and in America that's all that matters. Just don't try to tell me that one is better than the other, because they are all playing the same game.

# 8
# WHAT ARE BASEBALL PLAYERS REALLY LIKE?

QUESTION: What are baseball players really like?

ANSWER: They are like anyone else.

All right, I'll rephrase that—some baseball players are like anyone else. Some are even worse; a few are better. But for the most part it is far more agreeable to watch a baseball player on the field than share a dinner table with him, unless you don't mind your guest squirting tobacco juice into the coffee cup right before you serve dessert.

Baseball players have great hand-eye coordination. If a fly should appear during your meal with the player, don't worry; if the guy is a good hitter, he should be able to snatch the fly right out of midair and squash it with his hands. If the player is a bit primitive, he might even eat the fly. But he'll probably just wipe his hands on the tablecloth.

Exaggerating, you say?

Perhaps.

But I ask you this: Have you ever been in a big-league clubhouse?

This is a romper room for guys supposedly beyond the age

of reason. It's like when you were a little kid and you had a place to go where you could play with blocks and throw Lincoln Logs around the room. You could pull your friend's hair, call him fatso, and then roll around on the floor.

Actually, the baseball clubhouse is like a graduate school for the kids who were the biggest jerks in kindergarten. In the clubhouse, baseball players:

1. light each other's shoes on fire.
2. tie each other's clothes in knots.
3. throw hot dog buns at each other.
4. put hot stuff in each other's jockstraps.
5. sit on cakes.
6. have belching and farting contests.

As you can see, the clubhouse is a nice place if you have a severe case of arrested adolescence. In fact, even if you're a normal person, it is important that you act like "one of the boys" and nail someone's spiked shoes to the floor. This is like a rite of passage. Acting like a bozo gets you accepted in the clubhouse.

Tobacco chewing and spitting are indigenous to the game, which makes periodontists everywhere very happy. You know that tobacco chewing is solely a product of the environment. No one would actually do it by choice. It is too hideous and simply too messy for someone just to decide that he is going to stick a bunch of tobacco leaves in his mouth and start chewing it as if he were a cow munching on a cud. Players chew tobacco because baseball players have always chewed tobacco. You know that rookies have to be going off somewhere by themselves with a pack of Red Man and a cup so they can practice chewing and spitting. No ball player wants to be in the clubhouse with his friends and throw up the first time he reaches for the Skoal.

Baseball players like chewing tobacco because it gives them a legitimate reason to spit. They can spit on the floor, spit at your shoes, or if they are neat, they can spit into a cup. But the idea is spitting, and what fun it is to spit. It is just like the little kid who first discovers that he can perform this marvelous deed, so he climbs up some stairs and tries to spit at people walking below. But in the clubhouse, ball players spit at reporters and everyone laughs. Most of the time, they just miss the reporter. The idea is to let loose with a stream that makes the reporter jump to get out of the way, causing him to appear graceless and foolish in the process.

Actually, a ball player will tell you that he chews tobacco to relieve the tension. So he has the tobacco in his mouth, and it's rotting his guts and gums. The periodontist is smiling and rubbing his hands with glee. Even the guy who does chemotherapy on jaws is happy. Of course, the undertaker is taking an interest. The entire medical profession must be pleased whenever a player shoves that cancer into his mouth. It's good for business.

I will say that there are fewer bums in baseball today than there used to be. They don't run around quite as much, and they don't drink as much. But they still run around and drink a lot more than the average guy. Also, they have drugs, something those from Babe Ruth's era missed.

There are even "intellectual" ball players. Sportswriters love these guys. They can put two sentences together. They read hardback books instead of paperbacks, Stephen King instead of *The Sporting News.* The intellectual ball player is a guy who watches one soap opera a day instead of three. He can do about half of a crossword puzzle, and can even spell some of the words right. He frightens the guys who spend every free hour in the bar, the chapel meeting, or smoking dope. They think he knows something, and they probably think he knows more than he actually does.

In other words, he has normal intelligence, but in the baseball world that makes him a freak.

The latest group to take hold in the clubhouse is the religious freaks. Now I have nothing against God or going to church. A sincere Christian such as Andre Thornton deserves and receives my utmost respect. That's because Andre Thornton doesn't say it was God's will when he pops up with the bases loaded.

But for the most part the religious freaks are bad for the game. They turn the clubhouse into a revival meeting. You ask them about hitting a curve and they quote Matthew, Mark, Luke, and John instead of Charlie Lau. They won't throw at a player's head unless they think God told them to. The religious freaks don't play hard, they won't get down and dirty and play the rough and tough baseball of the Ty Cobb mold. They spend too much time saving souls instead of saving games.

The Cleveland Indians' Andre Thornton, who is a real Christian, once said, "Who says you can't believe in God and still play hard?" It's a legitimate question, and if you ever saw Thornton deck a second baseman to break up a double play, you know exactly what he is talking about. But as I said, so many of the religious freaks aren't sincere, and they use God as an excuse for a poor performance. If there is one thing no one should accept, it's lame excuses.

So far we have discussed three kinds of players—the blood-and-guts tobacco chewer, the intellectual reading Stephen King, and the religious freak.

But what about the minorities?

Baseball is mostly a white game, and it's getting whiter every year. That's because more and more blacks are being raised in the cities, and basketball is the city game. Drive through New York and try to find a baseball diamond anywhere but in Central Park. But there are playgrounds and hoops on every corner.

The black baseball player likes the money he is making, and he usually likes playing the game. Down deep, most black players know that baseball is a pretty good gig. But these guys seem to be the target for the radicals, who fill their heads with notions that they are slaves and the white baseball establishment is the plantation owner. Over and over, they are told they are exploited and it is time to rebel. A lot of these radicals also offer players drugs to help them cope with being under the owners' thumbs. But the truth today is that the good black player makes as much as anyone, and the owners dump on anyone they can, regardless of race, color, or creed. When it comes to taking advantage of players, the owners are an equal-opportunity exploiter. Most black players ward off the dopers and the radicals. They literally keep their noses clean, and they keep playing. When they retire, they should be set for life.

The Latin baseball player is a much different story.

He was signed when he was 15 and brought to America from the Dominican Republic or somewhere like that. Most rookie leagues are in Florida, which is the easiest place for them to assimilate. But there also are rookie leagues in Montana and upstate New York. Imagine what a 15-year-old from Costa Rica thinks of Butte or Batavia. And think of what the folks in Butte or Batavia think of this kid who doesn't know better than to order a cheeseburger and french fries three times a day.

Like any 15-year-olds who are uprooted from one culture and dropped into another, they are homesick, scared, and suspicious. That's why I am baffled when I hear baseball people ask why all the Latin players hang around together. Well, whom are they supposed to go out with, the tobacco chewers? All those guys will do is laugh when the Latin kid orders a cheeseburger and french fries for the millionth time. As for the black players, their life in Watts or Harlem is as different from the Latin's as the tobacco chewer's background is from El Segundo, California.

So most of the time the Latin player is understandably unhappy. He doesn't know English, and he often assumes that the guys in the clubhouse are making fun of him. And you know what? He often is right. He lives to go home in the off-season and play in the winter leagues. It is only there that he receives the respect and adulation he believes he deserves.

Regardless of his background, baseball players have a strange existence, a lifestyle where they are being paid millions to do the things they did as boys. They catch the ball, they throw the ball, they hit the ball. Then every two weeks they get a check for 10 grand. Consider the incongruity of that. No wonder so many baseball players are maladjusted.

It's surprising that more of them haven't gone Fruit Loops.

Yes, some of them can talk, some of them read, and a few of them can even write more than their autograph. Many, of course, can't.

Steve Carlton is the classic example of a guy who has become famous for not talking. When Carlton finally did speak, we found out he had very little to tell us other than he likes to stick his elbow in a barrel of rice. In the world of baseball, an elbow in a barrel of rice is mystical. The other reason Carlton started to talk was that his career was coming to an end. That happens with a lot of these guys—they want to say hello to the press when it's really time to say good-bye.

Because of its individualistic nature baseball breeds prima donnas. In no other sport is a player's won-loss record so valued as it is for the pitcher. It is almost like the pitcher won or lost 20 games without help from anyone on the team. And hitters sometimes pay far more attention to their batting average than the standings.

I will say that baseball players are under as much pressure as any athletes. They play more games than anyone else, and this means more travel and more opportunities to mess up. It may be a negative way of looking at it, but every time a player takes the field he has just as much chance to fail as he does to succeed. The .300 hitter makes outs in 7 of every 10 at bats. The best pitchers still average nearly one base runner per inning, three runs per game.

On one level, baseball is a very simplistic sport. All the fans have played some form of baseball, even if it was just whiffle ball in the backyard. To play basketball, you have to be a giraffe. To play football, being built like a rhino is a big help. And most Americans have no idea what it takes to play hockey other than a couple of quick fists.

But even little girls play baseball, or at least softball.

The game is nicely centered. It always starts with the pitcher throwing and the hitter having to react to the pitch. It all looks so easy, at least to the fans. So we hear things like this in the stands:

"Why can't that joker on the mound throw a strike? When I was in the fifth grade, I never had control problems."

"Why can't that clown with the bat hit Jack Morris? I played against guys with better stuff in high school."

"How could that guy drop a fly ball? I played baseball for four years at Spitoon College, and I never dropped a fly ball like that."

This fan mentality confuses the ball players. They are the only ones who can truly appreciate how difficult it is to play this simplistic game. They are the only ones who know the true extent of the talent in the majors. The players were the chosen ones, the cleanup hitters and star pitchers in high school, and often the same player filled both roles. If they went to college, they had batting averages higher than the national debt. They have spent their lives throwing, hitting, and catching a baseball, and the last thing they want to hear is how Sheldon Stein was a star at Spitoon College and he would be in the big leagues today if it weren't for his trick knee.

Baseball players have little time for people telling them they could have made it if . . .

That's because baseball players know how hard it is to reach the majors, and they know that the Sheldon Steins never would have gotten through their first month of pro ball in Utica, New York.

To make it in any sport, tunnel vision is a necessity. But the guy who "eats and sleeps" baseball is not exactly a well-rounded individual. Pitchers tend to be the worst because they become obsessed with their arms. A little twinge in the elbow, an ache in the shoulder, and it's over. No million-dollar contract, no trip to Bermuda, no Mercedes—nothing but a lot of time in a doctor's office. So pitchers wake up in the middle of the night and move their arms in a circle to assure themselves that their arms did not fall off when they went to sleep.

The bottom line on baseball players is that they always want something. They aren't sure just what; all they know is that they want more. Another Porsche, another house with

18 rooms instead of 14, another girlfriend, more press clippings, more people telling them that they are the greatest thing since Louisville Slugger made the first baseball bat.

The average baseball player makes about $500,000, and he can stay at that level for 5 to 10 years. But a half million isn't enough. Guys want a million a year. If they make a million, then they want two million. The money ceases to mean anything except to the IRS and the players' accountants. It becomes a moral issue. A player thinks, Fred over there makes $750,000, and I'm better than he is. So why am I getting only $600,000? I'm gonna hold out. This isn't logic, it isn't the real world, and it really isn't sports. It's Looney Tunes, but that's what baseball has become.

In the past, a player looked at his career as one stage of his life. A player would think, If I'm lucky, I'll last 10 years with the Yankees, and then I'll use my name to go into the insurance business. Maybe I'll be able to sock away enough dough to open a used-car lot. But the modern player believes that he should earn enough in a few years in the majors so that he doesn't need to work for the rest of his life. For a lot of these guys, that's exactly what happens. The players will tell you that this is good, the way it should be. I can't blame them for getting all they can—that's the American Dream—but it has changed how baseball players think and play, and the game isn't better for it.

No matter how much money they make, baseball remains what it always has been—theatre. To understand it, you need to know the actors and what roles they are trying to play. Since baseball is the most traditional sport, it is also the most predictable. Knowing what to expect and actually getting it are a part of what makes baseball so popular, but there is more to the game than what you see on the tube or from the bleachers. There is life backstage, life in the dressing room and the boardroom. That's why it is time for Franklin's tour through the typical baseball organization.

## GENERAL MANAGER

In a world that is as political as the Senate, the general

manager is the master of the smoke-filled room. He is a guy who has it made. He has the job he wants. He gets to hire and fire the manager and to suggest strongly that a manager hire a certain coach. Remember, when a general manager strongly suggests anything, that means "*Do it.*" The general manager has only one boss, and that means he needs to con only one guy—the owner. That is why people such as Gabe Paul and Spec Richardson were general managers for years despite records both on the field and on the trade front that were pretty damn lame. The Gabe Pauls know how to handle the owners. The general manger's wife gets to know the owner's wife, and they start playing bridge or golf. The ideal situation for a GM is to find an owner who not only knows little about baseball, but also is aware of his ignorance. Then the GM can put his arm around the money man's shoulder and say, "I know that you've made millions in the shoelace business. Believe me, I respect that. I respect any man who has risen to the zenith of his field, and when people think of the shoelace industry, they think of you. But you also are intelligent enough to recognize that baseball is different from shoelaces. The goals are still the same—to win, to make a profit, and to be the best. With your business acumen and financial resources, I know you'll end up where you want to be with just a little guidance. I can supply that. I've spent a lifetime in the game, and I'll teach you what you need to know."

What does the GM teach the owner?

That no one knows more about baseball than the general manager.

So the smart GM sets himself up as a genius in the eyes of the dumb owner. This way, he can blame all sorts of people for the team's failures—the manager, the players, even the writers—and for a long time the owner will buy it. After all, the general manager has spent a lifetime in the game, and he has been so nice and patient to explain everything that the owner feels a bit of loyalty toward the man.

That's why backslapping and butt kissing are two of the major skills of a baseball general manager. But at the same time there must be a little firmness. Mr. Shoelace is happy just to watch the game from his private box and go to the winter meetings and maybe get to shake Sparky Anderson's hand. Mr. Shoelace knows that he is Mr. Shoelace, and a shrewd general manager will make sure that the owner keeps that lesson in mind. To bring it home, the GM always mentions—just in passing, of course—that he has "spent a lifetime in the game."

Spending a lifetime in the game is supposed to mean that you know something. Sometimes it even means that. But sometimes it just means the GM's greatest talent was to con one owner after another into hiring him.

Traditionally, the GM was a player, even if it wasn't in the majors. But he never was a great player. That is the source of one of baseball's myths—great players never make good managers or general managers.

That's because the guy doing the hiring, the GM who was a can-of-corn utility infielder, needs to maintain another myth—the worse the player, the deeper the understanding of the game. The argument is that if a guy can't play, he has plenty of time to sit on the bench and listen and learn. He also gets the wonderful opportunity to sit next to the manager, who in his day also was a can-of-corn infielder.

The next stop is as a minor league manager. GMs love to hire guys who were terrible players to manage in the minors. After a few years of beating the bushes, these bushers graduate to first base coach, where their main responsibility is to assist the batboy in picking up any batting helmets that were dropped on the ground.

After a few years as a coach, one becomes a manager. After that, he's promoted to the front office and ends up running the team. This seems to be a good system for keeping third-rate talents around so one day they can tell Mr. Shoelace, "I know you went to Harvard, and I know you've made more money than the Hunt family, but baseball is a very intricate business. Believe me, I know, because I've spent a lifetime in the game."

It would seem that most general managers are frustrated players, and often frustrated managers. They hire a guy to manage their team, then they second-guess the poor bastard to death. Former Indians general manager Phil Seghi was hell on managers in this respect. He would sit in the press box and openly question the moves his manager was or wasn't making, right in front of the press. But since the press box is supposed to be like the clubhouse—"What you hear and see here stays here,"—no one ever wrote about it. Besides, Phil was a nice, likable man as long as you weren't his manager.

Gabe Paul and Phil Seghi both loved to say "I hired this guy to manage because he is his own man. He's got guts."

What they really wanted was a guy who had enough guts to go into the clubhouse and tell the players what stupid decision had just been made by the front office and then follow orders. In other words, they wanted a guy who had guts in the dressing room but was a wimp in the boardroom.

Another prerequisite for a general manager is a selective memory. He may have made 50 trades, and more than half were grounds for dismissal. Those are forgotten. But the deals that did work, those are remembered and recalled for writers and owners with relish and in great detail.

Actually, a GM has several balls in the air. The biggest one he can't afford to drop is the owner. He must keep Mr. Shoelace happy. Next, he needs the writers on his side. If the GM and the writers are on good terms, then the writers will blame the manager when things go wrong. This sets the stage for the GM to can the manager, and it buys him good press and more time to keep collecting paychecks from Mr. Shoelace. For this guy, survival is the key. He needs to say "The buck stops here" on one hand while he is passing the buck with the other hand.

In the past, GMs had a lot of personality. People such as Frank Lane, Gabe Paul, and Phil Seghi may not have been very good, but they had a certain entertainment value. But as more conglomerates buy baseball teams, the corporate mentality seeps into the front office. This is breeding a generation of executives who still may have been former players but act more like they have MBAs. They all wear the same dark, boring three-piece suits, and they talk a lot about upsides and downsides. And you know what? They know no more about the game than the lackeys who came before them.

## SCOUTS

Scouts are the last hope for baseball. They are the throwbacks, the prospectors mining for gold. They have lively personalities and awful wardrobes. They wear white shirts and white belts. They wear sportcoats that look like Purina checkerboard squares. They think colors like blue and kelly green match. They smoke cigars that smell like donkey farts. They have either gray hair or no hair. They must have a face that looks like a 25-year-old first baseman's mitt. They must squint so that everyone knows they have spent a lifetime in the sun searching for talent on some dusty diamond in Paris, Texas.

Like the general manager, they were crummy players. They peaked when they hit .280 at Oshkosh and were named to the 3-I League All-Star team. They always have yellow newspaper clippings in their wallets, proving beyond a reasonable doubt that they did indeed hit .280 at Oshkosh, as if someone really gave a damn.

Also like the general manager, the scout needs a selective memory. He has signed 250 prospects, and only 4 have made the majors. Three of those guys were can-of-corn utility infielders who will soon become scouts. The other was a pitcher with a good fastball who blew out his elbow in the middle of his rookie year. They don't like to talk about the fact that they told the GM to draft Willie Weakelbow instead of Eric Davis. Nor do they want to admit that the first time they saw Hank Aaron, they thought he was too small to be a power hitter.

The real skill of being a scout is trying to live on the pittance they pay you. The only people in baseball who collect more generic receipts and know where to find more free meals than the writers are the scouts. It's a rough night when a scout and a writer go out for dinner, because hell will freeze over before either one of them reaches for the bill.

Scouts love their mystique. They want you to think that they are "the backbone of baseball." They would make you think that there would be no players if there weren't any scouts. They talk a lot about their sources, their "bird dogs," who are gas station attendants and American Legion coaches in Nowhere, North Dakota, who call the scout with a tip on where to find the next Jim Palmer.

Of course, that tip usually is Arizona State, where 50 other scouts already are watching him, but who cares? A tip is a tip.

Scouts are the master of the cliché:

"He can play."

"He's a player."

"He has a chance."

"He might have a chance."

"If he plays, he has a chance to be a player."

This drivel goes on and on, getting more ridiculous with each passing sentence. Then they come up with one of my favorites:

"The kid has a good face." What the hell does that mean, the kid isn't cross-eyed? Is he scouting for a baseball team or a Gillette commercial?

"He's got a good makeup." Maybe good makeup is how a kid gets a good face.

"He comes from a good family." I suppose that matters if you're breeding horses, but ball players? I doubt it. If that were the case, we'd have a new generation of stars who have the same last names as guys already in the Hall of Fame.

"He's a piece of work." That means he just went after his mother with an ice pick.

"He's a sleeper." That means he's a stiff beyond belief, and you could fire an M-1 right next to his ear and still not wake him up.

"He's got a good first step." But the second step is a real problem.

"He's got good hands." In fact, one day he'll make a great safecracker.

"He knows how to pitch." That's because no one has coached him yet.

"You can't teach anybody how to hit." Well, don't tell the batting coach that.

"He's got a live arm." I suppose that's better than having a dead arm.

"He's a big-assed pitcher." Scouts love big-assed pitchers, and by this reasoning Jackie Gleason would have had his number retired.

## MANAGERS

Managers are dedicated men, very dedicated indeed, and their sole goal, their only reason for being on the face of this Earth is the following:

*To keep their jobs.*

I can't accent that enough. To a manager, nothing else matters. The first rule of managing is: Screw the players, screw the writers, even screw the coaches, but do what you must to keep working. That's because managers are hired knowing that it won't be long before they are fired. They are hired knowing that they will be held accountable for everything that goes wrong, including idiotic trades made by the boss, that bozo of a general manager.

Managers also understand their vulnerability.

First of all, they can't even pick their own players. That falls to the general manager, who makes the trades, and to the farm director, who is in charge of the minor-league system.

Second, the manager can't play the game for his players. All he can do is put them in the game and tell them to play.

Third, the manager knows that the players and general manger are making more money than he is and that they often have longer contracts. This says little for a manager's job security.

Fourth, the manager is the point man. When something goes wrong with the team, the writers turn first to the manager for an explanation. The old adage about a manager getting far too much credit when things go right and too much blame when they collapse is so true. I've done a million talk shows in my life, and I can count on one hand the number of times fans wanted to fire the front office. But every night someone wants to kick Manager Glutz into the street.

A good manager is a tobacco chewer and a liar. He works on the Red Man so he can spit at the writers who are giving him a hard time. As for the lying, he does that to the writers he likes. One of the keys to surviving as a manager is to convince the writers that you have no talent and it is a miracle on the level of the loaves and fishes whenever you win a game. Casey Stengel would sit in the dugout and say things like "I've been very pleased with what I've been able to get out of Mickey Mantle this season." Of course, Casey got nothing out of Mantle, who was going to hit his 40 homers and drive in 100 runs even if Mary Martin were the manager.

The manager also finds himself in the middle of daily controversy. A player will pop off about being on the bench, then the writers will come running to the manager to tell him what the player said. Then the manager will say something about the player, and the writers will go back to the player to tell him what the manager said. Of course, the player responds, and it's back to the manager again. In Baltimore, Jim Palmer and Earl Weaver did this for a dozen years. They both needed it for their egos.

In most cases, when the stories finally appear, both parties are unhappy because the accounts are full of half-quotes, misquotes, and just plain dumb quotes. It is like playing telephone as a kid. One kid would whisper a story into anther kid's ear, and he'd do the same. By the time the story got to the last kid in the room, you couldn't even recognize it. But this activity does help pass the time on the baseball beat, and Lord knows there is plenty of time to kill.

Nonetheless, entertaining the writers, keeping them occupied, is one of the manager's major duties. If he is smart, he'll keep the writers a little off balance. One day he'll tell the writers that Lefty Lewis has a chance to win 20 games. He'll say that for the record. But off the record he'll tell the writers that Lefty Lewis had better get his head out of his butt and listen to the pitching coach, who is trying to teach Lefty a change-up. Then the writers will do stories about Lefty, quoting the manager about his 20-game potential, but also hinting that Lefty needs a change-up.

Managers also have their list of clichés to be used for various occasions:

"Good pitching stops good hitting."

"Good hitting can stop good pitching."

"The pitchers are ahead of the hitters."

"The hitters are ahead of the pitchers."

"We're not consistent."

"Pitching and defense win games."

"If you don't hit, you don't win."

"Walks will kill you."

"Home runs will kill you."

"Our pitching is killing us."

"Our hitting is killing us."

"Can't you see what we're trying to do here?"

None of these things mean anything, but pick up the sports pages any day during the baseball season and it's a safe bet that you'll find one of these lines coming from a manager.

I also love managers' rationalizations:

"We had only one bad inning." That's what a manager says after his team gives up 14 runs in the third. But last time I checked, all the innings counted. You don't get to throw out the worst one.

"The guy had good stuff in the bullpen." Of course the pitcher did. No one was standing at home plate with a bat.

"That one strike call cost us the game." This comes after the manager lost 11–0, and he's decided to blame the umpire for the whole debacle.

On and on it goes. You get the point.

As you see, it is crucial to lie. A manager has to tell the press that "The decision to move Hunt from the bullpen to the starting rotation is purely mine." The manager hands the press this line 15 minutes after he has just walked out of a meeting in which the owner and general manager ordered him to make Hunt a starter.

Managers have different styles, but avoiding the truth is a common trait.

Leo Durocher hated everyone and everything. He was totally ruthless and liked to destroy everyone. He never met a ball player he liked.

Sparky Anderson loves everyone and everything. He never met a ball player he didn't like.

Both guys were good managers, but both guys were totally full of crap. A good manager can make a difference in a team. He can keep the players from killing each other and keep them somewhat interested in playing well, which isn't easy over a 162-game season. He can figure out what players perform best in what roles.

Let's put it like this: more significant than that a good manager can win a lot of games is that a bad manager can lose a lot. The bad manager does things intentionally to cause conflict with the players. He asks guys who can't bunt to bunt, and he tells guys who can run not to steal bases. He forgets about using the guys on the bench or the guys in the bullpen. He becomes very predictable, either continually slamming doors and kicking tables to chew out the players or never making a scene. Variety not only is the spice of life, but it is the stuff of a good manager.

## COACHES

These are the manager's friends and drinking buddies. Of course, coaches aspire to be managers so they can surround themselves with their own group of bobos. Coaches go to the hotel bar with the manager because the manager always makes the hotel bar off limits to the players so he and his coaches can get drunk in peace. In the bar the coaches tell the manager exactly what he wants to hear—that it is a remarkable achievement that he has taken a team to only 17 games out of first place despite the fact that it has more talent than the 1961 New York Yankees. After they are through trashing the players, they move on to the guys in the front office and give them a pounding. The manager says something; the coaches agree and perhaps even embellish the point. The manager is the king, and the coaches are his court. If the manager plays cards, they play cards. If the manager drinks, they drink. If the manager has taken up running, they run. If the manager eats chili and raw onions at two in the morning, so do they. Any coach who forgets this rule doesn't stay a coach for long, and a coach wants to keep his job because—what the hell?—he might end up being the next manager.

Coaches do have titles:

### Bullpen Coach

He counts all the baseballs and makes sure the players aren't stealing them and giving the balls to the bimbos in the stands. He also makes sure that the players don't set the bullpen on fire during the game. He basically is a babysitter.

### First Base Coach

This is one of life's really dull jobs. The first base coach gets to say hello to the opposing first baseman and the first base umpire. He also might hear about a new restaurant this way. The first base coach also is in charge of telling the base runner the number of outs. When there is a runner on first base and the pitcher tries to pick him off, the first base coach yells, "Back." This is a defense mechanism. In case the runner is picked off and the manager asks the first base coach what happened, the first base coach can honestly say, "I don't know, Skip. I yelled for the guy to get back. I saw the throw coming." When a guy gets a base hit or a walk, the coach pats him on the rear and says, "Nice going." It is a very taxing job.

### Third Base Coach

Along with the pitching coach, he is the royalty of the

coaching staff. He gets to pull on his nose, jerk up his belt, and scratch between his legs. He even can pick his nose in public, all because this is how he is supposed to be giving signs to the hitters and runners. The third base coach spends a lot of time complaining that no one can remember the signs. So after five minutes of pulling his ears, scratching his chest, and hopping on one foot, he calls time-out and has a conference with the batter in which he says, "Just bunt the ball, will ya?" The third base coach also gets to decide if he should send a runner home or hold him at third base. He often is second-guessed, and if he works for George Steinbrenner, he'll get fired if he tries to score a runner and the guy is thrown out. After a number of years as a third base coach, a man invariably develops a number of twitches, which makes him very uncomfortable to be around.

### Hitting Coach

This is the guy you can always find when the team is hitting well. He is a star, telling everyone how he got Don Mattingly to stop dipping his shoulder or how he convinced Dave Winfield to try to pull the ball more. But if the team is in a slump, you couldn't find the hitting coach with six bloodhounds. The guy wisely disappears. The hitters have gone from "my guys" to "them."

### Pitching Coaches

This guy is the team's mother hen, because he is dealing with 10 neurotics. Pitchers are all unbalanced, and they need Freud more than a new curveball. Pitching coaches are a lot like hitting coaches. They are fun to be around when things are going well. When the staff is getting bombed, they seem to be on a safari. But the bottom line on coaches is the same as on managers. They are survivors, and they'll do and say whatever it takes to keep their jobs.

## OUTFIELDERS

The key to a good outfield is the centerfielder, so we'll

discuss him last. But keep that in mind—the centerfielder can make or break an outfield.

That's because the leftfielder couldn't catch a whiffle ball with a butterfly net. He usually plays against the fence, because he can't go back on a fly ball. That way, everything falls in front of him, and hopefully he can pick the ball off the ground and hold the hitter to a single. He spends most of his time between pitches swinging an imaginary bat at an imaginary pitch. Ted Williams did this a lot, and everyone had the good sense to stay out of his way.

The rightfielder may not be able to run much faster than the leftfielder, but this guy is supposed to be able to throw. But like the leftfielder, he spends most of his time trying to figure out what went wrong during his last at-bat.

Now the centerfielder is the athlete. He needs the whole package—the legs, the cannon throwing arm, the reflexes, and the ability to judge line drives and fly balls. Not only must he cover center field, but he has to make sure that the right- and leftfielders don't kill themselves trying to make a play. Managers tell centerfielders, "Catch anything you can reach." That's because managers know that if the centerfielder doesn't catch it, no one will reach it.

Sometimes, you hear a guy called "a fleet-footed centerfielder." This was Rick Manning. This was Jim Landis and Paul Blair. This was a guy who couldn't hit his weight, and he weighed 109. So he not only should be fleet-footed; he should cover all three outfield positions because he is killing his team every time he comes to the plate.

But most good teams have great centerfielders—Willie Mays, Mickey Mantle, Duke Snider, Joe DiMaggio—all Hall of Famers, all centerfielders.

These are the guys who do carry teams, because they are hitting the homers, driving in the runs, hitting .300, making diving catches, and throwing to the right base. If you have no centerfielder, you have no outfield.

As a breed, they are closely attuned to meteorologists. They worry about the wind and the high sky. I always like that last phrase, *the high sky.* What other kind of sky is there? So outfielders spend an inordinate amount of time watching the flag blow, throwing blades of grass in the air, and watching those things blow around. They like to put burnt cork under their eyes. Supposedly, this cuts down on the glare from the sun, but I really think that they want to look like Rambo, or maybe they think they are Indians putting on war paint. Beats me. All it really looks like is that these guys want to play ball with dirty faces.

## THE FIRST BASEMAN

The first baseman is a big galoot who was too clumsy for left field, which is a real indictment. At best, scouts say he lacks mobility. That means he needs to take a cab to reach a ball hit five feet to his left. First basemen all have nicknames such as Rock, Boog, Gorilla and Stonehands. Most look up when someone says "Clang." The first baseman is a big stiff, and since the beginning of time, big stiffs have played first base. He can't run, can't field, can't even bend over. Actually, he can't play first base, but if you're in the National League, you've got to put him somewhere.

That's because this guy's real position is batter. He hits a lot of homers. There is a formula for first basemen—the more homers they hit, the fewer balls they have to catch. When they come to bat, the announcer always says, "And here come Big Boog Powell." It's always "Here comes Big Somebody." In another time, the first baseman would have been the guy who did not need tools to be a blacksmith.

## THE SECOND BASEMAN

The second baseman is usually the smallest guy on the team. He plays second because he can't throw and he can't hit. He often grew up as a social outcast and made an art form out of being a brat. Ring a bell? Yes, second basemen are the future managers and coaches. Just check Billy Martin and Eddie Stanky for references.

The second baseman typically has a lot of spirit, which means he really knows how to whistle through his teeth, and he never forgets to hold up fingers to let everyone know how many outs there are. Of course, everyone already knows the number of outs, and if they don't know, they'll look at the scoreboard before they'll look at the second baseman. But none of this bothers our spirited hero. He pats guys on the butt and yells encouragement to the pitcher. He shouts, "Come now, you tall drink of water. Bull your neck, big fella. Nothing but strikes, right down the old shoot, yes sirree . . ." Then he goes back to holding up his fingers and whistling because he knows it looks good to the manager. Well, it should look good since the manager indulged in the same stupid, time-consuming garbage when he was a second baseman.

The second baseman also is the complainer. He usually likes to tell the groundskeeper how to do his job, and the infield never suits his taste. It is either too hard or too soft; the grass is too high or too low. There is too much sand or too much dirt. He is enthusiastic when he throws the ball around the infield, and he resents the fact that the third baseman traditionally receives the ball last and gets to rub it up before handing it to the pitcher. The second baseman would love to have that job since, in his mentality, rubbing up the ball is a form of leadership. That's why second basemen often like shortstops, but they have little respect for third basemen. Secretly, the second baseman believes that the third baseman has no idea how to rub up a baseball.

So we are talking about a feisty little guy, which is a nice way of saying that he's a jerk. He does know more baseball clichés than anyone else. He likes to start fights and then get the hell out of there when the heavy action starts as the benches empty. He gets demolished when turning a double play, but doesn't care. He's happiest when his uniform is dirty and when he maybe is bleeding a little. He thinks that's what it means "to do the little things." Well, a second baseman better be able to do the little things, because almost sure as hell he can't do the big things—such as hit, throw, and run.

## THE SHORTSTOP

Often, the shortstop is the best natural athlete on the field.

The only player who is close is the centerfielder. A lot of centerfielders such as Mickey Mantle even started their careers at short. This is a guy with terrific hand-eye coordination. He can bend down to pick up grounders, but he also has the ability to range far to his right to make perhaps the most challenging play on the diamond—backhanding a ground ball in the hole at deep short and then throwing the runner out at first base. If a guy can make this play, he can earn $1 million even if he can't hit, and I point to Ozzie Smith as an example. As the centerfielder can make or break the outfield, the shortstop dominates the infield.

## THE THIRD BASEMAN

This guy is a future first baseman or leftfielder. He has the range and body of a refrigerator. He's a cement block with legs. His best play is to let the ball pound against his chest. Then he picks up the ball and throws it to first base. Announcers see this and praise him as being gritty and not being afraid to put his body in front of the ball. Well, he has no choice since he's too big and too slow to get out of the way. He has a football brain-set. Like Dick Butkus, he'll play with a broken leg and relish the pain. If Jake LaMotta were a baseball player, he would have played third. In other words, this is a guy who can take a punch.

There are some third basemen who were terrific glovemen—Brooks Robinson and Billy Cox are two examples. But for the most part, these guys are there to hit. If they make a great play, it is done out of self-defense. They throw up their glove so that a line drive doesn't embed itself in their forehead. The hot corner is aptly named, and the guy playing this position does need great powers of concentration. If he goes to sleep one moment, he could be getting fitted for dentures the next day.

## THE DESIGNATED HITTER

This guy started as a third baseman or a leftfielder. But he was such an embarrassment with the glove that he was moved to first base. When that didn't work out, he was shipped to the American League and made a DH. This is a player whose position actually is batter. He has to think about only one thing—hitting. Half the time, if he gets on base, they take him out for a pinch runner.

Do you realize how much this man has to work?

I'd say about three or four minutes a night, and he knocks down about $750,000 a year.

All he does is bat, and most guys hit only four or five times a game. The rest of the time he walks back and forth between the dugout and the clubhouse. In the clubhouse he might swing the bat a few times, or he might just sit down with a cup of coffee and watch the game on television. Some of these guys eat candy bars during the game, making them the only player in the lineup who actually can gain weight during a baseball game. But this guy does hit the ball out of the park. He tells people that he would like to play first base or left field, but he is very content hitting because swinging the bat is all he ever wanted to do in the first place. For the DH, hitting the ball has always been easier than catching it.

## THE CATCHER

The catcher is an ugly man.

The catcher is a man with gnarled fingers, and he likes to show them to you.

The catcher is a man who always aches.

The catcher is a man to whom the world doesn't look right unless he is squatting.

The catcher is a man who always needs a bath.

The catcher is a man who always needs a knee specialist.

Basically, the catcher is not a well-balanced individual.

He spends his life squatting with a fat umpire such as Ken Kaiser leaning over his shoulder. He has to wear all these pads and a face mask that weighs about 100 pounds, and he puts on all this garbage and walks onto the field in Kansas City or Cincinnati where it is 110 degrees on a Saturday afternoon. In the bullpen the guys are bored, and they are frying eggs right on the turf. I mean, they just crack the egg, drop it on the ground, and let the sun go to work. But on a day like this the catcher is wearing 100 pounds of equipment, dealing with an umpire who is leaning and sweating all over him. Furthermore, there is a chance that he might get hit in the head with a bat. He has to crouch down in the mud and dirt. He has to put his body in front of stupid curveballs thrown by stupid pitchers who can't even remember if one or two fingers is the sign for a breaking pitch. He also is supposed to block the plate when a Godzilla like Jim Rice or Steve Balboni tries to score.

This job is so tough that half the time the catcher has no idea where the ball is. He is looking up in the air when it is by his feet. Or he is looking to the left for a pop-up, and it went to the right. Foul tips are breaking his fingers, all the squatting has turned his knees into swiss cheese, and he has to do this 140 times a year.

The catcher is either a hero or an idiot—I'm not sure which.

But I do know that the catcher is supposed to be the smartest man on the field, the team leader. And he also is the guy suffering from heat prostration. He has to be the middleman between the pitcher and the manager, both of whom he thinks know nothing about pitching. He has to talk to umpires, which is something I don't wish upon anyone. He also has to remind pitchers that one finger is a fastball, two is a curve, and so on. I also don't envy that chore. About all I can say for certain about the catcher is that he is the one man on the field who really earns his salary.

## THE PITCHER

Pitchers are not baseball players. I can't stress that enough. I refuse to call them players because they really don't play. They don't or can't hit. They can't run. They can't even bunt. If you hit the ball back to them, it's considered a miracle if they catch it and then make a decent throw to first base. No one expects them to do anything athletic.

What you need to remember is that pitchers are an isolated breed. They are to baseball what the prima donna is to the opera. You won't find the diva mixing with the rest of the cast. They hate hitters. Hitters are their avowed enemies. The hitters on their own team never score enough runs for them. The hitters on the other team are always lucky when they score off the pitcher.

The pitchers on a team huddle together. They have their own language, even their own science and their own cures.

In the old days pitchers were more like ball players. They didn't put their arms on ice. They thought a rotator cuff was something on a tire. They thought tendinitis was the name of a dinosaur. They did know that throwing a baseball was unnatural and that when the body does something unnatural it hurts. But they still threw 300 to 400 innings a year, which is far more than anyone does today. And one day their arms just hurt too much, so they quit. And that was that. No mystery, no arm specialists. Just take the ball and throw until you can't throw it anymore.

Now medical science has taken over pitching. Suddenly all we hear about is ulnar nerves, rotator cuffs, and calcification problems. These guys spend far more time in a doctor's office than they do on the mound.

Pitchers also are primary sources of excuses. You know that when they were kids pitchers were always telling their teachers that the dog ate their homework.

When a pitcher gets beat, you hear the following:

"The wind was blowing out, and the ball just carried."

"The ball was too slippery."

"The defense needs to make better plays behind me."

"The mound is too high."

"The mound is too low."

"I didn't want to throw that pitch, but the catcher called it."

"That was a cheap home run."

"That was a cheap single."

"The umpire was squeezing the plate on me."

"The manager won't let me start."

"The manager won't let me pitch enough."

"The manager makes me pitch too much."

These guys are amazing. They give up a ball that is hit halfway to Calgary, and they talk about a cheap, windblown homer.

Pitchers have no concept of reality because their existence is unreal, even by baseball standards. Now a manager only asks them to throw 100 good pitches or go six innings. There are long relievers, middle relievers, short relievers, spot starters, and who knows what else since new euphemisms are added daily.

After a guy starts a game and maybe even lasts five innings, he can't even throw for two days. On the third day he tosses lightly. He sits again on the fourth and finally goes back to work on the fifth day. Pitchers are supposed to do a lot of running to keep their legs strong. But some coaches such as Johnny Sain said running wasn't important. That was one of the reasons that pitchers loved Johnny Sain. He used to say that pitching was all a matter of confidence, so pitchers would sit around the bar and tell each other how great they were. Ah, the wonders of group therapy.

Relievers are a little different, since some of these guys pitch every other day. I do have a little more respect for these guys, because they at least are supposed to finish the game. Every night they pitch under pressure, which is why a reliever's greatest attribute is egomania. He needs to think he is the greatest, no matter how often he gets his brains beat in. He can't be a very intellectual guy. He should be like Sparky Lyle, who is happiest when he is naked, sitting in a cake, and belching. The biggest question on his mind is if Lite beer tastes great or is less filling. He likes the bullpen, where he can spend the early innings sleeping or looking at the bimbos in the stands. In the fourth inning he can have someone sneak him a hot dog and a beer. Once in a great while the boys in the bullpen will find a mouse on the loose, and they'll throw a baseball at it. Rodent killing is great fun.

Basically, this is a man of little substance. He has to be sort of dumb to pitch 70 times a year with the game on the line and not really care if he wins or loses. You don't want Einstein in the bullpen. A good relief pitcher should have only one pitch, and he throws it again and again. The moment he starts to experiment, he's finished. But without a good reliever a team is finished.

## UMPIRES

In a game filled with characters who aren't tightly wrapped, the umpires may be the most warped of all. A kid who grows up dreaming of being an umpire is the same kind of person who wants to be an embalmer. This is the person who begins life with an inferiority complex, a person who really believes that he is not as good as everyone else and then sets out to prove it. This is a guy who wants to be stigmatized. So this person becomes an umpire, and the following happens:

He is booed unmercifully.
Billy Martin kicks dirt on him.
Earl Weaver shoves him.
He is told he is blind.
He is told he is stupid.
He is told that he is deaf, blind, and stupid.
He is pelted with garbage.
He is called dirty names.
His mother is called dirty names.

What else could you want out of life? Not much if your goal is to become an umpire.

## TALKING BASEBALL

Baseball is something I can talk about endlessly because there really is so much to talk about. There have been many January nights in Cleveland when it was 15 below zero and Lake Erie was frozen so solid that you could walk across it to Canada. But I always am able to crank up the hot stove. We put on the "Talking Baseball" theme song, maybe get a general manager or even a sportswriter on the show, and boom, we blow four hours in January on baseball. No other sport has such an appeal, because there are so many topics.

And you better believe that Pete Franklin has opinions about baseball. Here's Franklin's trip around the diamond:

## The Designated Hitter

When the American League went to the DH, I never thought I would like it. I was a victim of my conditioning. I grew up watching baseball without a DH. I welcomed progress in about every avenue of society except this stupid game I love so much. I said it would take strategy out of the game—do you let the pitcher bat or send up a pinch hitter? I said it would lead to one-dimensional players, almost like slow-pitch softball with fat guys swinging for the fence. But as I watched the American League, the DH grew on me. I liked seeing Andre Thornton and Reggie Jackson hit home runs, and I realized that watching them hit was a helluva lot more fun than seeing Dean Chance at the plate, waiting for him to bloop his one single every two years. As for taking strategy out of the game, I'm basically in favor of anything that takes strategy away from the managers. Those bozos make enough moves already, and the DH is not about to change the fact that most of these egomaniacs already over-orchestrate the game. So, I give the DH the nod. In fact, the National League should have it, too, so baseball can stop confusing us.

## Domes

I'm not like some purists who insist that baseball should always be played outside, always on grass, and preferably in the daytime. Sometimes you just need a dome. If they ever put a big-league team in Phoenix, they better have a dome, or the players will feel like an upside-down cake that has just been baked at 400 degrees. In July and August, the heat is so bad in those places that even the Apaches said the hell with it and moved to the mountains in Prescott. The same is true of Dallas and Houston. Washington and Baltimore also need a dome because the humidity there is so bad. Minneapolis is the land of 10,000 lakes, but it's also the land of 10,000 feet of snow. It has all this beautiful scenery and everything, but who wants to watch a baseball game in Minnesota during the spring? In April, they've got a foot of snow up there. So Minnesota was smart to build a dome. Cleveland also could show some brains by following suit. Instead, you get some people in Cleveland who say, "There is nothing better than baseball down by Lake Erie on a beautiful summer day." Well, that takes care of three home games, so what about the other 78? If you want beautiful weather all the time, put a big-league team in Hawaii. That would be great because I like nothing better than baseball under the sunshine. But most of the cities in this country have extreme weather problems, and domes can alleviate the trouble.

### Computers and Consultants

This is another sign of the egomania that has slipped into baseball. I suppose a computer is fine if you're hard up and can't get a date. Then you can go to one of those places and get the phone number of someone who is as ugly and desperate as you are. But as for managers having computers in the clubhouse and the dugout, you gotta be kidding. Last time I checked, each inning was three outs, a walk was four balls, and a strikeout was three strikes. Talent also still won games, and I don't care if you have IBM in the dugout. You don't need computer programmers and consultants; you need guys with 90 mph fastballs.

### Mascots

All right, I'm not enthralled with all the featherbrains and assorted other creatures wandering around ballparks, but I do like the San Diego Chicken. I like people who entertain. I'm an entertainer, and I know what is a good bit and what isn't, and the Chicken's act ain't half bad. I don't want to see it every day of the week, but nothing is great every day of the week, not even sex. But once in a while the Chicken is fun. He knows a little about baseball; he has a good sense of timing. As for the rest of the mascots, forget it. They don't know what they're doing, they don't even look funny, and worst of all, they're boring. Some of the best mascots are people who aren't mascots, just guys in the stands. There is a guy at Mets games who makes up all these stupid signs and waves them around. I like him. He's spontaneous. Forget the mascots on the public relations department payroll—give me the fans.

**Sparky Anderson**

Sparky has a handicap—the English language. He can't speak it, or at least he can't say anything reasonably close to what he means. Like all good managers, Sparky is a great fabricator. But he does it with a lot of charm. Every player is great, every kid has great potential, and everything that happens is great. No one, not even Sparky, believes a word of it, but a lot of that crap finds its way into the newspaper. On the field, I think Sparky knows what he's doing. He gets the most out of a mediocre pitching staff. He knows how to move the bodies around and keep the bullpen busy. He doesn't need eyes; he just listens to his stomach. When his ulcer acts up, that means it's time to go to the bullpen.

**Tom Lasorda**

This is a fat guy who one day is destined to gag on linguine and clam sauce. He likes the Dodgers, he likes the celebrities around the Dodgers, and he likes Italian food—not in that order. He is a master at slinging the bull, and when you have dinner with him you want to break a plate over his head when he starts up with all his Dodger Blue crap. Lasorda is an ex-pitcher, and he understands that baseball really shouldn't be called *baseball*; it should be called *pitching*. Pitching always will be what determines who wins and loses, and when Lasorda had Fernando Valenzuela and the rest he was a great manager. When his pitchers were in the tank, Lasorda felt Dodger blue.

### Dick Williams

This is an unhappy man whose goal in life is to make everyone around him equally unhappy. Like most managers, he was a crappy player who did learn a few things while sitting around the dugout. His miserable personality catches his players' attention for a short time, but it wears thin after a while. He has raised being an unpleasant individual to an art form.

### Frank Robinson

He was born to play baseball. He was a magnificent hitter, a killer on the base paths, and he had such an intense drive to win that it rubbed off on his teammates. He is my definition of a winning player. At times in his career he has been a winning manager, a guy who can be delightful and charming, but in the next breath he can turn arrogant and odious. When he managed the Indians, he tended to lose patience quickly, and if there is anything a manager in Cleveland must have, it's patience. Frank was the first black manager in the majors, and I desperately wanted him to succeed. I was very critical of him, but I actually held off my criticism for some time because I so wanted him to cut it in the dugout. I will admit that when I first knocked Frank, I felt a little guilty because he was black. But I eventually realized that all managers should be treated the same, and when they screw up, Pete Franklin is going to let them know.

### Dave Johnson

He learned well from Earl Weaver, who was one of the best managers of all time. Johnson was an infielder with the Orioles when Weaver was winning pennants in Baltimore.

The general manager was a guy named Frank Cashen. Cashen knew that pitching was what wins, so he collected pitchers in Baltimore, and now he's doing the same with the Mets, only his manager is no longer Weaver, but Johnson. So, I basically like Davey Johnson, but I do wish he'd take his computer and shove it where the sun doesn't shine.

### Mickey Mantle

Mickey was supposed to be faster than a speeding bullet. He was signed as a shortstop and was once clocked running to first base at 3.1 seconds, supposedly the quickest time ever. He was a switch hitter with tremendous power. He played in New York, which made him an instant legend. He also came after Babe Ruth and Joe DiMaggio, but he wasn't in their class. Yes, Mickey would sometimes hit a home run that would come down in the Hudson River, but for the life of me I can't figure out how some people could say he was as good as Willie Mays. He wasn't even in the same league as Mays. If he had played in Cleveland or Detroit, no one would have mentioned him in the same sentence as Mays. I don't mean to say Mantle lacked greatness, but some of that aura had to do with the Mantle mystique. He was always hurt, always had leg problems, and people would say, "The guy is good, but what if he had been healthy?" Or even, "What if the Mick had stayed home at night? He would have been a better player if he hit fewer watering holes and spent more time hitting in batting practice." Because about all the males in his family died by age 40, there was a death watch around him, but did that make him one of the greatest players ever? No way.

### Joe DiMaggio

He may not have been our best player ever, but DiMaggio was the most stylish. He had the perfect stance, the perfect swing, the perfect long, loping stride, and even married the person we thought was the perfect example of the American woman—Marilyn Monroe. DiMaggio never threw to the wrong base, he never swung at a bad pitch, and he never missed a sign. DiMaggio playing baseball is like Arthur Rubinstein playing Chopin on the piano. To this day, DiMaggio has that great, classy image, even when he's doing those Mr. Coffee commercials, and when you look classy while hustling Mr. Coffee, you've really got class.

### Ty Cobb

I rate him the second greatest baseball player of all-time, right behind Babe Ruth. Thank God this man played baseball, because he had a very demented streak. But this maniacal side of his personality is also what made him a great player. He could concentrate every minute for 24 hours a day on beating the other team. It was beat the other team, beat the other team—he said it over and over—and in the end he found a way to do it.

### Babe Ruth

He was the quintessential baseball talent and the realization of America's dreams. He was an orphan—a fat, ugly orphan at that. The other kids made fun of him and said he looked like an ape. But he went from a social reject to a man who revolutionized the game. First he was a great pitcher with the Boston Red Sox, then he showed everyone the power of the home run with the Yankees. He made a ton of money and blew it all. His life was a quest for more—more booze, more broads, and more home runs. He was a good-natured guy who did what he always wanted to do. Babe would tell the manager to go to hell, and he'd take a nap during batting practice. He'd eat 14 hot dogs a day because they tasted good, and he drank gallons of liquor. He was like a beach bum who had this incredible gift for the game. No player had more of an impact on baseball than Babe Ruth, both on and off the field.

## Roger Maris

This is the man who committed the most heinous of all baseball crimes—he broke Babe Ruth's single-season home run record—and no one would ever let him forget it. Unlike Ruth, he wasn't fat, he wasn't jolly, and he didn't like to smile for the camera. He came out of North Dakota, where life is short and hard, and that was how Roger Maris approached baseball—as if he expected something terrible to happen to him. And in his greatest moment, the breaking of the record, it did. America acted as though someone had spat on the flag. Was Roger Maris a great player? No. Does he belong in the Hall of Fame? No. But he was a man who had a great year, and he was a man who deserved far more respect than he ever received.

## Hank Aaron

This is another man who broke Ruth's record, this being the lifetime home run record. And in the process Aaron became another man who spat on the flag in the eyes of many fans and writers. He was not a colorful player or a great personality. All he did was play hard and hit home runs . . . lots of home runs, year after year. He had star statistics but was more of a plugger. He endured, and his nickname, "the Hammer," was perfect because what he did was hammer out home run after home run almost like a guy making tables. A great player, of course, but he does not rank up there with Ruth and Mays.

## Lou Gehrig

He was strong, an awesome superstar. He once drove in 184 runs; he played in over 2,000 straight games. He truly was the Iron Horse, and the tragedy of Gehrig's career was that he played on the same team with Babe Ruth. Gehrig's quiet, businesslike personality was lost in Ruth's giant shadow. Only after he retired, and after he left his deathbed to say "I'm the luckiest man alive" during Lou Gehrig Day at Yankee Stadium, did we fully come to appreciate his greatness.

### Steve Garvey

A good ball player whom we will one day be calling Mr. President. I'll give him this much—he knows how to keep his hair well-combed.

### Johnny Bench

Some people have called Bench the greatest catcher ever. Some people are incredibly wrong. I agree that he is the best catcher to come along since, say, 1970, but I have a hard time putting Bench in the same class as Roy Campanella and Bill Dickey. Bench is a legitimate Hall of Famer with a great arm who also hit for some power. But to place the mantle as the best catcher ever on his shoulders is going way too far.

### Willie Mays

In every aspect of the game, Mays was a great player. He came to the majors with the New York Giants, and he played under Leo Durocher, who immediately pronounced Mays the greatest player anyone has ever seen. Leo wasn't far wrong. Willie was fast, and we loved it when he ran out from under his cap. He had a childlike innocence and was labeled the "Say Hey Kid." The Giants then were playing in New York, and they desperately needed a hero. Mays filled those immense shoes. He could run, throw, hit for power and average. He made truly amazing catches, and his glove, as much as his bat, could turn a game around. He did everything, and he did it with style and pizzazz. I rate him a close third of all time behind Ruth and Cobb, and as great as Mays is considered, he is still underrated by many baseball people. Willie Mays, not Mantle, was the premier player of his generation.

# 9
# BASEBALL AND BLACKS

I am convinced that the reason a man excels in sports is environment. The greatest basketball players are black because no one plays as much basketball as the blacks. The greatest golfers and tennis players are white because those are country club sports, and country clubs are white. If you were to fill the ghettos and the housing projects with whites and move the blacks into the country clubs, basketball would be primarily a white sport, while blacks would dominate golf and tennis.

This is a lesson people need to learn, and I'm talking about everyone from Al Campanis to Jesse Jackson.

I suppose we should thank Al Campanis for putting the issue of race at the forefront of baseball. Mr. Campanis did it very unintentionally, of course, as he shot off his mouth on Ted Koppel's "Nightline." Mr. Campanis basically said what most men of his generation believe—that blacks make great players but lack the "necessities" and "buoyancy" and basic intelligence to be managers or to run baseball teams.

It is very true that Branch Rickey broke the color line in

baseball when he signed Jackie Robinson to a contract with the Brooklyn Dodgers. Rickey was in charge of the Dodgers, and in the end, signing Robinson was his decision. But Rickey's right hand man was Al Campanis, and Campanis lobbied for the signing of Robinson. For his time, Al Campanis was a pioneer in the field of race relations in baseball. He always was a close friend of the Jackie Robinson family. Al Campanis is no redneck. He doesn't believe in lynching or in separate drinking fountains for the different races.

This is not a defense of what Campanis said. But some background is necessary. Campanis is a man with good intentions and a runaway mouth. Campanis obviously believes that blacks are as good as anyone on the field of play. The Dodgers have always been at the forefront of signing minority players, and Campanis has had a strong hand in that policy. But he also probably believes that blacks like watermelon, that they have natural rhythm, and that they can't swim. It would never occur to Campanis to hire a black to a major front office job. That doesn't make Campanis a vile, evil man. He is a product of his generation and his environment, which has passed on stupid, ignorant views. In fact, it would not surprise me if Campanis believed that blacks are inherently better athletes than whites, that they are superior physical specimens. But the danger in making such a supposition is that there is the flipside—if blacks are bigger, stronger, and faster, then whites are smarter. That is exactly how most men of Campanis's generation see the world.

All of this controversy has been very good for the politicians. Jesse Jackson is black, and he's running for president. He also has been one who looks for a cause and jumps right in, seeking headlines and racial justice at the same time. So Jesse Jackson leaped upon Campanis's remarks and set himself up as a guy who is going to pressure baseball into correcting all the racial inequalities. He has conferred with Commissioner Peter Ueberroth, who also has presidential ambitions, and these two candidates are getting a lot of mileage out of Campanis.

Does Jesse Jackson really care about trying to integrate baseball front offices?

Well, he never did until Campanis became a national controversy.

Would Jackson continue to talk about it if the media didn't quote him? I'll let you answer that one for yourself. All you need to know is that Jesse Jackson is a politician. Like any politician, white or black, he needs issues that will keep him in the papers. That's why I don't get very excited about what Jesse Jackson has to say about baseball.

So what is the true story about blacks in baseball?

On the field of play, all men are created equal and the managers are color-blind. That's because managers are terrified of losing—not just a game, but their jobs. They will play the best man, and they don't care if he's Latin, black, or a ranting KKK racist from Mississippi. If you look at the pay scale for baseball players, you will find blacks right near the top. The better the player, the more money he makes. Show business is the same as sports. If a man is producing, if he is winning and bringing in the dollars, he is a star, and stars come in all shapes, sizes, and colors.

Now there is truth in the statement that white stars receive better treatment from the media than black stars, and this happens for a very simple reason—95 percent of the media is white. White writers usually come from middle-class suburban (read: all white) neighborhoods and schools. The writers usually have other writers as friends, and we end up with white writers hanging around with other white writers. When they are confronted with a black player, they are uneasy. Now, if the black player is outgoing, if he has a fun personality, he will be treated well by the media. Reggie Jackson is a perfect example. The man can talk; he knows how to con the writers and keep his name in the news. The white media seeks out Reggie because he is cooperative and colorful, regardless of the color of his skin.

But another black star such as Jim Rice sometimes has problems. Rice is from rural South Carolina. He has been known to be "sullen" and "moody," according to the writers who have covered him. He is a big man whose size and looks can intimidate. In the case of Rice, I believe he has been hurt by being black because the writers won't take the extra step or grant him the extra patience they do a white player.

Furthermore, black players tend to hang around with black players; and white players hang around with whites. It's that way in the real world, so why wouldn't it be the case in the dressing room? In fact, race relations are better in the dressing room than about anywhere else because the players, both black and white, know that they are dependent upon each other to win. They also know that the more they win, the more they make, and money is what they are all after. But there still is a division between blacks and whites, and that is due to a number of environmental factors. Basically, blacks grew up with blacks and whites grew up with whites. Nothing profound here, but it is a fact of life.

Often, you can tell if a player is black or white just by how he is described on the radio or in newspaper stories.

For example, name one "scrappy" player who is black. Every scrappy player is some little white guy, probably a second baseman or a catcher. Rick Dempsey was scrappy. Billy Martin was scrappy. But you know who played harder and was "scrappier" than any player I've ever seen?

Jackie Robinson.

That's right, Jackie Robinson, as in Jackie Robinson the first black player in the majors. It also is Jackie Robinson as in a guy who would do anything, and I mean anything, to beat you. He'd steal a base, knock over an infielder, lay down a bunt, or even start a fight. He was perhaps the most aggressive player in baseball history.

Now who is a player described as "intelligent" or "crafty"? Those guys, too, always are white. But the "natural athlete" is black. The guy with "great athletic skills" is black. It often seems that whites are smart, blacks are athletically gifted. Whites usually are the overachievers, blacks are the underachievers. We hear it and read it every day. But I have seen just as many smart players who were black as white. And I've seen just as many white players dog it as blacks.

We come to sports with our own prejudices. We expect the white player to be scrappy and smart, and when he hustles or makes an astute play we call him "intelligent." We expect the black player to be athletic, but dumb. So when the black player throws to the wrong base, we say, "What else would you expect? He's all natural talent, no brains."

All of these labels are a bunch of crap, but that crap is dished out every day of the week, and it explains why white players get more and better press than black players. Never forget that the media is white and is more comfortable dealing with white players. Also, white players usually are more public relations–conscious and less suspicious of the media. Why less suspicious? Because they are white, and so are the writers.

In other words, baseball has yet another "problem" in dealing with the racial question—the media. Newspapers, radio stations, and television networks have been under great pressure to hire minorities, but so far they have come up incredibly short in their attempts to find qualified people or at least people they deem trainable and/or qualified. So far, they have been as unsuccessful as baseball, but that's another story.

So how come there are no blacks as managers and in the front office?

Let's go back to the perception of players. Remember, it is the white guys who are scrappy and smart. Most managers are supposed to be scrappy and smart, so the managers come from that pool of former scrappy and smart players. And never forget that those doing the hiring were once players—smart, scrappy, and white players, to be exact.

Which brings us to the crony system. Let us now hoist a toast to the crony system, because hoisting a toast and pounding the Bud is what the crony system is all about. We are talking drinking buddies, drinking buddies who hire their drinking buddies.

It is the same system that exists in the military and in corporate boardrooms. Friends hire friends. Friends take care of friends. The guys who went to Harvard Law School together keep in touch for the rest of their lives. When one of them gets canned, the old fraternity buddy is there with a job to "get Blinky back on his feet."

Let's start right at the top. No black owns a baseball team. No black is a president of a baseball team. Only one black—Hank Aaron—is a farm director.

Who hires the front office personnel and the managers, in both the majors and the minors?

The owners, presidents, general managers, and farm directors.

If all of them are white and their friends are white, just whom do you think they will hire?

Also, remember this: once you have been a manager, then you have *experience.* Baseball people love to talk about hiring a guy with *experience.* It doesn't matter that the guy's only experience was messing up some team. The argument is that the guy has done the job before, so he can do it again. The fact that he didn't do it very well the first time is not discussed. This is how incompetent people go from one job to the next. It is much easier and safer to hire a retread than someone brand-new. When you are asked why you hired the retread, you can bring up the word *experience.* In sports, you can be absolutely terrible at your job, but if you drink with the right people and cultivate the media, you can get hired again and again.

The experience argument means you would hire the captain of the *Titanic* to navigate your ship because he has done it before. Besides, maybe he even learned from his mistakes.

What crapola!

The biggest obstacle facing blacks who want to get into baseball management is that they have no crony system. There is no old-boy network for them to fall back on. It is not a question of color or ability but opportunity. When put in the position, blacks can con the media and make friends in high places just like anyone else. But they need that entry level job to gain access to the movers and shakers in the business.

How is opportunity created?

Sometimes it takes an incident such as the beleaguered Al Campanis shoving both of his shoes down his throat. And it might take someone such as Jesse Jackson making noise.

It also takes—and this is a dirty word to most of the population—affirmative action.

If you are white, you probably have no use for affirmative action. It offends the majority of our population, because the majority is white, and affirmative action will not help whites. But something must be done to right the wrongs. Blacks have been stepped on and shunted aside in this country for over 100 years. They have faced discrimination, and they can't hide because they are black. Those are not excuses, but facts borne out by history.

That's why I see nothing wrong with affirmative action, so long as affirmative action means opportunity. If you are going to have a race for a pot of gold or for that treasured piece of the American economic pie, let's start everyone at the same spot. Let's not put these three guys 10 yards ahead because they used to drink with the boss and let's not make these two guys run with refrigerators strapped to their backs because they happen to be black.

On the playing field, I don't believe racism exists, because a premium is placed on talent and winning. But in the boardroom, blacks have been denied opportunity and entry. You'll hear about a young white guy who gets the chance to "grow into the job," but seldom is that said about a young black. Now I loathe taking a person who isn't qualified and putting him in a high position because he is black. That is humiliating and embarrassing for the people who did the hiring and the guy who was hired. But often, you'll be surprised how most people of reasonable intelligence and character can "grow into the job."

I have watched sports for a lifetime, and I know that there are blacks who would be fine managers and executives. I also know that some white executives would be very uncomfortable with a black in the boardroom. Some whites just act abnormally in front of blacks, and they start saying things such as "Some of my best friends are blacks." We've all heard the lines. In this case, it means that the old white executive probably has a bigger problem than the new black executive. Well, this is a problem that the white executive will just have to work out, just as some of the white players on the Brooklyn Dodgers had to learn how to deal with Jackie Robinson. But when a man is given a chance, and when he can perform like Robinson did, attitudes change. They have on the playing field, and they will in the front office.

# 10
# BASEBALL AND THE MEDIA

Art Linkletter made a mint by pawning off the myth that kids say the darnedest things. Well, I'm here to tell you that baseball fans say the dumbest things, but I'll also maintain that it isn't always their fault.

The tip-off for one of these ventures into idiocy goes like this:

CALLER: "Pete, I really think that Manager Glutz is doing a great job."

PETE: "Yes . . ."

CALLER: "I mean, he has been in the game for 25 years, and 22 of his teams have won the World Series."

PETE: "So?"

CALLER: "Obviously, he has spent a lifetime in the game and knows what he's doing."

PETE: "Despite all that, you know more than Glutz."

CALLER: "What's that, Pete?"

PETE: "You've told me what a great and intelligent guy Glutz is. You've told me that he wins, he is a pillar of society, his wife raises millions of dollars every year to save the manatees, and all of his children have gone to law school and now only work for minimum salaries as they fight for the civil rights of the oppressed. You have told me that when Glutz goes to that great dugout in the sky, he will be seated at the right hand of the biggest manager of all."

CALLER: "I don't get it."

PETE: "All I'm saying is that you're getting ready to deliver the 'But' line."

CALLER: "What's that?"

PETE: "Oh, you know, the 'but' line. You tell me what a great guy Glutz is, then you say, 'But . . . .' "

CALLER: "Oh . . . yeah . . . well . . . I was gonna . . ."

PETE: "Go ahead, turnip head, say it. Give me your incisive observations and insightful comments about how Glutz is screwing up and you know more than he does. That's what you really want to say, isn't it?"

Then the caller says something about Glutz not bunting in the fifth inning of a game that Glutz's team ended up losing 13–3.

Usually, I don't just hammer a caller like this right away. If I'm in a patient mood, and we all know that patience is one of my many virtues, then I let the dummy talk because I know he will hang himself. And 99 percent of the time, these kinds of callers, the guys who think they know more than Manager Glutz, reveal themselves to be embarrassingly dense. It really comes down to egomania. Everyone from the president of the United States to the crapper cleaner at the White House thinks he can manage a baseball team. They're always telling me that one player is better than the other or that the manager is so misguided that he needs a road map to find his toes.

QUESTION: So why don't the fans know anything about baseball?

ANSWER: Because the media really doesn't tell them much.

One day I was in the press box, and this gorgeous blonde was there. She was one of those television news blondes, the kind that you think only exist on the tube or in magazines.

Well, all the boys in the press box were getting very distracted. They were kind of moving around in their seats, and a few suddenly developed twitches. There could have been a machine gun murder at home plate and no one would have seen it. The blonde was asking us questions like "Who is Jack Morris?" and "What did he do before he got to Detroit?" You know that all the guys wanted to answer her and offer her some popcorn and a Coke, too. But only a few actually spoke up. These questions and answers went on and on for a few minutes, and it became obvious that the blonde knew a lot more about makeup and hairdressers than baseball. But after the game she goes down on the field, grabs a microphone, and starts telling the world about what a great pitcher Jack Morris is. Of course, in the middle of her report, she stares directly into the camera and calls Morris a left-hander, but hey, who is really listening, anyway? I mean, everyone watching the news can't hear a thing that she's saying. We're all just staring, if you get my drift.

Okay, this is an extreme example. But my point remains. Part of the reason fans are so dumb is that the media is so dumb, and it is a much deeper problem than just sending a blonde to a ball game once a month.

*Fact 1:* The public relies on the media to be its eyes and ears on the field and in the clubhouse.

*Fact 2:* The difference between the blonde and some of the guys reporting baseball—on television, on radio, and in the newspaper—is that the blonde has better legs.

*Fact 3:* Fans believe what they read in the paper and hear on the air.

*Fact 4:* The most important thing about a story is who wrote or reported it.

I get calls all the time from fans telling me that they read a story that said this or that.

PETE: "Who wrote it?"

CALLER: "Duh, I dunno."

PETE: "Where did you read it?"

CALLER: "In the paper."

You get the idea. But if you want to know if what you read

is right, you need to know something about the guy who wrote it. Since I've been in the media for a million years, I know about everybody. I know which guys are dumber than dumb, which guys may as well be on the team's payroll, and which guys at least have a chance of getting the story right. Let's face it: in every press box there are guys who can quote accurately and others who should be novelists since every quote they write is pure fiction. Some guys have a perspective and a feel for the game; others are hopeless.

In order to sort out the truth, it's vital that you know who's doing the reporting. It is the same as going to a restaurant and not knowing about the chef or the business's reputation. The building may look great, but the food could rot your gut.

## PLAY-BY-PLAY ANNOUNCERS

When it comes to baseball, you are exposed to the guys on radio and television more than anyone else. They give you the score, tell you what happened, and are a link between you and the players.

But never forget this: these guys are lackeys hired by the ball club. They are owned by the team and work at the discretion of the team. Some of these guys are willing to buck the power structure. They have been around long enough and have enough juice with the public to speak their mind without getting canned, but these guys are very, very few.

Suppose you are one of the few people in the world who know that Keats and Byron aren't ball players but poets. And suppose you even know that every sentence should have a noun and a verb. And suppose you listen to Phil Rizutto yelling "Holy Cow," for the 800th time in 60 seconds and suppose that offends you. Well, so what? It doesn't offend the Yankees, and it sure as hell doesn't offend George Steinbrenner. That's because the old Scooter is making the Yanks sound good; he's selling tickets and keeping the hustle going full-blast.

Now there's nothing wrong with listening to the games on radio or watching them on television. I do it. It's entertaining, and at least you find out who won and lost. I mean, these guys won't lie about the score. Some ex-jock is liable to get the score wrong, but that's not intentional; it's just because he is incompetent.

Just remember that the announcer is an extension of the team's public relations department. He's telling you about bat day and painter's cap day and reminding you to get your tickets early. If it's raining, he tells you not to fear, because the weather will clear. In fact, this rain delay is a blessing in disguise because it gives you more time to get down to the ballpark and buy tickets and hot dogs. They give you the infamous line "There's still plenty of baseball action left tonight," and they are saying this just as Hurricane Mildred is settling over second base.

For the most part, the guys in the booth break down into two categories.

There is the pro broadcaster, who really is the second banana to the ex-jock. But you need the pro, or the ex-jock would never be able to remember who is pitching, what is the score, or even where the game is being played. He basically is an accountant. He gives you East Coast scores, West Coast scores, and minor league scores and reminds you that the team has a lot of talent down on the farm just ready to burst upon the major-league scene and give us a brighter tomorrow. Seriously, that's the kind of pap they feed us. These kids all have "a bright future ahead of them." Where else is their future supposed to be, behind them?

It isn't easy being the pro broadcaster, because you've got to do all the commercials for the club, you've got to do these inane dugout interviews without asking one probing or even interesting question, and most of all, you've got to carry the ex-jock. Making matters worse is the fact that the ex-jock makes more than you do.

That's because people like the ex-jock. He was somebody as a player, and as the years have passed, his career looks better and better. At least to the ex-jock and to the people who introduce him at banquets, that career certainly has gained a lot of luster for no discernible reason.

But as an announcer, the ex-jock is often sad, and his work is garbage. But ex-jocks sell. People like them to do commercials, even if they need 48 takes to say "Coke is it." Broadcasting executives like ex-jocks because they have immediate name recognition. The ball clubs like ex-jocks because they know that the ex-jock still remembers that old clubhouse rule, "Whatever is said here, stays here, and whatever you hear or see here, stays here." In other words, the ex-jock knows to tell us how all the guys on the field "are terrific people with beautiful wives and charming children."

So when Johnny Bench retires, someone with power says, "Let's give Johnny a job in the booth. Why not? He kept his mouth shut, and he only took us for about $5 million during his career, and he likes to sign autographs."

Suddenly, Johnny Bench is behind a microphone. Half the time, they don't even bother to try out the ex-jock; they just put him on the air and figure the pro broadcaster will "work with him." Well, the pro broadcaster has about as much chance of making Johnny Bench into a topflight broadcaster as Bench would have trying to teach the broadcaster how to become a Hall of Fame catcher.

Now and then there is a pro broadcaster such as Joe Tait, Ernie Harwell or Chick Hearn who is articulate, knowledgeable, and can keep the ex-jock to a minimum of bumbling and babbling. But believe me, it ain't easy, because some of these ex-jocks go through life half-bombed. They may not remember who's playing and where they are, but they can always find a good watering hole, and they know the name of the bartender.

The truth is that the ex-jock knows as much about what is happening on the club as anyone. The manager, the players, and the coaches all talk to him. They give him all the gossip, but the only reason they tell the ex-jock things is that they know that the ex-jock is a wimp behind the microphone. He is not about to tell us the good stuff. If he does, he won't survive.

## BASEBALL WRITERS

Believe it or not, these guys are our only real hope of finding out what is going on with a baseball team. The public relations flacks and the broadcasters often think that the beat writer really is a guy who should have been in the French Revolution running around with a hatchet looking for someone's head to lop off. Then other writers are viewed as being owned by the club.

So you have the headhunters and the housemen, and both of those guys do you about as much good as the network boys—they tell you nothing you need or even want to know. One guy splatters blood; the other one apologizes.

There are some decent, hardworking guys on the baseball beat. They are few, and they often don't last long, but they do exist. I'll talk more about them later.

Generally, baseball writers spend a lot of nights on the road schmoozing and boozing with the manager or a coach or anyone who can stand to have a writer schmooze and booze with him. That is especially true if the manager or coach is willing to pick up the writer's tab. So many beat writers think that the way to get inside information is to get drunk with someone on the team. Well, even if he does get something, which is very doubtful, he'll probably be too hung over to remember it.

For most baseball writers, the job is the manifestation of a childhood dream. They get to go to games free, they get to travel with ball players, and they even get to stand on the field during batting practice and go into the clubhouse after games. Any 12-year-old boy would want the same thing. And everyone would live happily ever after if the writer stayed like that 12-year-old boy.

Suddenly, the baseball writer discovers that he is traveling with people in a completely different socioeconomic class. These guys are five times as dumb as the writer, but they make 50 times as much money. The players are the celebrities; the writers are celebrities only in the sense that their names are on the stories in the paper and they have access to the players. But they are not really celebrities—they just live with them. By the time a player is 25, he has agents, accountants, and investments. If he has hired the right people, he'll be set for life if he can play until he's 30. At 30, the writer has a wife who bitches at him because he's never home. He has a couple of kids who can't recognize him because he's never home. If he has an accountant, it's to tell him how to make two house payments, take care of a second mortgage, and put aside money for the kid's education without having to file for bankruptcy. Even the ex-jock and the pro announcer earn at least three times as much as the baseball writer.

For many guys, the baseball job is a dream that becomes a nightmare.

Ideally, a baseball writer should have a basic knowledge of the sport. He should know how to keep a scorecard—you'd be shocked at how many guys in the press box really don't score a game correctly. He should know the rules of the game—just ask a writer to explain the infield fly rule or the save rule and see what you get. That is the minimum. I also believe a baseball writer should have a passion for the game and its history. He should be able to put things into perspective and realize that there were good pitchers before Dwight Gooden stepped on the mound. You get a lot of baseball writers who say that if it didn't happen before 1960, or even 1970, they're not interested in it. That's like a history professor saying "If it happened before World War II, who cares?"

So many of the baseball writers not only have a limited outlook on the sport but also aren't from the community where they work. Furthermore, they make no effort to learn the history of the franchise they cover and how it has related to the city. The Yankees are as much a part of New York as the Indians are a part of Cleveland, and both franchises tell us a lot about the towns where they are located. The Yankees as we know them could never have existed in Cleveland, and it's doubtful that a team depressed as long as the Indians could have been tolerated (and even loved) had they been in New York.

I'm not saying that a writer should come at people with a

dazzling display of facts. That's just showing off and, in many cases, showing a writer's ignorance and insecurity. But he is traveling with the team, and he has superb access and the time to learn. Ask the coaches about pitching and hitting, and most will be glad to explain the game to you. They like their jobs and they like to teach. Suppose you were assigned to go to Amsterdam and write about diamonds. Most writers would find someone in the business and bombard the guy with questions. But the baseball writer often thinks there is no need to do this, because—what the heck?—he grew up playing the game and everyone knows about baseball.

Yet, so many baseball writers are caught off base when a kid is called up from the minors or when a trade is made that brings in a player from the other league. Hell, they don't know if the player is right-handed, left-handed, or what. Writers have 10 billion hours a year of free time on the road when they can read reports and talk to the experts, but most guys spend their time drinking and eating on someone else's tab.

I find this lack of dedication and historical sense offensive, because a writer is paid to be an expert. If he's not when he gets the job, he should do his homework and become one.

In defense of the baseball writer, I'll say that his job may be the most demanding on the newspaper. The poor guy doesn't have a chance of being well-dressed. Even if he could afford nice clothes (which he can't), he still isn't one place long enough to keep them clean and pressed.

### The Expense Account

This is the one place where the baseball writer does his best and most creative writing. He'd better if he doesn't want his family to starve. The key to a great expense account is blank receipts. Say you eat at Howard Johnson's, and all you get is a corn toastie and juice for breakfast. The bill comes, and it's two bucks. You drop a quarter on the table for a tip, and you're out of the door spending only $2.25. But if you were able to rip the tab off the bottom of the bill, and if you did it before the waitress had a chance to write the final total on the tab, you can put down $8.25 for breakfast. That's a $6 profit. As far as the newspaper accounting office knows, you had bacon, eggs, hash browns, juice, and anything else that came with the breakfast supreme. If a writer is really smooth, he can ask the waitress if she has any other extra receipts sitting around, and then he can take those. This becomes the ideal situation whereby a writer is able to turn in a receipt for a meal when he didn't even walk into a restaurant. Also, if the writer has friends (granted, that is a doubtful prospect), they can collect receipts for him.

Travel also creates financial opportunities. Suppose the writer is one of four guys in a cab from the airport to the hotel. All four guys split the $20 fare, meaning it cost the writer $5. But if the writer is bright, he'll have the cabby write him a receipt for the full $20 and come away with a $15 profit. He also should know where all the free meals can be found, such as in stadium press rooms.

There are other tricks of the trade, but I'm afraid that some accountant from a newspaper office will read this and make life even more miserable for the baseball writer. Let's put it like this—the expense account is crucial to the existence of any baseball writer. Whatever he is able to make off this paper-pushing he deserves, because if newspapers had any class they would pay him the big-league per diem in cash so he could be on the same level as the ball players at least when it comes to eating.

## Drinking

A baseball writer must decide if he is going to drink, and this decision is crucial to you as a reader. It determines whether the guy writing about the games will be drunk or sober.

Now some writers drunk are still better than other writers sober. After all, getting soused is a great newspaper tradition. At larger papers there is a copy boy who is in charge of doing nothing but dispensing the Bromo-Seltzer to all the gin-soaked sportswriters and police beat writers. These are the guys who saw *The Front Page* once too often.

Baseball always was and always will be a drinking sport. Every night after a game, there is beer in the clubhouse and press box. That's 162 days of free beer, not counting six more weeks of spring training. Too many players and writers get into the habit of having a few beers at the park and then settling down to some real drinking, Jack Daniels and the rest, later on that night at the hotel. It's almost as if the beers didn't count. Well, you may not be counting them, but your liver is. If the writer doesn't drink much, he is viewed with suspicion. What's wrong with the guy? baseball people ask. How come he doesn't want to wake up each morning sick to his stomach with his chin hanging over the edge of the toilet like we do?

## Old-Time Baseball Writers

Dan Daniel was the typical old-time baseball writer. He covered the Yankees when Babe Ruth hit 60 homers in 1927, and he covered them when Roger Maris hit 61 homers in 1961. In between, he wrote countless features about players, yet he barely interviewed anyone. When Dan needed a quote, no problem—he just made it up.

But all the quotes were wonderful, and the players liked Dan Daniel's quotes. Even they knew that Dan Daniel made them sound better than they ever thought they could. Besides, Daniel seldom knocked anyone. All the players were great guys and faithful husbands, the manager was a genius, and the Yankees were always right. Daniel got to play cards and drink with all the great Yankees as they made long train trips.

And when it was over for Daniel, he was named to the Hall of Fame.

Are you kidding me?

A writer has as much right to be in the Hall of Fame as the guy who sweeps out the men's room at Fenway Park. The only reason writers are in the Hall of Fame is that writers are the voters. Consider this: one year Ted Williams batted .400, and a writer didn't vote for Williams for MVP. I'm not saying he didn't put Williams first, but the bozo didn't even have Williams among the top 10 on his ballot. You mean to tell me that there were 10 players in the American League better than Ted Williams in a year when Ted Williams hit .400? No, this bozo of a writer was mad at Williams because Williams wouldn't talk to him or something, so he left Williams off his ballot.

Not all baseball writers are petty, small-minded, and spiteful, but too many are exactly that, and some of these people are voting for who goes into the Hall of Fame. Isn't that wonderful?

### Writers and Television

Television forever changed how baseball was covered in the newspapers. In the Grantland Rice era, the writer often was an extension of the public relations bureau. Management and players were his friends, and the team's actions or motives were seldom questioned. Game stories were nothing more than play-by-play accounts of what happened on the field. There were no quotes unless the writer made up some perfectly harmless ones.

Then came television, and the fans already knew the score and how both teams scored before they opened up the morning paper. In fact, the people watching television often see the game better than the writers because they have the benefit of close-ups and instant replays. Most official scorers rush to a television set to watch a replay before deciding if a play is a hit or an error. In other words, the best way to score a game is to watch it on the tube, not at the park. That's an impact.

Television also changed radio coverage. Bill Stern was considered a great announcer, and one day he was doing a game and had the wrong guy scoring a touchdown. Realizing his error, Stern simply told the audience that one player lateraled the ball to another player, who then scored. That's how he corrected the error, and as long as no one saw it, Stern was able to pull his ass out of the fire. But with television, there can be no phantom laterals. Mistakes end up being exactly what they are—bloopers.

Where television had its greatest effect was in race relations in this country. TV did more for civil rights than Martin Luther King, Jr., and John F. Kennedy, and that's because television showed a black, Jackie Robinson, playing baseball with whites. To the average American who happened to worship baseball, seeing Robinson with the Dodgers was a startling revelation. Robinson entering baseball gave blacks more exposure and caused whites to think more about integration than ever before. On the baseball diamond, where the best man was supposed to win, Jackie Robinson, a black, was winning. That made white America pause and take notice.

So television and baseball not only helped civil rights, on a lesser level, they have demanded more accuracy and truth from both radio and newspapers. The media must do more behind the scenes. More interviews and more interviews with depth, more analysis pieces and more columns and pure opinion. In the late 1950s, television gave birth to the chipmunk school of writers, as the players called them. These guys like Dick Young who ran around asking tough questions, probing into the players' personal lives (at least to a greater extent than ever before) and writing stories that were critical. For writers and players, the game has changed.

## Writers vs. Players

Players and writers have ceased being friends, and what has resulted is an uneasy truce between the media and the players today. They may be acquaintances, and they certainly use one another, but they seldom are friends as Dan Daniel was with Babe Ruth. Jimmy Cannon, the late New York columnist, correctly characterized the nature between players and writers as adversarial, and it always will be.

Baseball writers spend more time with their subjects than they do with anyone, including their wives. A writer doesn't cover a baseball team, he marries it, and that means there will be ups and downs and lots of tension. In this case, you better believe that familiarity breeds contempt. By its very nature, baseball is a cloak-and-dagger sport. Managers are doing everything in their power to remain managers, and that includes telling writers just how lousy the players are so that the writers will be aware of what a great job the manager is doing with so little talent. Players on the bench are subtly lobbying for spots in the lineup, thereby putting pressure on both the manager and the player starting in front of them. Front office people often leak rumors to writers just to see if they can get a player traded, and then they turn around and deny those rumors to another writer. This is a sport of prima donnas, lunatics, third-rate operators, and frightened young and old men. Jim Bouton gave us a glimpse into this world in his now infamous *Ball Four*, where Mickey Mantle and the legends of our time were climbing onto the roofs of hotels so that they could peak into a window and watch a woman undress. There are plenty of stories of players stepping out on their wives, of players having two girls at the same time, but in different rooms.

This is the stuff a baseball writer can't report—not if he wants to remain a baseball writer. So compromises are reached all the time. A guy is too hung over to play, and everyone around the team knows that he spent the night pouring everything but Mr. Clean down his throat, but the club announces that Larry Lush will have to sit out the game because of a virus. The announcers say Larry Lush has a virus, the writers write that Larry Lush has a virus, and everyone, especially Larry Lush, is happy. Most of the other players don't object to the cover-up, because they know that there will be a day they'll be suffering from a virus, too.

Everything goes all right for a writer until he writes something bad about one of them. Suddenly, he becomes the enemy. The guy he has written about may be the biggest scumbag since Attila the Hun, but he is really shocked that someone would dare to mention in print that he has a lousy arm. Players expect public praise because that's all they have ever heard. They are not grateful when it comes their way, because theirs is a life of being spoiled, coddled, and idolized and of having talcum powder thrown on their precious fannies from the time they first touched a baseball. Just because a ball player has a 90 mph fastball, he expects everyone to write that he has the smile of Cary Grant, the acting ability of Richard Burton, and the mind of Thomas Edison.

What if something goes wrong?

Most players are ready with the alibi. They lost the ball in the lights, or they slipped on some wet grass, or the umpire screwed them. A player will complain when he hasn't pitched for a few weeks. Then he gets a chance to pitch, he gets bombed, and he tells the writers, "How was I supposed to get them out when I haven't pitched for two weeks?"

You read these ludicrous alibi stories every day. I remember one player saying he was in a slump because he recently had a baby and the infant was crying at night, keeping him up, and he wasn't getting enough rest. And the writers just nodded as they took the notes and wrote stories about it for the next day.

I'll admit that not all baseball players are these kinds of egomaniacs, just as most baseball writers aren't blabbering idiots, but a helluva lot of these people are exactly as I describe. A baseball writer is going to spend a lot of hours with people he doesn't like and people who don't like him. It's a lonely job, and a lot of guys have gotten very bitter doing it.

The amazing part is that writers and ball players haven't taken to shooting at each other with rocket launchers.

The reason is that ball players and writers need each other.

When a new writer goes on the baseball beat, the manager and the more astute players will try to get the guy in their camp. They know that the writer will be there every day, and he will be writing about them every day, so it's best to get off on the right foot and keep that ink positive. The players and manager figure out what they can tell a writer and what they can't, what the writer is interested in and what he is not.

After a while, the baseball people like to have an idea when the writer will zonk them, and as long as the writer's actions are predictable, he will survive. In effect, a comfort zone is created.

But eventually the writer steps out of line, at least as far as the players are concerned. The writer is like a puppy who has been trained to stay in the backyard and to wag his tail when he is petted and slink away when he is bad. But when the puppy becomes a dog, he barks, he wanders out of his yard, and when someone gets mad at him, he bites back. So the writer rips a player, and what you have is a feud.

Sometimes a writer and a manager will just get sick of each other. The writer will blame everything from a .210 team batting average to cancer on the manager. The manager will freeze out the writer and tell the other writers things like trade rumors and who is in the lineup and who is out. Both parties have decided that the other is a son of a bitch, and they plan to fight this cold war until one of them disappears. Believe me, this happens all the time.

Writers get the reputation of being "positive" and "negative." A positive baseball writer is a guy who writes a story exactly as the player would have written it about himself. The positive writer also is the master of the alibi story. The negative writer sometimes is a guy who tries to tell the truth and often is a guy who is just so sick of all the crap that comes with covering baseball that he just lashes out at everyone and everything. He spends every waking hour trying to find someone who will say something bad about someone else. The fact is that baseball people are constantly at war with media people, and then they hop right into bed with them. One week this player hates this writer, and the next the player and writer are getting drunk together, but the player is ready to kill another writer. And this carries over into the media, where certain writers have been covering the same team since the Civil War and they haven't spoken to each other since Warren Harding was president. The writers trash each other to the players, who find this skullduggery very amusing.

## Baseball Writers: The Facts

For the most part, baseball writing is better now than it ever has been. That may not be saying a lot, but there are a number of guys on the beat who at least try to get things right.

As I said before, it's a lousy job. You'd never catch me doing it. If a writer has survived a few years, he knows how to make money off his expense accounts, how to pack his suitcase in five seconds, and how to keep the players from trying to break his right arm in six places. He knows how to drink without getting too drunk, and he has the remarkable ability to write the same story over and over without thinking twice about what he is doing. He knows people really don't like him and that they wouldn't even look at him if he weren't a writer. He has no friendships, just business acquaintances. In the clubhouse, he is viewed as the enemy. Baseball is an "us" and "them" world, and the baseball writer will always be among the "them."

Yet baseball writers are a little more literate than before. They certainly are more educated and once in a while they even think before they write something. A few have enough guts to write a critical story and yet are smart enough to stay out of the petty feuds that surround the beat. But the modern baseball writers are far too preoccupied with statistics. Bill James made some quick coins with his *Baseball Abstract.* Now everyone wants to cover the game as if it were a calculus problem. Only about 10 percent of the baseball fans understand what most of the statistical categories mean; the other 90 percent can't tell one number from another and don't care enough to find out.

So what is the bottom line about baseball and the media?

What you see is seldom what you read or hear. There is a lot of sidestepping of the truth, a lot of shading of this or that. But any writer or announcer who hopes to make a career on the baseball beat learns how to walk all the tightropes between truth and lying, and what the fan hears is usually a little of both.

# 11
# WHY I HATE THE YANKEES BUT STILL LOVE BASEBALL

Let's begin with the negative. I don't like the New York Yankees.

I really don't.

Not much at all, in fact.

I try to be logical about the Yankees. I try to find the source of my discontent. I try to put emotions aside and speak not from the heart but from the head. Then I remember that the Yankees are in New York. So that means I not only must try to be logical about the Yankees, but I must do the same about New York City. But I keep thinking about the combination—the Yankees and New York City. And slowly, my brain says over and over, "The New York Yankees, the New York Yankees . . ." That's when I can no longer control myself.

You see, *I hate the Yankees.*

There, I feel better. Only there's more:

*I've always hated the Yankees.*

I don't mean to scream. I don't make a practice of screaming. I am a very quiet, well-adjusted guy. But:

*I'll always hate the Yankees.*

What can I say? That much is true.

*The Yankees are scumbags.*

What else can I say? That much also is true.

Perhaps my feelings are not rational. Perhaps I need a doctor in a white coat smoking a pipe and speaking with a German accent. Perhaps I need someone to say, "Vell, Herr Franklin, this ding about deese Yankees . . . where did it all begin?"

Well, I'd tell the quack this: "It began at the beginning—where the hell else would it begin, you Nazi schmuck?"

That's because my feeling about the Yankees did begin at the beginning. Even when I was a kid, the Yankees represented the most dominant team in the history of sports. There was an old joke about rooting for the Yankees being the same as rooting for U.S. Steel. I didn't find it funny, because it was true, and it made me loathe the Yankees even more. It goes back to the fact that the Yankees always won. They were the symbol of power and strength, and the rest of the American League was a living testimony to human frailties. In other words, the Yankees won and about no one else did. Year after year, the Yankees won. The more they won, the worse they got. After a while, they got to be so damn smug I don't even know how they could like themselves. They certainly didn't treat each other very well, and this comes from a guy whose favorite player was Lou Gehrig, one of the greatest Yankees of all time.

Gehrig and Babe Ruth were the Yankees who made that franchise the Yankees. They hit more home runs than anyone else,. and a strong case can be made that Ruth ushered in the era of modern baseball. But think about Ruth for a moment. When he stopped playing, he had only one goal. He wanted to manage the Yankees. That's all he asked. He would have done it for nothing. He did everything but get down on his hands and knees and lick the owner's shoes.

But the Yankees never made Ruth their manager, and the guy died with a broken heart. I'm still mad at them for that.

As for Gehrig, he died before they had a chance to figure out a way to screw him. But I'm convinced the Yankees would have turned their backs on Gehrig, too, if he had lived long enough.

The Yankees are a team that fired Casey Stengel in 1960, after he won a pennant but lost to Pittsburgh in the World Series. They also fired Yogi Berra—not once, but twice—as their manager. The first time it wasn't even George Steinbrenner who pulled the plug on Yogi. That was in 1964 when Yogi managed the Yankees to the American League pennant. They lost to St. Louis in the World Series, so they canned Yogi and hired Johnny Keane, the guy who was managing the Cardinals. Say what you want about Yogi Berra, but the last Yankee team to win a pennant in the 1960s was his club in 1964.

They didn't give a damn about Yogi Berra or anyone else. Any group of people so steeped in arrogance as the Yankees could have written the book *Looking Out for Number One.* That's because the Yankees are the epitome of New York hype. In New York, if a guy hits .250, the media makes him a star. If he hits .270, they put him in the Hall of Fame. The Yankees had great players, but not every one of their players was great. You'd never know that if you had read the New York papers.

When I lived in New York, I rooted for the Brooklyn Dodgers. Those guys were fun. Just think about the names of the two teams' facilities. The Yanks played in *Yankee Stadium.* The name just sounds stuffy, like Carnegie Hall or something. The Dodgers played at Ebbets Field, which sounds like a place where kids go for a pickup game in the park. The Dodgers broke baseball's color line with Jackie Robinson, Don Newcombe, and Roy Campanella. The Dodgers and New York Giants had these great feuds, and they were fighting all the time. These guys seemed like human beings.

The Yankee players were robots, like the people who work at the Honda plant in Tokyo, punching out one perfect car after another. Their best player was Joe DiMaggio, who never dropped a fly ball, never threw to the wrong base, never failed to come through with a big hit when it meant the most. For years, DiMaggio wasn't a player, he was a baseball machine.

An area where the Yankees did nothing to cover themselves in glory was that of race. It took them years to integrate the team, because not just any black man was good enough to be a Yankee. They supposedly searched for the guy with the right kind of temperament, the right kind of table manners, and who the hell knows what else. The Yankees spent too much time listening to Madison Avenue and worrying about their image, and in the process they did absolutely nothing for race relations in this country. Their first black player was Elston Howard, an outstanding athlete and person. Like Ruth, Howard always wanted to manage the Yankees. The Yankees refused to give Howard, like Ruth, a chance.

When I came to Cleveland, it was a perfect town for Yankee haters. Cleveland was the only team to break the Yankee dominance during the dynasty years. From 1947 to 1958, the Yankees won all but two pennants—the Indians snuck in there during the 1948 and 1954 seasons. Thank goodness for the Indians winning those two pennants, or else the Yankees would be even more insufferable and even bigger jerks. I rooted for the Yankees to lose because they always won. And on those rare occasions when they did lose, such as 1948 and 1954, I was exhilarated. It was as if America had won World War II all over again, and I took sheer delight in the middle and late 1960s and into the 1970s when the Yankees not only didn't win but stunk up the joint. God bless you, Horace Clarke, you were my favorite Yankee second baseman. Suddenly, the word *Yankees* became associated with mediocrity, and that had a great appeal to me. That's why in Cleveland I hosted "I Hate the Yankees Hanky Nights," and we'd put 40,000 fannies in the seats to boo those bastards from New York and to wave Pete Franklin's "Beat the Yankees" hankies. It was terrific group therapy.

If you think I hated the Yankees when I was a kid, it has

been worse since George Steinbrenner came along. Before he became owner of the Yankees, George Steinbrenner tried to buy the Indians and was rejected. This was very painful to Steinbrenner, who is from Cleveland and always wanted to be a local hero. So after the Indians didn't want his money, Steinbrenner turned to New York, where the Yankees had totally bottomed out. That should not have been a surprise when you consider who was running the Yankees. It was CBS, the broadcasting network. If you want something terminally screwed up, just let the television executives at it. Messing up the Yankees wasn't easy, and it took a lot of thought, so give CBS credit for doing it so fast. CBS did what few organizations could have done. It tore down the greatest organization in baseball history in about the wink of an eye.

It may surprise you to hear me say this, but Steinbrenner's buying the Yankees was a good thing. That's because anyone would have been a good thing after CBS.

New York is the perfect stage for Steinbrenner, who is a megalomaniac of the first dimension. He is a man of little substance or depth. He is happiest when he is making someone else miserable. He needs someone to humiliate, someone to bully, someone to fire. Steinbrenner reminds me of a guy who has never had to compete. He's always been the rich boy, and he's never had to work for a living. I'm not saying he won't or doesn't work, but Steinbrenner has never been in the position where he had to work or he didn't eat.

That is why winning is so important to him, and it's why being in the spotlight is even more important to Steinbrenner than winning. He needs publicity like a drunk needs Muscatel. He needs New York more than New York needs him. That's because New York feeds the insatiable appetite of Steinbrenner's ego. If he were in Indianapolis, his name would be Robert Irsay, just another klutz, another clown with a tiresome act.

So Steinbrenner has to be in the spotlight even when his team is winning. Remember during the 1981 World Series when the Yankees were playing the Los Angeles Dodgers? There was Steinbrenner supposedly having a fight with someone in an elevator. He said he "clocked some guys" to protect the integrity of New York and the Yankees. We never heard from or saw these guys. But we did see Steinbrenner walk around with his hand in a cast as if he had just punched out a hippo. The *New York Post* would go out of business without Steinbrenner, because he gets as much ink as the Son of Sam and Bernhard Goetz. In the *Post*, Steinbrenner is the boss. But in real life, this is a very insecure man.

That's why he always criticizes his players in the papers. It used to be Reggie Jackson. If Reggie had a couple of games without a hit, Steinbrenner ripped him. Next, it was Dave Winfield, who is a great athlete, a terrific competitor, and just a magnificent player. It takes a colossal jackass to rap Winfield, but that's Steinbrenner. Steinbrenner even has knocked Don Mattingly, who also happens to be a great player.

Sparky Lyle was right. The Yankees under Steinbrenner are the Bronx Zoo. The stadium is in the middle of the South Bronx, which has been forever burning down. The police district is called Fort Apache, because it is an area where no civilized man or beast should venture. Even the cops are afraid to go out. Anyone who plays in this part of New York under Steinbrenner deserves combat pay. If you play for the Yankees, you've got to block out Steinbrenner, and that's what most of the good players do.

Unfortunately, managers don't have that option.

No one knows more about Steinbrenner's insecurities than the manager of the Yankees. If you manage the Yankees, you really don't manage. You try to follow orders, and when you follow orders and they don't work, you are second-guessed. The owner tells you whom to play and not to play. He hires and fires your coaches; he calls you in the middle of the night to call you a jackass. He overrules you; he demeans you in the end, he'll destroy you.

This is not startling news. Anyone in baseball knows this.

Some guys manage for Steinbrenner because of the money. He'll give you a four-year deal for $1 million and fire you after a year. Nonetheless, you'll never work harder for $1 million than you did in that one year under Steinbrenner.

It is hard to work for Steinbrenner, because every morning you have to look in the mirror and know "I am owned lock, stock, and barrel by this guy who is happy only when he is making me miserable."

That's why I am amused by people who say that Billy Martin is his own man, that he does things his way. Billy Martin has worked for Steinbrenner more than any other manager. That tells you something about Billy, and it says little about him being a walking definition of a rugged individualist.

Billy Martin is a lot of things—a drinker, a marshmallow salesman attacker, a guy who often is late for work, and a guy who has less character than Steinbrenner, as mind-boggling as that may seem. Martin is obscene and he gets in fights, and the fans have been conned by all this. They think he is a fiery leader and all that crap. Nothing could be further from the truth. Just ask the guys who have played under him. After a year, Martin has to hide in his office, or else someone is going to dent his skull with a bat.

Steinbrenner has been searching all of his life for a guy like Billy Martin. You see, Martin is a big name. He was a banjo-hitting second baseman, but he was a banjo-hitting second baseman in New York, where the papers turned him into a deity. In public, Martin adopts a tough-guy posture. Behind closed doors, he cowers under Steinbrenner, and George loves it. Both of these guys are working out their psychological problems on each other.

Only in New York could these guys become heroes, which is why I so hate the Yankees.

It is true that Martin and Steinbrenner need each other, but baseball needs these two jokers about as much as New York needs another mugger.

So that's the worst about baseball, but the fact that it can survive Martin and Steinbrenner says a lot about the game.

There is so much right about baseball, or else baseball wouldn't be *baseball.* It would not have endured, and it wouldn't have found such a strong niche in the American psyche.

Baseball managers go on and on about the little things. The little things this, the little things that; the little things help you win, and the little things can make you lose. Well, the little things make baseball a great game, and I'm not talking about whether or not Ducky Duckbrain can bunt.

Instead, I mean things like the box score.

No other sport can be summed up in so little space. You look at the box score and it's all there—the pitchers, the hitters, the innings, who got the hits and who didn't. When the hard-core baseball fan grabs the sports page, the first thing he does is turn right to the agate page, where the box scores and the standings can be found. Stop some kid on the street and ask him who plays right guard for the New York Giants, and he'll have no idea. Ask the same kid who is the second baseman for the Yankees, and he'll tell you about Willie Randolph. That's because of box scores. Anyone who appears in the game gets his name in the box, and next to his name is where you'll find what he did and where he played in the field.

We understand baseball because we all have played it. Yes, that works against the players. It makes us less patient with them than we are with football or tennis players. With baseball, we don't have to learn the rules, because we already know them. We probably can't remember when we actually learned how baseball was played; we just knew. It is like fairy tales that are passed down from generation to generation; so is baseball.

Baseball is a simple game because it is right out there in the open. You never hear a manager say he didn't know what happened in the game because he needs time to check the films. That's a line football coaches often hand you. In baseball you can see every pitch, every hit, every catch, and every error. One guy has a ball, the other a bat, and the game breaks down like this:

1. The guy with the ball wants to throw it past the guy with the bat.
2. The guy with the bat wants to hit it.
3. When the guy hits it, there are other guys who want to catch the ball.

That's basically it—throw the ball, hit the ball, catch the ball. You have offense and defense in the most obvious terms. The bases are clearly defined and so are the foul lines.

Only mankind tries to make baseball hard. Everyone wants to be a genius, but what is there to be a genius about? This is baseball, the same game you played in the third grade, not the neutron bomb. I don't care what the managers and coaches say; there is no correct way to pitch or hit. What works for one guy probably won't work for another. Ted Williams had a classic, straight-up stance at the plate. Stan Musial coiled like a cobra. Both were great left-handed hitters. Dave Winfield is 6'7", and he hits a lot of home runs. Mel Ott was a foot shorter, and he hit a lot of home runs. Bob Feller had a high leg kick and could throw the ball through a carwash without getting it wet. Phil Niekro had no leg kick, and most of his pitches weren't fast enough for a speeding ticket. Both guys won big. Feller is in the Hall of Fame and Niekro will be. Every hitting coach and pitching coach has his own pet theory, but none of them really know what works. They only know what may have worked for them or for another guy, but they can't begin to guess what will work for most players.

I've seen more good, young players screwed up by coaches who, the first time the kid slumps, start tinkering with his swing or his grip:

"Hold the bat tighter."

"Loosen your grip on the bat."

"Your arm is ahead of your body."

"Your arm is behind your body."

"Your feet are too far apart."

"Your feet are too close together."

What crap they pass out as coaching. The best advice to give any younger player who is having a problem is *no advice.* Tell him that you love him and write his name in the lineup day after day. Either he will prove he can play or he won't, and the coaches have nothing to do with it. Yogi Berra was right—you can't hit and think at the same time. Either you can hit or you can't.

Can you believe that they have dragged computers into

the dugout? Is this the Star Wars defense system or a game between the Mets and the Cubs? Davey Johnson is in the dugout looking at printouts that tell him God knows what, and it won't matter to anyone. If Ron Darling has his good stuff, he doesn't need the computer. If he can't get the ball over the plate, the computer won't help him either. After all is said and done, the best pitchers still were the guys like Sandy Koufax, Walter Johnson, and Feller, who could take the ball and throw it so damn hard that no SOB could see it, much less hit it. Guys have won with curves and knuckleballs and screwballs, but the best way to win is to throw the damn ball hard.

As for hitters, the best are the power hitters. They are so strong that they can hit the ball where no one is allowed to stand. As Earl Weaver once said, the home run is the safest play in baseball. If you hit the ball halfway up the bleachers, nothing can go wrong. No one can catch it; no one can get thrown out. The guy who hit the home run can take six years to cover the bases, and no one will say anything. So God bless the power hitters. As for the "contact" hitters, you and I both know that these guys are wimps. The best they can do is hit the ball on the ground and hope it rolls between a couple of infielders for a single.

The game has been cluttered by managers, coaches, squeeze plays, double steals, hit-and-runs, pitches that break left or right, that rise or sink. But teams are still picked as they always were. Remember when you were a kid and the two captains at the park were looking over everyone who wanted to play. When they picked sides, a captain would say, "Give me Pinky; he can hit." The other captain would say, "I'll take Stinky; he can throw hard." Talk about wisdom from the mouths of babes.

Kids intuitively understand that is what the game is about—the matchup, the pitcher vs. the hitter, and the best man for that particular at-bat will prevail. This always was and always will be the essence of the game—the hitter vs. the pitcher. And the pitcher will always be the more important of the two. I'll say that again. *The pitcher will always be the most important man on the field.*

If you can come away with one message from this book, that should be it.

The pitcher can dominate play as no one else in sports. He always begins the action because nothing happens until he throws the ball. And if he throws it hard enough or with enough sneaky stuff, he will win. Remember, if a guy throws a shutout, he'll never lose. If you don't believe me, then ask the bookies. They set the odds on every game based upon who is pitching. In the early 1970s, the Phillies were a terrible team and seldom favored to win except when Steve Carlton was on the mound. Then, Philadelphia and Carlton were the team the bookies liked.

Great managers such as Earl Weaver and Casey Stengel won when they had great players, especially great pitchers, and lost when they didn't. When Weaver had Jim Palmer, Mike Cuellar, Dave McNally and the rest of those great Baltimore pitchers of 20 years ago winning their usual 20 games, Weaver was a marvel. When Weaver came back in 1985 and the Orioles pitching had gone sour, Weaver went right down the tubes and got fired. It is like an actor. When Sir Laurence Olivier had a good script and supporting cast, he was great. But when he was in a turkey like *The Betsy*, with no cast and no script, he was terrible, just like Earl Weaver trying to manage a team with no pitching. There is such a thing as a bad manager just as there are bad directors. They take talent and screw it up by using it wrong. But in the end, managers are dependent upon their talent, and so are directors. Movies and baseball and other businesses have that much in common. Either you have the horses or you're stuck with the donkeys. Keep in mind that the managers who have stayed in one place the longest have been with organizations that have tremendous farm systems to keep a steady flow of pitching talent coming to the big leagues, as was the case with the Dodgers and the Orioles.

But the fans don't want to hear about pitching because it's boring. Home runs are fun. Everyone stands and cheers, but pitching is methodical. Ground out, pop out, strike out. Inning after inning, it's ground out, pop out, and strike out. A good pitcher gets them out in that kind of machine-like fashion.

The funny thing is that even if our team loses we still love the game. I think it's because there is something special about baseball—there is no clock.

That is a tremendous asset because the damn clock is driving us crazy. The clock has us completely messed up. We are always looking at the clock so we can get to work or get to lunch at a restaurant or get home in time for dinner. The clock beeps at us, it rings at us, and it turns on our television sets and radios. We may not like it, but our lives are on the clock. So many of us literally punch in and out on the clock at work.

But baseball says the hell with the clock, almost as if it knows that the clock is eating up our guts and keeping the Maalox people rich. You can go to a baseball game and be there for a little over two hours or over four hours. You can decide if you want to get a sunburn or you don't, you want to get bombed or you don't, you want to argue with the moron sitting next to you or you don't. In fact, you can do all three—get bombed, get a sunburn, and argue with the moron—and still not miss much of the game. You can go to baseball games decked out in Brooks Brothers suits or wearing a pair of purple jockey shorts. You can be a bleacher bum in Wrigley Field or a millionaire in the loge at Yankee Stadium. And like Steinbrenner, the bleacher bum and the millionaire both think they know more than the dummy managing the team.

The egalitarian aspects of the game, how its popularity cuts across all racial and economic lines, is why it has survived. The game can glamorize a guy who was a drunk and whoremonger such as Babe Ruth because Babe liked children, ate a lot of hot dogs, and hit a lot of home runs. The game endured the Black Sox scandal in 1919, which is amazing. Baseball is the only sport where its biggest event—the World Series, for God's sake—was fixed. And baseball has had the longest strike of any sport. It has had more contract disputes, more deranged owners, and it even has had George

Steinbrenner, but it goes on, and the fans keeping buying tickets. Part of the reason is that most of the fans become unraveled when it comes to baseball. A crazy owner decides to give Billy Martin, who was a banjo-hitting second baseman and later a scumbag manager who can't keep a job, a place in the monuments in Yankee Stadium with Ruth, Gehrig, and Mantle. And what do the fans do? They don't throw fruit as they should, but they give the scumbag a standing ovation. That tells you what you need to know about the baseball fan. He loves his heroes, even if a guy has no business being a hero.

There have always been legends in baseball, and there always will be. No athlete from 50 years ago is mentioned more often than Babe Ruth. There are very few people still alive who actually saw Ruth play, but his name and his fame have been handed from one generation to the next like a prized family heirloom. During World War II at Guadalcanal, the GIs would hear the Japanese yelling obscenities about Babe Ruth, and that's because the Japanese knew that Ruth was a part of Americana, even if Ruth had already retired. His name was important enough to us for the Japanese to take it in vain in hopes of getting right to the souls of the American Marines. Remember that when World War II began and the best athletes were being drafted into the service Franklin Roosevelt said that baseball would continue, even if it had to be played by the old and lame. FDR said that baseball was crucial to the social fabric of our country. It gave the people at home something to follow; it was a relief from all the war news. It also gave the troops something to talk about, a subject other than the fear of dying. Countless soldiers talked about wanting to get home in one piece so they could go to Fenway Park or Yankee Stadium for a game. *The Sporting News* was shipped to the fronts in Europe and the Pacific so the troops could keep up with news about their teams.

Being a fan—I don't care if it's a Mets fan, a Yankees fan, a Cardinals fan, or even a Cleveland Indians fan—has always meant something. We wear the shirts and cap; we wear the colors of our team. For baseball, it always has been like that.

Now the game has gone to Latin America, where it is a religion and where some of our best shortstops are being produced. After we defeated Japan in WWII, we rebuilt the country and gave the Japanese baseball. Now the Japanese sign some of our players.

The game is so great that it seems to be impossible to destroy it. It has so much charm, so much personality. I've never gotten tired of baseball. Sure, I've gone through spells when I've become bored, when inning after inning goes by and I can't remember what happened, but then something happens on the field and I'm back into it, my attention once again riveted on the game. And it has nothing to do with the guys playing the game, because they can be tiresome and obnoxious beyond belief. Rather, it's the game itself that has captured my imagination and the soul of America. Think of our language:

"I don't know what chance I've got. There are already two strikes on me."

"Today I'm going for the home run."

"I can't make lunch. We'll have to take a rain check."

"I think our good friend Fred has lost his fastball. He just can't cut it around the office."

"Now it's time to bring in Joe. He's our cleanup hitter, and he'll close the sale."

I won't beat you to death with examples, because there are hundreds. But the point is obvious.

There are several other things baseball has going for it, such as spring training. That is a glorious time of year because all the clichés are true. Every team has a chance, the kids look pretty good, and the sun is out. Baseball is played during the day before retirees in Florida and Arizona. The players are friendly, the skies are blue, and the world seems right. I love going to spring training because it seems like baseball in its purest sense, the same game we played as kids. The scores don't mean anything; no one cares about the standings. It's just the game that matters. I also believe that this is why newspaper stories from spring training are so well read. They are crap, of course. A guy who has hit .242 for the last 12 years suddenly has a new stance and thinks it will really make a difference, and the writer does a story on it because—what the hell?—it is spring training, and he has to write something. The writer knows that his guy will end up hitting .242 again. In the back of their minds, the readers know it, too. But we relish the charade. Spring training is the greatest public relations tool ever invented for professional sports. It makes opening day something special because, after reading six weeks of stories from Florida or Arizona, here is a chance to see this year's team and this year's rookies. It is spring training that makes OPENING DAY, a time of optimism, a time to feel good.

While spring training gets us into the season, it is the radio broadcasts that carry us along. Baseball on the radio makes a perfect background, almost like a musical score for a movie. We can listen to it and not listen to it. The announcers who have done it for a long time such as Ernie Harwell and Vince Skully become like old friends, telling us what is happening. We become used to their vocal style and know when their voice reaches a certain tenor that it is time to pay attention and listen because something important is happening on the field. That's another key to baseball on the radio. Just as we can see everything on the field when we watch a game, we can easily picture the game as we hear the game on the radio. It is just the ingenious manner in which the game is played and the diamond is designed.

Baseball still clings to its strong rural roots. Many announcers such as Harwell and Red Barber had soft, southern accents. We don't like our play-by-play men to sound like game show hosts or used-car salesmen. The game is leisurely, and a good announcer is like a front-porch storyteller. No other game lends itself to this style of announcing. That's why radio broadcasts of baseball games can be on in stores, in cars, about anywhere. They don't intrude. Football and basketball are much different because those games have so much action that is so extreme.

Of course, baseball is the only sport with its own song. More people know the words to "Take Me Out to the Ball Game" than know the words to the national anthem.

The only objection I have to "Take Me Out to the Ball Game" is that it is very hard to buy Cracker Jack in most parks. Cracker Jack is in the song, and it should be at the concession stands. If I were commissioner of baseball, I'd send out an edict ordering that Cracker Jack be made available at every stadium. Food is a very important part of baseball. I mean, where else do we buy a hot dog other than a baseball game? Who goes into a restaurant and orders a hot dog? Who makes hot dogs at home? But if we go to a baseball game, we usually order a hot dog. Same thing with peanuts. Nobody eats them at home or orders them for dessert at a restaurant, but if we're at the park, we often get peanuts. It's subliminal. At the park, we want hot dogs and peanuts. Anywhere else, who cares?

I have found that baseball games just make me hungry. I think it has something to do with the pace of the game. If we are watching it on television, we know we have time to get up, make a stop at the bathroom, raid the refrigerator, and get back in front of the set without missing anything. That's because there is a break between innings, even a break at each half-inning. There are breaks when they change pitchers and even when a pinch hitter is used. It gives us time to think about our stomach. When I'm at games, I'm in the press box eating the free food, and I mean I eat it. Peanuts, popcorn, hot dogs, and I'd like to say Cracker Jack, but they don't have any. If all the food is gone, I eat the plate. Baseball has that kind of effect on me.

There is one other aspect of baseball that has ingrained it into the mainstream of American life. It's the number. A lot of people just love numbers, and baseball has more numbers than the phone company.

If you want, you can keep score. You can keep track of what every hitter and every pitcher did, and you can come up with your own symbols and system. If you are a nervous person and don't like to eat for three solid hours during a game, keeping score gives you something to do. It's better than twiddling your fingers. Keeping score also gives some people the feeling that they are a part of the game. They can look at their scorecards and know what Don Mattingly did in every at-bat. They can know when Ron Guidry went out of the game and when Dave Righetti came in. If they are very meticulous, they can even tell you who is the umpire at which base. I know people who save all their scorecards and have 50 years' worth in their desk drawers.

I've never kept score in my life. Not once. It bores me. I can see what is going on; I don't need a card to tell me. I don't need to write down what I've just seen. If it's important, I'll remember it. If you keep score and it makes you happy, wonderful. If you think you can be some kind of anthropologist by saving your scorecards, go right ahead. But it's not for me. During a baseball game, I need my hands free so they can help me feed my face.

The numbers freaks have taken over the game. We have batting averages, ERAs, RBIs, home runs, runs scored, batting averages before the seventh inning, and batting averages after the seventh inning. We have saves, although they are always changing the rules about what exactly is a save.

Then a guy like Bill James comes along, and you wonder who ever let him out of calculus class. The 9,000 statistical categories we already have aren't good enough for James. He has to make up 9,000 more. And you know what? All the numbers freaks out there are nodding their heads and saying "That's good, Bill. I always wondered what the Mets' record was when the sun goes down before the second inning." There is a playwright in Las Vegas who has had a couple of shows done off-Broadway, and one of his plays is called *The Box Score Family.* It is about a family whose life revolves around baseball numbers. For a lot of people, that's not art but reality.

The numbers freaks play games with cards and dice based on mathematical probability such as Strat-O-Matic board games. There are mythical cards and dice games where the

1927 Yankees play the 1961 Yankees. Now we even have these fantasy league baseball games and the rotisserie leagues that are all based on stats, and people keep elaborate records, spending hours on them daily.

Of course, there are the baseball card collectors, the guys who pay $500 for the 1931 Bing Miller card.

The point is that baseball keeps growing, and the interest is stronger than ever. There are more books about baseball published now than ever before. The attendance is higher than ever. The radio and television rights are worth more than ever before. That's because baseball is a simple game, but it can be viewed on an intellectual level. The pennant races grab us, cause us to wait up late for scores from the West Coast. Then there's the World Series. It seems like the country just stops during the World Series. It's the major topic of conversation, even for the casual baseball fan. People plan their vacations around baseball. They go to Arizona or Florida during the spring. During the summer, some people set up a vacation by going from city to city and stadium to stadium to watch games. No other sport has such a grip on us.

# 12
# WHY I LOVE THE NBA

Some people in the media and some sports fans are beyond dumb. I hear them talk, and I ask myself, "What's dumber than an idiot?"

The people I am talking about are those who knock the NBA. Not those who say they don't like basketball—I can accept that. If you don't like basketball as a sport, there is no reason for you to like the NBA. But the morons who say "I love basketball. High school basketball, college basketball, I just can't get enough of it. But the pros, you can have it. I can't stand to watch the NBA."

That's like saying you're a music fan but you really prefer Grandma playing a washboard to Duke Ellington and Chopin. Or else it's like saying, forget the lobster, forget the steak, give me the Big Mac because that is really the essence of dining.

If you truly are a basketball fan, and if you really understand and appreciate the sport, the NBA is Mecca. In the last 35 years, no sport has evolved quite as much as the NBA. We've gone from a center jump after each basket and two-handed set shots to the fast break, the slam, the three-point jumper. Things the Harlem Globetrotters did 25 years ago that were considered magic are now done every night by Magic Johnson and the rest. There is something about watching Magic Johnson, Michael Jordan, Larry Bird, or even a kid such as Ron Harper that has to get you excited, assuming you realize that a basketball is blown up and not stuffed.

Nonetheless, there are those basketball fans, alleged basketball fans, who knock the NBA. Here are some of the reasons:

1. *"You need only to watch the last two minutes."* That's like saying "Why not skip the first 200 pages of an Agatha Christie mystery and turn to the last 25 pages because none of the good stuff happens until the end?" Hey, all we really want to know is if the butler did it. Of course, if you open a book and it says that the butler did it on the first page, who cares? You don't know what the butler did or why. It is the same thing in the NBA. If you see only the winning basket, it has no impact. How the game got to that last stage often is as interesting as the last couple of shots. If you like the game, then you want to see the passing, the guys hitting the boards, how the coaches use their bench, and when they call time-outs. Basketball is a marvelous game from the opening tap to the final buzzer.

2. *"The players are too good."* That's like saying the artist is too good or the writer is too good. "By God, I don't want quality! Give me mediocrity!" This kind of mentality is scary. It is the "settle for less" thinking carried to the ultimate. Not only do you settle for less, but that's all you want. Good becomes bad. Sure, I enjoy a high school or college game, but when it comes to basketball I'd rather see Kareem Abdul-Jabbar shoot a hook shot than anyone else. I'd rather see Magic Johnson play the point or Isiah Thomas go to the basket than some acne-faced kid from Hayseed High. I like to watch the pros shoot the lights out and jump over the rim for rebounds, just like I prefer a steak to a Big Mac.

3. *"The game is played by physical freaks."* And pro football isn't? Ninety-nine percent of the athletes in the three

major sports are bigger than the average guy, who is about 5'9" and 160 pounds. I do understand how some people have trouble relating to pro basketball players because they are not only so big but so gifted. But the one saving grace for basketball is that about everyone shoots hoops. There is a hoop at the playground down at the corner and a hoop on the garage. So the 5'9" guy can be shooting in his driveway, believing he is Larry Bird even if he is a foot shorter. Actually, the only sport played by "normal"-sized people is baseball. Football has elephants, and basketball has giraffes. That's just a fact of life.

Basically, I don't see any problem with the NBA as far as these three arguments go. The image of the league is better than it ever has been. The drug plan is pretty strong, and every year a few junkies get kicked out of the league, which is a good idea. The players are conscious of public relations. Some of the most cooperative athletes you'll find in dealing with the fans and press are basketball players. They truly love their game and love being pros, and that enthusiasm shows.

But there is a danger in the NBA.

Overexposure on one hand and underexposure on the other.

That sentence sounds like a contradiction, but it's not. The underexposure comes from network television. On the game of the week, all we see is:

- The Celtics
- The Lakers
- Michael Jordan

It's like the league is made up of two teams and one guy, and it will get worse with the retirement of Julius Erving. At least we used to see the Good Doctor and Philadelphia once in a while.

The NBA has become a two-team league with the Celtics and the Lakers trading off as champions. The league would love to have a strong team in New York, but half the time the Knicks don't know who is the coach or the general manager.

When they do have a GM, he trades a number one pick for Jawaan Oldham.

As for the overexposure, too many rinky-dink tank towns have teams. Salt Lake City, Sacramento, and Portland will never be big-league cities. Now the NBA is expanding to Charlotte, another third-rate town. The NBA is running the risk of losing us as the National Hockey League lost us, by expanding into too many cities. You end up with so many teams and so many conferences that you can't name half of them. I don't care if Portland and Charlotte are basketball hotbeds. If that is the thinking, why not put French Lick, Indiana, in the league?

Ten years ago, the league was on its deathbed. It wisely stopped the expansion, cleaned up its act in the front office and on the court, and became healthier than ever before. But now, with the addition of four new teams by 1990, the dilution of the talent will put the game in jeopardy. If you watched some of the Continental Basketball Association games on ESPN, then you saw what could be the future for several NBA franchises. I don't know about you, but I sure as hell wouldn't shell out 20 bucks a ticket to see Jawaan Oldham be the starting center for the Minneapolis Timberwolves.

The NBA is great. I love it. I just hope they don't mess it up. It is a league that understands the star factor, and as long as it remembers that people want to see the stars, not the mundane, that most people want the steak, not the Big Mac, then it will be all right.

And on the theme of stars, here is a look at my all-time NBA team:

## GUARDS

1. *Magic Johnson:* I love Jerry West and Oscar Robertson, and 10 years ago it would have been hard for me to imagine putting anyone ahead of those guys, but that was before Magic. I think guards will be divided into two categories—Before Magic and After Magic. That's because Magic Johnson is the most dominant player of my lifetime, and the guy

can play any position on the court. Never forget that the Lakers won a world championship with Magic filling in for Kareem Abdul-Jabbar at center. It is true that Magic can't shoot with Jerry West, nor is he quite the passer that Oscar Robertson was. But he is very close in those categories, and in terms of running a club, getting the right player the ball at the right time, and setting the tempo of a game, Magic Johnson is the best who has ever played. Every year he gets better. He came into the league without an outside shot, and now he has developed one. Next he added a hook shot. Where it will end, no one knows. But I would not be surprised if at the end of Magic's career, when his knees are hurting, he switches from point guard to power forward and still makes the All-Star team.

2. *Oscar Robertson:* When he had the ball, Oscar could find more people than Sherlock Holmes. He was the best passer—ever. Oscar also could score at will, and he never missed an important foul shot. Kareem never won a world title until the Milwaukee Bucks traded for Oscar Robertson. In fact, Kareem used to say that Oscar was the greatest guard he ever played with. Now he says that about Magic. Robertson or Magic? You can't go wrong.

3. *Jerry West:* He was perhaps the greatest clutch player in the history of the league. West had that line-drive jumper that seemed to have no chance of going in, but it always seemed to go in. In the last 30 seconds of a game, West was like Alfred Hitchcock. He loved the suspense and played to the pressure. I just loved to see him with the ball with the clock ticking down and the score tied because I knew Jerry West was going to find a way to win the game.

4. *Lenny Wilkens:* A lot of people will be surprised by the choice, but that would not be the case if Wilkens had played in New York, Boston, or Los Angeles. The worst thing about Lenny's career was where he played—St. Louis, Seattle, Portland, and Cleveland. None of those places are media centers. Not only is it hard to become a national star in Seattle or Cleveland; it is quite easy to be ignored because you play in those places. Lenny was a great point guard. He had a terrific set shot. If you played up on him to take away

that shot, Lenny would drive around you, and he had a million different little hooks and other driving shots. He was a brilliant basketball mind on the floor and the consummate point guard.

5. *Walt Frazier:* Now here was a guy who was a creation of the New York media, but he was still pretty damn good. Clyde and Lenny Wilkens were neck-and-neck in my mind, although they were considerably behind the big three—West, Robertson, and Magic. Frazier had the clothes, the nickname (Clyde), the quick hands, and the knack for making the crucial steal or the big shot. He also blended in very well with his teammates on those great New York Knicks teams. Yes, the man had an immense ego, but he also had a sense of teamwork and what it takes to win, and it was that approach to the game that made him a great player.

## FORWARDS

1. *Larry Bird:* He has changed how we view pro basketball. Bird can't soar, he can't run, and he doesn't even have the deceiving quickness that scouts like. But he is a big man, 6'9" and 225 pounds, and he uses his body well under the boards to make himself one of the best rebounders in the league. He is a tremendous shooter, whether you are talking about from three-point range or from the foul line. With the ball, he continually astonishes you because he seems to have about six sets of eyes. He always knows where to find everyone on the court. For that reason most teams won't double-team him. If Bird has two men guarding him, then he knows someone is open under the basket, and he usually finds that someone with a pass that leads to a lay-up.

2. *Elgin Baylor:* Elgin was the grandfather of the Dr. J generation. We often hear that Julius Erving was the man who brought the high-wire act into basketball, but Baylor was doing the same stunts when Dr. J was in junior high. Elgin was a midair magician, and when he was on his game, Elgin Baylor was the most exciting basketball player I've ever seen.

3. *Julius Erving:* The sad part of the Doctor's career is

that he spent some of his best years in that backwater league known as the old American Basketball Association. It didn't matter how many times he jammed that red, white, and blue basketball for the Virginia Squires; no one saw him do it except the hard-core basketball fans. It wasn't until he came to the NBA with Philadelphia that the Doctor attained the legendary status he deserved. He had all the tricks and pizzazz, but what made Erving great is that he could play solid, fundamental basketball when the situation called for it. Furthermore, his personality was a tremendous asset to the game. He is my choice for the next commissioner of the NBA.

4. *Bob Pettit:* Pettit was a big goon who could do the things that big goons weren't supposed to do—get up and down the floor, hit the 15-footer, and show some nice moves around the basket. He played in the late 1950s and early 1960s, and at 6'9" Pettit was considered a monster. Pettit redefined how a forward was supposed to play, he was a forerunner to Larry Bird in some respects, and in the context of when he played the game Pettit was a great player.

5. *Rick Barry:* I can't stand to listen to him as an announcer, but that does not diminish the fact that Rick Barry was a great player. Sure, he was moody. Sometimes he was selfish. But he could shoot the lights out and also was perhaps the greatest foul shooter in the history of the league. When the mood struck him, he could pass as well as Larry Bird.

## CENTERS

1. *Bill Russell:* He was the most significant player in NBA history because he showed the world that rebounding and defense are what really win games. Certainly he was fortunate to have played in Boston, but that does not change the fact that Russell could shut down the other team like no player ever has. It was his defense that changed games. He was totally unselfish and the definition of a winning player.

2. *Kareem Abdul-Jabbar:* He really is like Old Man River because it seems that Kareem keeps rolling along, and his

team keeps winning. He's not the player he was at 25, but he's still pretty damn good, and the man is 40 years old! No one has ever shot the hook as well as Kareem, and when he is 150 years old and in a wheelchair, I still have a feeling that he'll be able to drill that hook shot from 15 feet. His passing is solid. He doesn't rebound as well as he once did, but Kareem still comes up with the clutch rebounds. Overall, I think his defense has been better than people have said. For much of his career, Kareem worked at being unhappy. He raised being sullen to an art form, and this hurt him with the press and fans. Now that he has loosened up at least a little bit, the fans and press are responding to him, and he's receiving the accolades he deserves.

3. *Wilt Chamberlain:* He probably was the greatest raw talent ever to play the game. One year he averaged 50 points a game. In another season he led the league in assists. When the mood struck him, Wilt scored 100 points in a game! The problem was that Wilt was never sure exactly what he wanted to do. Perhaps the game came too easily to him and it wasn't enough of a challenge to keep him interested. But for whatever reason, Wilt Chamberlain will always be known as a great talent that was never quite realized.

4. *Nate Thurmond:* Nate came very close to rivaling Bill Russell as a defensive center. He viewed the game the same as Russell, and he understood the importance of rebounding and blocking shots. When Nate Thurmond played center, the key belonged to him. Kareem Abdul-Jabbar often has said that the toughest center he faced was Nate Thurmond, and that expert testimony is enough to convince me that Nate belongs on the list of great all-time centers.

5. *George Mikan:* If George Mikan were to play today, he probably would be good, perhaps like Bill Laimbeer, but nothing great. But during the 1940s and early 1950s he dominated his sport. He was 6'10", 250 pounds, and the first significant moose to play in the middle. He showed the world exactly what size meant to basketball. He was a pioneer. Sure, he was slow and uncoordinated, but George Mikan was another player who changed how we viewed the sport, and for that reason he belongs on this list.

# 13
# THE TRUTH ABOUT PRO FOOTBALL

Want to know who really understands football? Just ask some kid down at the schoolyard who is on the field with about 10 of his friends. First, watch them play. What do you see?

There is one guy with the ball, and he is trying either to run or to pass it over the goal line. Then there are about 48 other guys trying to tackle the kid with the ball and then make him eat it.

And if you ask the kids about football, they'll tell you that one guy has the ball, and he wants to get it over the goal line. Meanwhile, 48 other demented bastards are chasing him, intent on breaking bones and spreading his brains across the field.

That, folks, is the essence of football, and I don't care what level you happen to be discussing.

As kids, we know this. But when we get older and we start watching football on television and reading about it in magazines and books, we become distracted. God save us from the "expert" commentators, whose main contribution to the sport is to complicate it and muddle it to the point that most fans no longer know what they are watching. So forget all the other crap you have heard and read. Forget John Madden drawing Xs and Os on your screen and screaming "Oink" and "Doink." Forget whatever the latest bozo on "Monday Night Football" has to say. And whatever you do, don't pick up one of those *Guides to Pro Football,* those books they sell on the paperback book rack at the drugstore. You'd be better off buying the *National Enquirer,* because that has about as much truth in it as those football guides.

Consider the typical pro football press conference, which is where most people in the media get their information. Remember, if that's where the writers and broadcasters are getting their scoop, then that is also where you are getting yours.

Pro football conferences are extremely dull by design. The owners and public relations people like the press conferences because they give the writers something to write, and all the writers get the same thing, so no one complains.

That is correct. They all are getting the same thing—nothing.

Coaches despise press conferences. The last thing they want to do the day after a game is talk about it with a bunch of writers who don't understand the first thing about the game. Writers and broadcasters usually think that all you need to win are a good quarterback and some fast backs. Writers and broadcasters who usually think like that are idiots. The coaches know it, I know it, and now you know it.

Well, the coach stands in front of the writers, and it goes like this:

WRITER: "Coach, about yesterday's game."

COACH: "What about it?"

WRITER: "You lost."

COACH grunts.

WRITER: "What went wrong?"

COACH grunts again.

WRITER: "Could you be more specific?"

COACH: "We couldn't run the football."

WRITER: "Why not?"

COACH: "We didn't execute the things we had to execute to run the football and win the football game."

On and on it goes, and the coach is right. His team didn't run the football, and it didn't execute. But what he means is that his offensive line didn't pull the switch on the defense. When the coach says "execute," he means execute as in murder.

COACH: "We just have to go on and put this game behind us."

You hear a lot about putting games "behind us" at press conferences. Of course games are put behind; they've already been played. You can't play the damn thing again.

COACH: "We'll just have to play them one at a time."

No kidding, Einstein. I've never seen a team play two games at once. But this is the garbage coaches pawn off at press conferences, and everyone writes it down as if it were Moses revealing the Ten Commandments for the first time.

At some juncture in the press conference, the coach decides to have a chalkboard lesson. He draws a million Xs and Os on the board and starts putting up arrows and lines of all kinds. Then the coach says, "We were trying to influence traffic blocking on the dog screens, but it broke down in the red area."

There isn't one writer who understands what the hell the coach is talking about, but they all nod and write it down. The writers are afraid to look at each other because they don't want the other guy to know that they have no idea what the coach is saying.

This is the point of the press conference: the coach is showing the writers why he is the coach and reminding them that they will always be civilians and will never be privy to the inside world of football. But it's all semantics and useless nomenclature. They have 10 different ways of describing crunching a guy's skull.

Meanwhile, the media is at the team's mercy. No sport denies access as much as football. The players are kept away from the writers; the writers are kept away from the dressing rooms and the practice fields. There is only a certain time of day when the writers are allowed a few moments to talk to the players. The coach usually speaks only in a structured press conference. It is the complete opposite of baseball, where the writers are allowed to hang around the dressing room and the dugout all the time and where the manager talks with the writers for hours, and I really mean hours.

The football writer is in a much different situation. His job is akin to watching paint dry. He can't get access to the players or access to the coach. Every week he has to write a story saying the opposing team is made up of 45 Hall of Famers because that's all the coach will tell him. The fans don't want him to be negative, unless it is to rip the coach for not passing enough. Fans never think a coach calls enough passing plays. The writer also can knock the quarterback, but only if the team is losing. But he must be kind to everyone else. The NFL does a great job of managing the media. It is best at handling the writers and keeping them in line. No other sport even comes close. The NFL does like to give the writers a few things to do. It hands out a ton of press releases with one team saying the other team is composed of 45 Hall of Famers. The league likes to set up telephone interviews that are conference calls. The writers ask boring questions, and the coach or players give boring answers. If a writer asks a tough question, he usually gets no answer at all, so he learns to ask boring questions.

Football coaches have the greatest dodging techniques in the world. After a game, you can ask a coach what happened on that interception, and the coach immediately says, "I won't know until I see the films." Ask him about a botched field goal, and the coach says, "I won't know until I see the films."

It is true that it is hard to see everything on the field. There are 22 guys out there trying to snap each other's spine. But most of the time, the coach does know what went wrong. He just doesn't want to say, so he brings up the films. And if you see him a few days later—after he has seen the films—and ask him the same question, he'll just mumble and still refuse to answer. When a coach starts up about seeing the films, you know that the rest of the interview is going to be a waste because he doesn't plan to tell you anything about anything, and this makes the boys running the NFL very happy.

At the Super Bowl, the NFL supplies bus rides between the stadium and the hotels for the writers. It wines and dines the media and has lots of boring press conferences. The league has its public relations act together. They all say the same things, dress the same way, and imitate the KGB.

But no one tells you anything about the game. Not the writers, not the broadcasters, and certainly not the league itself.

So what is the main thing to know about football? What is the difference between a good team and a bad one?

Defense, baby.

Just as baseball should really be named *pitching*, football should be called *beating the crap out of the other guy*. It is a physical sport in every sense of the word. Of course, there are trappings of finesse and positions that demand great skill such as wide receiver and quarterback.

But the game always comes down to beating the crap out of the other guy. The team that does that better and more often will win. There are no exceptions to this rule.

I don't just think, I *know*, that games are won and lost in the trenches. The most important thing is not your running backs or your quarterbacks; it is the line play. If your offensive line is beating the crap out of their defensive line, your running backs will have monstrous holes, and they'll all look like Jim Brown in his prime. If their defensive line is handing your offensive line its collective head, you may have Jim Brown in his prime, but he'll look like Barney Fife carrying the ball.

This carries over to the passing game.

If your offensive line can hold, and I mean literally hold, the defensive line, then your quarterback will have all day to stand in the pocket, and eventually he'll get the ball to a receiver. But if the defensive line is leaving footprints all over your offensive line, you better hope that your quarterback has his Blue Cross paid up.

Never mind the plays and never mind the guys in the backfield. If the offensive line stinks, the offense stinks. If you don't have animals in the trenches who like to hold and hurt the defense, it is pointless to discuss the rest of the offense because the backs will never have enough time to show their skills.

So what about strategy?

Of course there is strategy in football, but it's not the kind of strategy you think. What coaches really talk about is how their guys can best beat the crap out of the other guys. I may be sounding redundant, and you may not believe a word I'm saying. That's because it's more fun to talk about sweeps and post patterns and nickel and dime defenses. But I won't give you two cents for all that unless you've got a line.

It all goes back to defense.

The Dallas Cowboys had the great four-three defenses with such animals as Too Tall Jones, Jethro Pugh, and Bob Lilly on the line. When the Rams were great, they had Merlin Olson and the Fearsome Foursome. Minnesota had Jim Marshall and the Purple People Eaters. The most dominating team of the modern era was Pittsburgh, and the Steelers had a great quarterback in Terry Bradshaw. But the reason the Steelers won was the Iron Curtain defense with Mean Joe Greene, L. C. Greenwood, and Ernest "Fats" Holmes. I liked Fats Holmes. He was my idea of a defensive lineman. When he wasn't trying to skull a running back, he was out shooting his gun at passing cars. At least he had that hobby until the police told him to stop and took away his bullets.

What a great defense will do is set up the offense. The defense goes on the field, and you hardly see it. Three plays and the great defense is on the bench because the other team did nothing and was forced to punt. The great defense keeps giving the ball to the offense, usually in pretty good field position. And eventually, no matter how inept that offense happens to be, it will find a way to score because it has had so many chances. Field position determines most games, and even if you have Kirby Klutz at quarterback, you can score if you have only 40 or 50 yards to go. A great defense in football is like tremendous pitching. It covers up so many mistakes.

I'm not saying that pro football players are dumber than a pile of dirt, although intelligence is not necessarily a prerequisite for athletic greatness. The guys in the NFL did go to college, if you consider places such as Texas, Oklahoma, and Georgia colleges. They usually belonged to fraternities where they learned such useful skills as opening beer bottles with their eye sockets, then drinking the beer through their noses. If a guy was exceptionally talented, he then would take the empty bottle and eat it. A number of our nation's leaders were former football players. Gerald Ford was a center at Michigan, which explains why he kept falling down later in life. Richard Nixon played end at Whittier College—end of the bench, that is. But once he became president, he drew up a play for Miami coach Don Shula to use in the Super Bowl.

So football is great training for politics and beer drinking. It also keeps doctors, surgeons, hospitals, and manufacturers of Novocain busy.

The thing a football player never forgets is that there are thousands of guys out there who want his job. If he's Walter Payton or Joe Montana, he doesn't have to worry. He is a great player, he knows he's a great player, and most importantly, the coach knows he's a great player and that the team needs him to win. But your second-string linebackers and wide receivers can be replaced as easily as one phone call. In terms of average players, the talent pool is deeper than the Pacific Ocean. The guys keep coming into the NFL in waves.

To keep a job, a football player must learn to play with pain. This is no meaningless cliché. The day after a game, football players are in agony. Yes, they are great physical specimens, but these tremendously conditioned athletes just spent three hours beating the crap out of each other. Believe me, they don't pull any punches. Most guys perform on each play as if it were their last, because they know if they fail they will be on the waiver list within 24 hours. The job of the football player may not be to kill, but it is to win. The way to win is to maim the opposition.

Peter Gent is one of the writers who captured this part of the game. His novel, *North Dallas Forty,* was terrific, and it was made into a fine film. Gent got right to the heart of football—the pain. Playing with pain. Living with pain. Nick Nolte limped and groaned throughout the entire movie, and that's how it is for most guys. They are interchangeable parts, and they know it. Most got their jobs because the guy in front of them was injured, and that is one lesson they will never forget. There is one thing that the football player fears even more than pain, and that's the real world. He has been the pampered jock since high school. He got the dates with the prettiest girls and has a scrapbook full of glowing newspaper stories. But usually his father was a truck driver or a turnip farmer with a double mortgage and an ulcer the size of Utah in his stomach. The football player wants to keep the money coming, and he wants to get in one more year on the pension plan.

Also, football makes playing with pain a test of manhood. Those who take a shot in the knee on the trainer's table and then go out on the field, catch a pass over the middle, and take a shot from a deranged defensive back are portrayed as heroic. Those who disdain the needle and sit out the game are said to have "character problems." Teams don't like players with "character problems." Unless you happen to be a star, you won't last long unless you can play with pain. Some coaches seem to keep score. The more knee operations, the better. It is as if you are fighting a war and you are giving up your knees for God, country, and motherhood. You might even say that you are doing it for the fans, but remember, if you go out there with a bad knee and fumble, those fans won't care about how much you hurt. They'll just boo your ass off the field.

With the exception of boxers, no athletes better fit the description of gladiators than football players. They even wear helmets and pads just like the gladiator had his suit of armor and shield. To the American sports fan, football is war, and the players are warriors. Fans expect blood to be shed, bones to be broken, and players to be carried off the field. And remember, players are taken off the field in something called the "Meat Wagon," and that really says it all when it comes to how both coaches and fans perceive the players.

In general terms, that is what football is all about. Now I'll be more specific as I show you how to build a football team. I'll tell you what a coach wants from players at each position and what those players are really like.

## DEFENSIVE LINEMEN

The defensive linemen are the most important men on the field. They are encouraged to gouge, slash, and crack spines. When they commit one of these atrocities on a quarterback, these marvelous, well-adjusted people like to dance, much like an Indian who has just slain a buffalo with a spear. Then the NFL, being humorless as usual, banned sack dancing.

I want to know one thing:

Doesn't the NFL have anything better to do than to worry about 270-pound linemen making like Pee-Wee Herman? The league says it is fine to pick up a quarterback and pound him straight into the ground, headfirst, as if he were a stake. But if the lineman wants to dance about it, then that is reason for a fine.

Hey, Pete Rozelle, what the hell is going on? Either you want these guys to hit or you don't. If you want them to hit, let them dance and make noise and do whatever else they want to do as a little celebration for preparing yet another quarterback for a spinal fusion. I say, let the big boys dance. They ain't Fred Astaire, but the football field is hardly Carnegie Hall. The fans like it when the big boys dance, because they can boo and cheer.

But the league said no dancing.

And the league said no spiking the football into the ground.

The league said there are too many hot dogs in the game and that all this spiking and dancing was giving the NFL a bad image.

I can just hear Rozelle saying "We don't want the fans to think we've got a bunch of thugs on the field."

If they aren't thugs, they won't win. I've explained that much already. Besides, fans like thugs, and they like to see quarterbacks killed and thugs dancing. Let the big boys do what they want. Who cares? The defensive linemen all have their brains scrambled anyway. If they didn't wear helmets, their brains would just roll out of their ears and onto the ground. The fans come to the games with hatred and violence in their eyes. They cheer when a quarterback gets carried off the field. You know why? Because the fans look at that player who was bent in half and think, better him than me.

And the reason they are carrying that guy out is because someone probably nailed him with a cheap shot.

Dirty football?

You bet.

But the first rule in the NFL is dirty football is dirty only when you get caught. The difference between a good hit and a cheap shot is the official's flag. If there's a flag, it was cheap. If there are no flags, just a limp body on the ground, it was a good hit.

If the police decided to enforce the law during a football game, there wouldn't be enough linemen left to play the second half. It's all out there—assault, battery, manslaughter, and head slapping.

Oh, head slapping is something else that the league has banned. I understand that the NFL thinks that head slapping is almost as bad as sack dancing.

It used to be that a nose guard would rush the quarterback, and a tackle would try to block him. No problem. The nose guard would just whack the tackle across the side of the helmet with his hand. The tackle would feel as if he had just endured a lobotomy.

But now they say you can't do that.

Of course, they also say you can't use groin shots, and that's still a favorite move because it is enforced sporadically. Defensive linemen revel in the groin shot. As the nose guard rushes the tackle, he keeps his hands low. When the tackle stands up and tries to block, the nose guard just punches the tackle between the legs. Suddenly, the tackle doesn't feel like blocking for a while, and he starts speaking in a much higher voice. Even though these guys wear athletic cups, a groin shot still feels like getting hit with a sledgehammer in man's most vulnerable area.

You might think that the defensive linemen reading this will become upset at Pete Franklin and accuse Pete Franklin of cheap-shotting them. But those guys know what goes on. I'm not telling them anything new. Right now they have been reading this and nodding, and they probably have three or four other dirty tricks that they want me to write about, but I think you have the idea.

I once did a banquet with Lyle Alzado, who admits to being deranged and has turned his craziness into a lot of bucks by acting nuts on commercials. Anyway, I introduced Lyle, and he charged up to the podium and sacked me. The crowd roared. And why not? So what if what happened was one guy in a business suit tackling another one? That's football.

What else is there to say about defensive linemen?

They drink a beer and then eat the mug. Sometimes they eat the mug first and wash down the broken glass with a beer. They are dangerous people, potential psychos. On the field, they are the nastiest, crudest people you'll ever meet. Off the field, they are . . . well . . . off the field you're just better off not meeting them at all.

## LINEBACKERS

Linebackers are not as big as defensive linemen, but they

are just as crazy. They want everyone to know that they are mentally ill, and they are unhappy because God didn't let them bulk up to 260 pounds, despite taking enough steroids to gag Man O'War. So they have to settle for being 235 pounds and standing a few yards away from the line of scrimmage. But they compensate for this by shaving their heads, wearing earrings, and making animal noises. They are happiest when they hit someone and hear the cracking of a vertebra. Put a raw T-bone steak in front of them, and they would eat it all with their bare hands, even the bone.

## DEFENSIVE BACKS

These guys are smaller than linebackers, but they bark and growl more. They are 5'10" and about 180 pounds. They can run pretty well, and they better be able to run, because they have to cover wide receivers—who also are little guys who can run. The difference between a wide receiver and a defensive back is that the receiver wants to catch the ball while the defensive back wants to catch the receiver's head and rip it off. The defensive back has one purpose—to dish out punishment. He also has one goal—to keep receivers from going over the middle of the field. The defensive back doesn't care if the receiver goes into the middle once, and he doesn't even worry if the receiver manages to catch the football. That's because the good defensive back knows that the receiver will never make another catch. It's hard to play end when you are in the paraplegic ward. Defensive backs like to be obnoxious. They bark, they point, and they say dirty things about the receiver's mother. They like it best when they hit a receiver and they know the guy is headed straight to an oxygen tent.

## OFFENSIVE LINEMEN

If you want a good offensive line, you want monsters. These guys are safes with arms and legs. They don't have necks. Instead, their heads rest on redwood tree trunks.

They eat everything in sight, and they keep eating because their goal is to be bigger than Shamu.

This may be hard to believe, but there is some psychology involved on the offensive line.

Shrinks have interviewed linemen, which just goes to show that some people will risk anything in the name of science. Anyway, the head doctors discovered that offensive linemen have to be a bit passive. Yes, they want to hit. But no, they don't want to kill. Their mission isn't as much to destroy as to protect.

*Protect the quarterback.*

That's all offensive linemen are taught.

*Love your quarterback.*

That's the message, and it leads to these guys having to let their bodies take incredible beatings from the lunatics on the other side of the line. Defensive linemen charge in, and the offensive linemen are there to hold them off. The offensive linemen also are receiving the groin shots and the head slaps.

Once in a while an offensive lineman gets his revenge. It occurs on a sweep when the 265-pound guard gets to run, and he puts down his head and levels a 180-pound defensive back. The guard smiles as he sees the back's head on one side of the field and the rest of his body on the other side.

Any quarterback or running back with more than a single-digit IQ knows that he must keep the offensive line happy. That's why about the first thing out of a quarterback's mouth is praise for the offensive line. If the offensive linemen love their quarterback, the quarterback worships the offensive linemen. He takes them out to dinner and buys them beer. The quarterback introduces the linemen to all the members of his sister's sorority.

So 24 hours a day the quarterback will praise the linemen. He will become their best friend, and he will tell them how important they are. Of course, the fans can't name five offensive linemen in the league, but that doesn't matter to the quarterback. He knows all their names, because he calls them brother.

What quaterbacks know and you should remember is that the only thing that stands between your favorite quarterback and the emergency room is the offensive line.

## CENTER

You know and I know that playing center is not a good job. But did you know that it's the worst job on the football field?

QUESTION: Would you want your son to grow up to be a center?

ANSWER: I suppose it depends upon how you feel about your son.

Anyway, the guy spends an inordinate amount of time bent over looking back through his legs. I think this is what is known as an unnatural position.

And what does he see between his legs?

A pair of hands.

Someone else's hands, to be exact.

I don't care how anyone explains it or what rationalizations are used—this is not a healthy situation.

And some of these quarterbacks have problems, too. They stick a rag in the center's belt so that it hangs down over the center's butt. Then the quarterback uses that rag to wipe his hands—while the center is bent over and, obviously, the rag is still tucked into the center's pants. I refuse to even speculate upon the psychological implications of that.

So the center spends his time looking at life ass backwards; this is even before play begins.

Then he snaps the ball to the quarterback, and the fun starts, because six monstrous animals come at him and the following happens:

1. A couple of 300-pounders leave footprints on his back.
2. His face is shoved into the mud.
3. Once he is facedown in the mud, another 300-pounder steps on the back of his head to make sure he stays facedown in the mud.
4. He is blamed for every fumble.

The center is a man who knows that life is really about suffering and sacrifice. He is never credited for anything that goes right, because even in the ideal situation he does get the ball to the quarterback, and he still ends up on the bottom of a pile.

But when the quarterback juggles the ball, it's the center's fault. When a kicker misses a field goal, it's the center's fault because the snap wasn't quite right. When a punter has his punt blocked, that also is the center's fault. Bad snap, of course.

I don't know about you, but I'm always amazed when these guys accurately snap the ball around 10 to 15 yards through their legs. It requires years of scientific study and depth perception, like a space shot at Cape Canaveral. I give these guys credit, even if everyone else just gives them blame.

## QUARTERBACKS

Everyone wants his son to be a quarterback because the quarterback is what everyone wanted to be. He's the best-looking guy on the team, and even if he isn't, people think he is because the quarterback is *supposed* to be good-looking. The dynamite broads all want the quarterback because they are *supposed* to want the quarterback.

Secretly, most of us don't like the quarterback, and we like to see one of the godzillas come in from the blind side and steamroll the guy. Make him hurt, make him pay. When Joe Theismann was demolished and they found an arm where his leg used to be and they never did find the missing leg, the crowd cheered. They loved it. Make pretty boy bleed. Way to go, Lawrence Taylor, we love you even if you have to do time in the drug joint. By God, we like it when the quarterback is dismembered, and don't you forget it.

Why all this animosity about the quarterback?

Because this is the guy who never had to study for tests. He got decent grades because he was the quarterback, and quarterbacks are *supposed* to be smart enough to get decent grades.

He got the best-looking cheerleader and didn't even have to buy her a damn box of candy. What the hell? The cheerleader was calling him, buying him candy.

He always had his name in the paper because the quarterback is *supposed* to have his name in the paper.

It all came so easily for them—the quarterbacks—while it was so hard for us.

To the outside world, the quarterback is the glamor boy. He has five guys on the offensive line whose main purpose in life is to protect the quarterback. When did we ever have five beefy guys looking out for us?

The root of the problem is jealousy.

Fans worship the quarterback when the team wins, and they despise him when the team loses. Like the coach, he's the weather vane for all the emotions during a football season. That is why the toughest test many quarterbacks face is off the field. They have to deal with all this crap from the fans, who want to nail him to a cross one minute and then resurrect him the next.

A classic case was in Cleveland a few years ago. When Paul McDonald was starting, the fans wanted someone, anyone, else. Then McDonald was benched and Bernie Kosar got the job, and the same bozos who had been booing McDonald a year ago wanted him to start and Kosar on the bench.

Often, the most popular guy on the team is the backup quarterback and he will stay that way until he becomes quarterback.

Fans love their quarterbacks to pass, as long as the passes work. If the pass goes to someone on the other team, then the fans not only want the quarterback to quit passing; they want a new quarterback on the field.

There are several misconceptions about the quarterback, one of the big ones being that he is perhaps the best natural athlete on the field. Sometimes a quarterback is a pretty good athlete, but he seldom is the best. Often, he is not that athletically gifted compared to the rest of the guys playing the skilled positions. His greatest athletic attributes are his throwing arm and his ability to run like hell away from the thugs who want to turn him into a box of Rice-A-Roni.

That's why quarterbacks often embarrass themselves when they talk to their offensive line. If the linemen want chocolate chip cookies, the quarterback gets up at five in the morning and bakes them. If the linemen like fine wines, the quarterback takes money out of his retirement accounts so he can afford to have the best wines imported from France. The mentality is "I'll give you guys anything; just keep those bastards off my back."

A good quarterback also does a psych job on his running backs, because those backs are also important to keeping the quarterback in one piece. If the backs can't run the ball, that means the quarterback must throw on every play. When the defense knows the quarterback must throw, the quarterback is not long for the game. I don't care if a guy is the greatest passer in the history of football; if he has to pass on every play and the defense knows it, the guy is destined to be hominy grits. That's why backs are crucial. If they are running the ball well, the quarterback can keep giving them the ball. Then the thugs can pound on the running backs for a while instead of the quarterback.

Receivers also have an interesting relationship with the quarterback.

We've established that a quarterback will beg his linemen to do a good job. Well, he threatens the receivers. When a receiver drops a pass, the quarterback can stare at him with disgust. Or the quarterback can throw up his hands to the heavens, asking God why he was given such crappy receivers. In the huddle, the quarterback can scream at the receivers, and the receivers have to take it.

Why?

Because the receivers are totally dependent upon the quarterback. Receivers are paid to catch passes, but they can't make catches if no one throws them the ball. Obviously, the quarterback decides where he throws the ball. So the receiver has to be nice to the quarterback.

That's why receivers don't complain about the quarterback. It also is why receivers are willing to take the rap when a play is broken. Ever notice when a receiver runs to the left and the pass goes to the right? The announcer never says that the idiot quarterback threw the ball in the wrong direction. Instead, the receiver ran the pattern wrong. Well, even if the receiver went the right way, he won't say it. Not if he wants the quarterback to keep passing him the ball. Because if the receiver blows the whistle on the quarterback, that receiver will soon be getting about as many passes as an offensive guard.

## RECEIVERS

We've already discussed the relationship between the quarterback and the receiver, at least in terms of the receiver's need to keep the quarterback content.

So receivers don't like quarterbacks who ignore them. They also don't like quarterbacks who throw the ball high and over the middle. The receiver doesn't mind jumping to catch a pass, but he doesn't want to go leaping at midfield, where every deranged defensive back can take a shot at him. The leaping receiver knows that as soon as he catches the ball, the defensive back will turn him into swiss cheese, and the moment of impact will be like Las Vegas when a slot machine turns up three sevens. Bells will ring, only he knows that the jackpot is being carried off on a stretcher, and a couple a months in traction.

There are two kinds of receivers—fast ones and slow ones.

The fast ones are burners. They just run past everyone. Throw the ball up and they'll run under it. These are the athletes.

The possession receivers are kind of slow and almost appear klutzy. They always catch the ball, and then they usually fall down as if someone had pushed them down a flight of stairs. They have nicknames like "Hands" and "Glue Fingers." They can't run away from anyone, so game after game they take a beating. They are Nick Nolte in *North Dallas Forty,* and quarterbacks love these guys because they won't drop the ball.

## TIGHT ENDS

The tight end is a cross between a wide receiver and an offensive lineman. He has the lineman's size and the receiver's hands. Sometimes he is there to block; other times he catches passes. He is a big, lumbering guy, and when he does catch the ball it usually takes about eight defenders hanging on his back to drag him down. Fans like tight ends because of this intriguing marriage between bulk and grace, the ability to be as big as anyone on the field and yet handle the ball with tremendous skill.

## RUNNING BACKS

Running backs supposedly are the glory boys. They score the touchdowns, and they get almost as much credit as the quarterbacks without having to endure nearly as much blame.

For the running back, everything is fine unless he fumbles. But when the back fumbles, you'd have thought he had gone after his own mother with a meat cleaver. The guy who fumbles the ball is sent to bed with a football for a pillow. He is made to carry the ball everywhere. So what if a ton of maniacs were trying to separate his right arm from his body? The man should not have fumbled the ball. But think for a minute about the running back. He is a relatively normal-sized person—6 '1" and 200 pounds. The running back takes the ball from the quarterback and runs smack into the line. That's smack into the five bloodthirsty pit bulls who happen to be disguised as defensive linemen and linebackers.

And who usually ends up at the bottom of a pile?

The running back, of course.

And the running back gets this privilege about 30 times a game. Take the ball, run about five steps, and have four guys who weigh a collective 1,000 pounds jump on your back.

Coaches love running backs, especially fullbacks. "The

guy will run through a brick wall for me," says the coach.

Well, the guy would be better off running at a brick wall. At least a brick wall isn't trying to snap his knee as if it were a twig. At least a brick wall won't try to nail him with a groin shot, and at least a brick wall won't fall on him after he is down. Supposedly, backs "run for daylight." The offensive linemen open up "holes," and the back is supposed to slip through these holes and then be free to spring away from the defense. Once in a while this actually happens—about one out of 20 times, to be exact. As for the other 19 times, the back takes the handoff, runs into the line, and ends up like corned beef hash.

Goal-line situations are the worst. Everyone is crowded into the middle of the line, and everyone knows that the ball is going to be run right up the gut of the defense.

So what does the quarterback do?

He hands the ball to the back and tells the back to run right up the gut of the defense. Why not just tell the back to lie down on the street and wait for the steamroller to show up? There would be less pain.

Backs have tried to figure out ways of getting that last yard at the goal line. They have taken to trying to fly without wings. They get a handoff and jump, hopefully over all the bodies that are stacked up on the line of scrimmage. Sometimes it works, but sometimes the pile is too high and the back feels as if he leaped headfirst into a brick wall. It is then the back learns the meaning of the word *whiplash.*

Even if the back does fly over the line, Newton tells us that there is a law of gravity, and that law states that what goes up must come down. So the back comes down, usually right on his head as if he were a spike being driven into the ground.

That's why a back's most salient characteristic is the ability to take punishment, much like a boxer is supposed to be able to take a punch. They all say, "Boy, that guy was a great one. He really could take a hit." And when that back is 45, he won't be able to take an aspirin without help, but so what if the guy can't find his own mouth? So what if not only his knees are gone but so are his brains? When he played, the man could really take a hit, and that's all that mattered.

## KICKERS

Field goal kickers are like relief pitchers in baseball. They come at the most crucial part of the game. They have one moment in which they will become either the hero or the bum. They work about one minute during the entire game, and that counts the time they are on the field for the kick-offs.

Usually, a kicker is expected to make the field goal. He really only hears about it when he misses, which is a nice way to develop an acute case of paranoia.

Kickers think the fans don't like them.

Kickers are right. The fans don't like them. Kickers are little guys who used to play soccer in Bulgaria. They can barely speak English, and they don't even kick the ball like an American. They stand off to the side. The joke about kickers saying "Hoo-ray, I kickee the touchdown" isn't far wrong. These guys are freaks. They can't do anything but kick, and I can't believe that makes them very well-adjusted individuals.

## PUNTERS

Punters usually are from the Southwest. Their job is to kick the ball high and far. Even though they are Americans, the rest of the football players don't think punters are athletes. Punters don't get dirty, they don't try to break someone's spine, and they don't even carry the ball. Their job is to get rid of the ball the moment they touch it.

So the punter feels isolated, and he usually is grouped with the kicker, which is no bargain. Remember, the punter is from Waco, and the kicker is from Bulgaria. Just what are these guys going to talk about? But they have one thing in common—no one notices them unless they screw up.

## COACHES

Here's what it means to be a losing football coach:

1. Someone throws garbage on your front lawn.
2. Someone kills your dog and throws it on the front lawn.
3. Someone stands on your front lawn and tries to throw a rock through your living room window.
4. Someone comes with a can of gasoline, spills it on your front lawn, and then lights a match.

Now you know why football coaches don't like to lose. What I can't understand is why many of them insist upon living in a house like a normal person. Fans don't want their coach to be normal. They don't want him to have a wife, a family, a living room window, or a front lawn. They don't even want him to have a car, unless he wins. A coach gets a car at the start of the season from a dealer in exchange for making a commercial. But if the team loses, the commercial is taken off air, and late at night a couple of repo men show up and take the coach's car away.

Not only don't we want our coaches to lose; we want them to be deities. We loved Vincent Lombardi. When this man died, and he was a sawed-off little man who screamed and berated everyone who ever played for him, the flags were flown at half-mast. We want our football coaches to be like George C. Scott in *Patton*. We want winners and we want men. We say we want a coach with integrity, substance, and heart. But really, those virtues are pretty far down the list. When we hear that Coach Brown spent the afternoon at the Veterans Hospital, we say, "Oh, that's nice." But in the back of our minds, some of us are wondering why Coach Brown didn't spend the afternoon in the film room getting ready for the next game. Now there is something that is really worthwhile and important.

Coaches usually are ex-players who knew how to take a hit. They are receivers who weren't afraid to go over the middle and leap for a pass. They are offensive linemen who endured groin shots for 10 years, and they are backup quarterbacks who came into the game when the whole world knew they were going to pass. These fine gentlemen knew how a tackling dummy felt.

Most coaches also had to come up through the ranks as they often began as college recruiters. That meant all those afternoons sitting in Ma's living room, eating her rancid apple pie, and trying to get Junior to go to good old State U. It meant either buying Junior or at least turning his back while someone else paid off Junior. Therefore, before he even becomes a head coach, our hero has had to deal with several unsavory aspects of this great American game. He resents having to eat Ma's pie and coddle Junior. He feels more like a magazine salesman than a coach. But if he does this well enough and makes enough friends among the alumni, he'll get to be the head college coach and then hire some other schmucks to go out and recruit. And if he wins enough in college, he can tell the folks at State U where they can stick their job and he can jump to the pros, where he doesn't have to recruit and where the players get paid by check instead of by cash in a shoebox.

That is why I find it laughable when someone talks to a pro coach and says, "That guy is paranoid."

Is the world round? Is the mosquito the state bird of Louisiana? Is Joe Namath a bad actor? Tell me something I don't know.

Of course coaches are paranoid. You would be, too, if they were killing your dog and dumping garbage on your lawn. That's why the coach surrounds himself with a million assistants whose job is to tell the coach he's getting more out of the players than anyone has a right to. The head coach wants a lot of assistants so when the owner says, "Our defense stinks," the coach can say, "It sure does, Mr. Moneybags, and I plan to get us a new defensive coordinator pronto." Then the head coach buys himself some more time on the job by canning the defensive coordinator.

The head coach also likes a lot of assistants to keep him company. No sport comes as close to having as many meetings as football coaches do. They meet 24 hours a day, and they want to have more meetings. Fans like to hear that the coach is having meetings, that the coach is watching films, and that the coach has a cot and once every three days he takes an hour's nap in his office.

## FOOTBALL FILMS, TV, AND INSTANT REPLAYS

If any sport were to use the instant replay effectively, it should be professional football. That's because football already has an affinity for film. I am tempted to say that football people have an understanding of television and film, but it is even more than that. An obsession is more like it.

Let's start with the effect of television on pro football. The sport always had a certain degree of popularity, then television discovered that it was the perfect package for fall and winter Sunday afternoons. The weather is bad, and the family is a captive audience in the house, just dying to watch something. By the afternoon, most of the television preachers have run out of gas. If it were summer, Dad might take the kids on a picnic or to the beach. But really, the old man usually wants to spend Sunday afternoon on the couch, eating cold cuts and swilling beer. Also, the old man usually likes to bet on something he sees on television, so gambling helped the football ratings.

CBS jumped on the NFL's bandwagon, and the trip turned out to be worthwhile. Oh man, did it ever. The NFL just annihilated the other Sunday programming, which often was old Robert Young movies and documentaries about the sex life of snails. With the increased ratings came profits from advertising rates, and football turned out to be the perfect television vehicle for advertising. The action was stopped after every play. There were four quarters and a nice, long halftime. When advertising executives first got a look at football on television, they drooled so much that they almost drowned themselves.

NBC was next. It needed football, and it found pro football in the old American Football League. When the NFL and the

AFL merged, CBS and NBC were left to cut up the healthy pie.

But that still left ABC on the outside, stuck with the black-and-white movies and the dreary wildlife shows. I mean, how many times can you listen to a guy with an English accent say "There is a decent and crucial difference between a snail and a slug"?

Finally, ABC came up with "Monday Night Football," and at last, all the networks were happy and, more importantly, richer.

Television made pro football the monster it is today. Television is perfectly equipped to show the same play from a dozen different angles in slow motion, fast motion and stop action. The sport also lends itself to such dissection, as the coaches discovered.

The only people who watch more football than the fans are the coaches. They even talk about watching football, giving us the infamous line "I can't say what happened for sure until I see the films."

Right after a game, coaches take the film and grade it. They watch each play 50 times, as if it might come out differently than it did on the field. Then these paragons of intelligence are stunned when they see the exact same thing on tape that they saw in the game.

Anyway, grading the films is big. The defensive coordinator grades his players, and the offensive coordinator does the same with his guys. One week they give a guy a 74; the next week he gets a 54. The coaches spend an inordinate amount of time discussing who gave a good hit and who took a good hit, which guys missed blocks and tackles and which guys "gave 110 percent." Of course, I'm still waiting for someone to give more than 100 percent, since 100 is supposed to be all you have. But these guys are like dictators and first grade teachers. They can grade any way they want, and no one is going to tell them that they are wrong.

After the film has been graded, it is shown to the team. The players and coaches are in a dark room. No, popcorn and Cokes aren't served. Once again, the same play is shown 50 times, and once again it hasn't changed. When Kneebreaker Smith blew a block, the offensive line coach shows the film in slow motion and says, "Now look, Kneebreaker. Lookee, here, boy. We was in a Red Dog 3, and you was in a Red Dog 2. You went left instead of right. That makes me wonder two things, boy. Either you don't know your right from your left or you can't count from two to three."

Everybody laughs at 288-pound Kneebreaker, who is trying to disappear.

By the end of the session, everyone has gotten it.

"Why didn't you pick up number 14?"

"How come you couldn't see the safety coming?"

"Smithy, how many fingers did you have up your butt on this play?"

On and on it goes. The coaches keep saying "Show that play again, show that play again." And they show it again, again, and again.

Most of the players are trying to stay awake during this, because after the first 47 hours of film, they get bored. Seeing Kneebreaker mess up once is funny; seeing it 50 times is deadly. The main thing the players try to do during film sessions is not to snore and to answer "Yes, sir," whenever someone calls their name. Snoring when you should be saying "Yes, sir" is grounds for being fined.

So films are of little use to the players. They played the game, they know the score, and they know who won or lost. Unlike the coaches, players never say they need to check the films to know what happened. Either they beat the crap out of the other team or the other team beat the crap out of them.

Once in a while, the film of a game is so brutal, so disheartening, that the coaches decide they can't show it to the players. It's like the film is X-rated, as if it might destroy the players' confidence if they were to see again how thoroughly they were demolished by the other team. But as I said before, the players already know exactly what happened. If they were slaughtered, they don't need the films to tell them that because three days after the game they are still bleeding.

So films are mostly for the coaches.

On another note, however, films may determine games. There have been a lot of people saying that technology has no business in football.

Well, when penicillin was discovered, the medical community didn't say "This is progress; we don't need progress screwing up our great business." The same thing with lasers. They didn't say "So what if the scalpel is more primitive? It has tradition going for it. Forget laser surgery."

I've always felt that since man invented the telephone, we should use it to call our neighbor instead of screaming out the window. Just as since man invented the automobile, I'd rather ride down the street than walk.

That's why I see nothing wrong with the inclusion of the instant replay in pro football. In most cases, it shows that the officials' judgment was correct. In those rare cases when the officials are wrong, it shows that, too, and then the error can be corrected. I no more accept human error than I do computer error. A blunder is a blunder. If you blow it, fix it. The point is not the advancement of technology or the officials' egos or the issue of man's eye vs. the camera lens. The point is getting the call right.

We want the best team to win, and we want the calls made based on what really happened, not on what the officials thought they saw happen. The fact is that one call can mess up a game, even a team's entire season.

So how should this work?

I propose that there be a soundproof booth away from both the field and the press box. There should be several television monitors in the booth. That is where three current or respected ex-officials would watch the game. They couldn't hear the crowd, the coaches, or the writers. There would be no audio on the game, just the video. These men should not only understand football, but they should be trained by the television networks about camera angles and other technical aspects of putting the game on the tube.

The officials would still have the right to stop the game and ask the guys in the booth for a ruling on a controversial play. Also, the guys in the booth would have the right to stop the game and correct an official's call. They would be the Supreme Court. The coaches couldn't ask them to rule on the play, and no one could question their final decision. What they'd say happened happened, because they would have the best means of making the call.

I think this system of instant replay is the inevitable product of the marriage among television, films, and football. The three have been in bed together for some time, so why not make the most of the relationship? It will give us a better, fairer game.

# 14
# THE GREATEST FOOTBALL TEAM EVER

Some people will tell you that they can rank the top 100 football players of all time in order. Well, some people are morons.

You can no more rank the top 100 football players than you can the top 100 foods. How do you compare a hamburger to a lobster, corn on the cob to a chocolate sundae? Well, tell me how you can determine who is more important to a football team—a back, a linebacker, or a center. In sports you can compare people, but only to others who have played the same position. Line up 10 cheeseburgers, and I'll pick the best one. The same in football. Give me a list of all the quarterbacks, and I'll pick a winner.

And that's just what I'm going to do, by presenting Franklin's all-time football team. This is the ultimate expert's ego trip, which is exactly why I'm doing it.

I haven't seen all the guys ever to play pro football, but I've seen a lot. As for the few I've missed, well, I've spent a lifetime studying the game, and I can make judgments on players who were part of the early days of football.

What I'm giving you is my team, the team I'd want if I had

a chance to pick from any players who have ever played. I've selected a defense based on the standard four-three setup, not with four linebackers as some of the donkeys are using today. With that in mind, here's the team:

## THE OFFENSE

### Wide Receivers

Paul Warfield and Don Hutson. The first and the greatest of them all was Hutson, a 6′1″ 180-pounder from Alabama. When Hutson was in college, the offensive end on the other side of the field was a guy named Bear Bryant. Hutson played before they wore shoulder pads, which means he was really a sitting duck for any cheap-shot artist. But Hutson amazingly stayed out of the hospital. He also stayed open, and I don't care if three guys were supposed to be covering him. The "umbrella defense" was designed to stop him, but all he did was take that defense and find the leaks. He was the greatest wide receiver who ever played the game, and I don't care if this was the 1920s and 1930s.

The other wide receiver, Warfield, had the misfortune of playing at Ohio State under Woody Hayes. Hearing the word *pass,* Woody would retch and call for another fullback dive up the middle. This meant that Warfield did not catch as many passes as you'd think, but that was because Hayes wouldn't allow his quarterbacks to throw Paul the ball. Warfield was the epitome of grace, as we all were to learn when he got to the pros with Cleveland and Miami. He could accelerate to get open, and he was a tremendous leaper. All a quarterback had to do was throw the ball up there, and Paul would find a way to get it. Warfield also was a great blocker, and that says something since he was only 6′ and 180 pounds.

### Offensive Tackles

Roosevelt Brown and Forrest Gregg. Brown was 6′4″, 260

pounds, and a late-round draft choice. The scouts just missed the boat on Roosevelt Brown, but the Giants did pick him and put him in the lineup, and he started for a million years.

The 6′4″, 250-pound Gregg played for Green Bay under Vince Lombardi, and all Lombardi had to say about Gregg was that Forrest was "the greatest player I've ever coached."

Both of these monsters understood what it meant to protect the quarterback. They would have thrown their bodies in front of a division of German tanks if it meant giving their quarterback an extra few seconds to get off the pass. On running plays, Gregg and Brown delighted in decking linebackers and beheading defensive backs.

### Offensive Guards

Jim Parker and Gene Upshaw. Parker was 6′3″ and took very good care of Baltimore quarterback Johnny Unitas. Parker kept Unitas out of the hospital and sent a few defensive tackles straight from the field to surgery. He was a huge man, a 270-pounder who was big enough to blot out the sun.

Upshaw has become better known as the head of the NFL Players Association than he was as a guard with Oakland. At 6′5″ and 260, Upshaw loved to get out and block on the sweeps. When defensive backs saw Upshaw coming, they immediately reached into their pockets and pulled out their rosaries. Upshaw was a nasty person on the field, and I like my linemen nasty.

### Center

Mel Hein. At 6′2″ and 230 pounds, Hein became the first offensive lineman to win a Most Valuable Player award. He also played during the days of two-way players and spent a good deal of time at linebacker. He played for the New York Giants in the 1930s and 1940s. He was one of the few centers who dished out more punishment than he received.

### Quarterback

Sammy Baugh. He was the greatest football player in history. That's right, I said the greatest football player . . . ever. He started as a single-wing tailback and became a quarterback when the T-formation came into vogue. He was 6'2", 180-pounds, and played for 16 years, starting in 1937. His passing was such incredible artistry that I have never seen a quarterback approach him. He dominated football as Babe Ruth did baseball. Baugh would stand in the backfield, lick his fingers, and wait for the snap. The defense knew where he was going to throw the ball, but it didn't matter. Sammy got it to his receiver, right on the money. Baugh not only was a great passer, but he was the last man ever to average 50 yards a punt, so he will also serve as the punter on this team. He also was the master of the coffin-corner kick, something that never shows up in the statistics. He had a way of kicking the ball out of bounds inside the five-yard line that just broke the heart of the opposition's offense because Baugh's punt had pinned its butt almost to the goal line. Slingin' Sammy's greatest tragedy was that he played before television discovered football.

### Running Backs

Gale Sayers and O. J. Simpson. Sayers was 6', 200 pounds, and the most electrifying runner I have ever seen. That takes in a lot of territory, because there have been so many great running backs. His highlight was scoring six touchdowns in one game for the Bears. He suffered a severe knee injury that shortened his career, which also was a major part of the plot in the fine football movie *Brian's Song.* When Sayers was healthy and doing his thing, my spine just tingled watching his magic while carrying the ball.

We all know O.J. from "Monday Night Football," where he gave Bill Russell a run for the title as the biggest mumbler ever to appear on network television. We also know the Juice from those Hertz commercials, and I have to admit that no one runs through an airport better than O. J. Simpson. But we tend to forget what a talent he was at Southern California. He was even a great player for Buffalo, and it's pretty hard to be great at anything in Buffalo. O.J. has always been a smart guy, and he praised his offensive line in Buffalo to the extent that the guys in the trenches became known as the "Electric Company," because they turned the Juice on. The tragedy of the Juice's career was that he played in Buffalo instead of Los Angeles or New York. The guy was 6'2", 215 pounds of dynamite and he deserves to be known as much more than a marble-mouthed announcer who dashes through airports and rents cars.

### Fullback

Jim Brown. No one was close to Brown in terms of durability and brute strength. When he was with the Browns and it was a third-down-and-two-yards situation, there was no doubt that the ball was going to Brown. There also was no doubt that Jim was going to get the first down. He could run the football 30,000 times a game and run it well each time. He never missed a play or a game. At 6'2" and 225 pounds, Brown was like a Sherman tank running over a grasshopper once he got past the line of scrimmage. He has since gone on to star in some of the worst movies ever made, but I don't hold that against him. When it comes to Jim Brown and movies, I like the ones where he carries the ball, not the ones where he is supposed to talk.

### Tight End

John Mackey. He was the first of the great tight ends, a 6'2", 225-pounder with the Baltimore Colts in the 1960s. He was a great blocker, a man dreaded by linebackers. Mackey liked to hit people, and he liked to see them lie motionless on the ground after they were hit. As a receiver, he had great hands. He had a way of getting open in the middle of the field, and if he got a finger on the ball, he caught it. He also was one of those tight ends who required eight defenders hanging on their back to bring them down.

### Kicker

Lou Groza. He is an offensive player because he kicks the field goals and extra points. Lou Groza was a superb player for the Cleveland Browns, not only because he could kick, but also because he was a very fine offensive tackle. His kicking put the kicker in the spotlight in the 1950s and early 1960s, which was before kickers were a hot media item. Seldom did the Toe miss a crucial kick.

## THE DEFENSE

### Ends

Deacon Jones and Gino Marchetti. David "Deacon" Jones was one of the key members of the Los Angeles Rams' fabled Fearsome Foursome. He was 6'5", 260 pounds, and he is the man credited with officially naming the quarterback "sack." Deacon bagged a lot of quarterbacks in his day. He was huge, but amazingly quick.

As for Marchetti, he was 6'4", 250 pounds, and during his glory days with the Baltimore Colts in the late 1950s and early 1960s was the best pure pass rusher the game has ever seen.

### Tackles

Bob Lilly and Merlin Olsen. Both of these guys have gone on to make commercials, which says something about the importance of defensive linemen. Lilly played for Dallas and was a God-fearing gentleman from Texas Christian University—at least until he got on the field. But for three hours every Sunday, Lilly went to war as few linemen ever have. He now hustles power tools on television. Before he played, he used to eat power tools.

Merlin Olsen was another well-behaved gentleman, a Mormon to be exact. He also was the exponent of the groin shot, a move that sent more than one lineman to the hospital. Now Olsen makes commercials telling us all to send flowers, which is something he has done for his victims for years. He also is a fine color broadcaster on the NFL games and not a half-bad actor. He was 6'5", 270 pounds, and another of the Rams' Fearsome Foursome.

**Linebackers**

Lawrence Taylor, Dick Butkus, and Chuck Bednarik. Taylor is the only active player to make my team. Yes, I know about the drugs and how he faked the urine tests and that he wasn't exactly a serious student at North Carolina. What the hell? Taylor put it all in a book and got over $200,000 for it, so he can't be all dumb. He plays for the Giants and is 6'3" at 240 pounds—a man who can destroy with or without cocaine. He has everything you want from a linebacker.

Another bad actor makes my team, and that's Dick Butkus. He was 6'3" and 245 pounds when he played like a raving lunatic as a middle linebacker for the Chicago Bears. He was so crazy that he played on one leg during the last few years of his career. His knee was gone, but that didn't stop him. He was too ill to worry about pain until one day they carted him off. Now he's back selling *Sports Illustrated* and Lite Beer.

The third linebacker is 6'3", 230-pound Chuck Bednarik. We can credit or blame—depending upon your point of view—Bednarik with giving us Frank Gifford, the broadcaster. It was Bednarik's crunching tackle of Gifford that knocked Frank out of football for a year and made him start seriously considering other endeavors of employment. Gifford did play after Bednarik crunched him, but Frank wasn't the same. Bednarik played for Philadelphia in the 1950s and 1960s, and he was the last of the great two-way players, as he also played center on offense.

### Cornerbacks

Herb Adderly and Dick "Night Train" Lane. Adderly was the main cog in the secondary for Vince Lombardi's great Green Bay teams. The 6'1", 200-pound Adderley was a fantastic talent. After you were covered by Adderly, you took off your jersey and expected to find him hanging onto your back. You just couldn't shake the guy.

Night Train was married for a time to the Empress of the Blues, Dinah Washington. But it was the players covered by the 6'2", 210-pound Night Train who really got the blues.

### Safeties

Emlen Tunnell and Larry Wilson. If there ever was a safety who could stop Sammy Baugh, it was Emlen Tunnell. At 6'1", 200 pounds, Tunnell was the leader of the Giants' famous umbrella defense.

Wilson, a 6', 195-pounder, was the father of the safety blitz, called the "suicide safety blitz" when Larry was in action. As a member of the St. Louis Cardinals, he rushed the quarterback as if he were going to kill someone or kill himself in the process.

## COACHES

Who should coach the team? There would be a lot of good choices, but these are the 10 men—in order—who I believe made the biggest contribution to pro football. Any of them would qualify to coach my team. The won-loss record is important, but so is the ability of that person to build a winner and get the most out of his talent.

## George Halas

He was the greatest coach of all time. Papa Bear also was the cheapest man to ever run a football team, but that's not why I picked him. As coach of the Bears, Halas developed the first great T-formation quarterback, Sid Luckman, whom he found at an Ivy League School, Columbia of all places. He developed the Monsters of the Midway, that huge group of blockers the Bears had. During the early days of the NFL, Halas was smart enough to move the team he owned, the Staleys of Decatur, Illinois, to a major market—Chicago. When he had Red Grange in the 1920s, he took the Bears on a nationwide tour so that the country could see Grange and get acquainted with pro football. He was an innovator as both a coach and an owner.

## Vincent Lombardi

He was a tiny man who intimidated people twice his size just by screaming at them. He was 5′7″ and he could scare the hell out of a 270-pound tackle. He was one of the Seven Blocks of Granite when he played at Fordham. When he coached at Green Bay, Lombardi understood that blocking and tackling were what wins games, not passing or computer-based offenses. Like Halas, he also had a short temper. I like my coaches to have a short temper.

## Paul Brown

He was the father of the Cleveland Browns and perhaps even the father of the modern era. He understood how to use a passing attack to its greatest advantage. He was always well prepared.

## Don Shula

He gets the maximum out of his team. When he has great talent, he wins. When his talent is so-so, he is still very respectable, and he knows how to rebuild a team quickly. The Miami Dolphins are a mirror of Shula's image—well organized and well schooled.

### Tom Landry

He was a brilliant defensive back with the New York Giants. He also was an assistant coach, along with Lombardi, with the Giants under Steve Owen. Landry has been the only coach in the history of the Dallas Cowboys. He employed the flex defense better than anyone else. Most of all, Landry has patience, which is crucial to putting together a young team.

### Steve Owen

The man who trained Lombardi and Landry. He was the father of the umbrella defense with the Giants.

### Chuck Noll

This man has no personality. In another life, he'd be in charge of the morgue. He has won four Super Bowl championships with Pittsburgh and has never been Coach of the Year because the media hates him because he never gives them a quote. He is the most colorless man ever to coach. He has total tunnel vision, and I admire his football expertise.

### Curly Lambeau

Lambeau Field in Green Bay is named after this man. He was a contemporary of George Halas. He was the man who best used Don Hutson's immense talents.

### George Allen

His claim to fame is that he has great wisdom on defense. He puts great emphasis on the pass rush and on his linebackers. His teams have always been characterized by old veterans who know how to play defense. He is a friend of Richard Nixon, but I won't hold that against him.

### Bud Grant

This is another boring man who does like to hunt ducks in his spare time. I mention the ducks only because duck hunting is as colorful as Grant gets. He had the Purple People Eaters in Minnesota, and he got the image as a loser because four times his team went to the Super Bowl and lost. Well, I'll take any coach who can get his team into the Super Bowl four times. That shows he knows something.

## TEAMS

Here, in order, are the top five NFL teams of all time. I know that I am comparing one era to another, and some people might find that impossible. But I view it this way—how did that team dominate its league? I measure a team's greatness by its ability to dominate.

### The George Halas Bears of the 1940s

Papa Bear had his greatest teams just as World War II was breaking out. These were the Monsters of the Midway. In 1940, the Bears lost a game toward the end of the regular season, 7–3, to Slingin' Sammy Baugh and the Redskins. A few weeks later, these teams played again, this time for the championship, and the Bears won 73–0. I guess you could say that George Halas had made a few adjustments.

### The Vince Lombardi Packers

This team had Bart Starr, Jim Taylor, and that great Green Bay defense. Until Lombardi went to the Packers, no one had ever heard of Green Bay, Wisconsin. Lombardi put it on the map and made it known for something other than cheese.

### The Paul Brown Cleveland Browns

After World War II, the Browns played in something called the All-America Football Conference, which was supposed to compete with the NFL. But the All-America Football Conference really was two leagues—the Browns and everyone else. After having the old All-America Football Conference for lunch, Cleveland moved into the NFL in 1950. Most of the NFL teams thought little of the Browns, who simply won a world championship their first year in the NFL. Brown was the coach, Otto Graham the quarterback, and this was a sensational team.

### The Chuck Noll Steelers

The Iron Curtain went to the Super Bowl four times. I don't think a whole lot of Pittspuke because I don't think much of emphysema, and Pittspuke and that disease are one and the same. But with Terry Bradshaw at quarterback and Jack Lambert anchoring the defense, this was a special team.

### The Sammy Baugh Redskins

These were the same Redskins who were knocked off by the Bears in 1940. With Baugh at quarterback, this was still a great team, just not as good as the greatest team of all time.

## SPECIAL MENTION

Who was the most overrated football player of all time?

That's easy.

Joe Namath.

You got it. Joe Namath, who is a bad actor who keeps acting—badly, of course. To this day, Namath has a southern accent even though he was born and raised in Beaver Falls, Pennsylvania. He went to Alabama and liked the way Bear

Bryant mumbled. He had a great arm, but Broadway Joe also had terrible knees and had only a couple of good years. The rest of the time, he was hurt. But he played in New York, wore white shoes on the field, had great-looking broads on his arm, has a lot of charm, and is a helluva guy. I can't say anything bad about him personally. But he is the classic case of a superstar created by the New York media.

# 15
# THE NFL DRAFT

Nothing is more important to an NFL team than the draft. The draft is where virtually all the players come from. It is the major talent pool. A good draft can carry a team for five years; a poor one can haunt a team for a decade. That's why NFL teams spend up to $500,000 a year on scouting and research for the draft.

But so many teams still mess it up.

That's because when it comes to the draft, some teams don't know what they are doing. Or the football people may have a clue, but the owner won't let them do their job. It happens every year in more organizations than we'd like to know about.

Here is a look at a typical meeting before draft day. We start with a list of characters:

*The Owner:* He would like to grow up and be Al Davis, so he always wears sunglasses, even to bed. He made his money the good old American way—through inheritance. He has never worked a day in his life and never will.

*The Son:* Horace is 20 and a junior at State U. He has

learned everything he knows about life, which is nothing, from his father.

*The General Manager:* Frank is 60, has been a general manager for four different teams in the past 20 years, and has never won a divisional title. His goal is one more four-year contract.

*The Coach:* Biff played for Vince Lombardi. He played for George Allen. He played for them all, and this is the fourth team he has coached. Last year, his team was 4–12. It had the top offense and the worst defense in the league. Like the general manager, his goal isn't the Super Bowl, but another four-year contract.

*The Player Personnel Director:* Sam was in charge of the helmets and shoulder pads for the general manager's teams in Cleveland and Detroit. He tells everyone that he has worked his way up from the bottom, which is at least half right. He was on the bottom, and he should have stayed there. But now he is the one guy in the organization who has scouted the colleges and watched more films than anyone else. His goal is never to have to pick up towels or be a high school football coach in New Jersey again.

*The Seven High School Coaches from New Jersey:* These are friends of the player personnel director, and they now serve as the team's scouts. They all were high school coaches in New Jersey back when the player personnel director had his only coaching job.

*The Scene:* The massive owner's office at the stadium. It opens like this:

OWNER: "Gentlemen, I want to thank you for all of your efforts in preparation for the draft. I'm sure that we have worked harder than any other team in the league. As you can see, I have asked my son Horace to sit in with us. As you know, Horace is a senior this year at State U, and his major is . . . is . . . well . . ."

SON: "Administration."

OWNER: "Right, administration. Administering what? Well, it really doesn't matter. He's my boy, and he comes from hardworking, solid stock. It's all in the genes, gentlemen. The boy is a thoroughbred. He even eats Quaker Oats for breakfast."

(The general manager starts to laugh at what he thought was a weak attempt at a joke by the owner, but the owner is serious and cuts off the GM with a sharp stare. The GM clears his throat and wants to crawl under the table.)

OWNER: "Anyway, Horace will be working for us after he graduates, and I thought a good starting spot for him would be as an assistant general manager. I realize that I haven't talked this over with . . ."

(The general manager is excited by this news. He sees a way to get that one last long-term deal.)

GENERAL MANAGER: "No problem. I'll be glad to teach the boy the ropes. After four or five years with me, he should be ready to take over."

OWNER: "Horace's job will be to watch and listen, to be a human sponge. As you know, Horace has football background. He has been a ballboy at State U for the last four years, and he also rooms with Bruce Bronson, who we all know is a fine young man and has set every passing record in the country during the last year. I think Bruce is a tremendous prospect and has a great future ahead of him, but that doesn't mean we should draft him, even though I do believe he will be available when our turn comes. But I have gotten to know Bruce pretty well, and confidentially, I made a few car payments on the boy's Corvette, but what the hell? That's how the game is played, right?"

(First the general manager nods. Then the player personnel director nods and is followed by the seven high school coaches from New Jersey. Meanwhile, the coach leans back in his chair, knowing that the draft is already shot to hell. The coach also knows that the next thing the owner will say is that he doesn't plan to try to influence the draft.)

OWNER: "I have all the respect in the world for everyone in this room. You people are the experts, the professionals. For me, football is, let us say, an avocation. I'm here purely as a fan, as someone who will support you, not try to influence you."

GENERAL MANAGER: "I respect you for that. You are never one to trample on another man's turf."

(The coach thinks, Too bad these guys aren't Pinocchio because right now their noses would extend from the Bronx to the Santa Monica Pier.)

OWNER: "So I turn the meeting over to you, Frank."

GENERAL MANAGER: "I'd like to thank our ownership for supplying us with the finances to do the scouting . . ."

(And paying the seven high school dumbbells from New Jersey, thinks the coach. Talk about good money thrown after bad.)

GENERAL MANAGER: "Since it is our player personnel director who is on the most intimate terms with the college talent, I defer to Sam."

(Frank doesn't want any part of this draft, thinks the coach. He's throwing the whole thing on the wimp player personnel director and his seven dwarfs from New Jersey.)

PLAYER PERSONNEL DIRECTOR: "I suppose it was painfully obvious to everyone that our greatest need this past season was defense, especially the pass rush."

OWNER: "I don't mean to interrupt . . ."

PLAYER PERSONNEL DIRECTOR: "Of course, feel free to inject any comments you may . . ."

OWNER: "I thought our passing game had some problems."

PLAYER PERSONNEL DIRECTOR: "We did lead the league in . . . well, I'm sure that your point is well taken, but we did lead the league in . . . ummm . . . well . . . passing."

OWNER: "Statistics can be deceiving."

PLAYER PERSONNEL DIRECTOR: "No argument from me on that."

(At this point, the coach knows that his dreams of adding Lucius "Groin Shot" Jones to the defensive line are over.)

PLAYER PERSONNEL DIRECTOR: "Well, my staff and I have studied the films, and we really like Groin Shot."

SEVEN HIGH SCHOOL COACHES FROM NEW JERSEY (chanting): "Groin Shot, Groin Shot, Groin Shot."

OWNER: "But our quarterback is getting old."

PLAYER PERSONNEL DIRECTOR (weakly): "Thompson is 29, and he was an All-Pro pick."

OWNER: "Need I remind you that he's represented by Howard Slusher?"

(There is a pall over the room as the most vile, obscene name in sports has been mentioned.)

GENERAL MANAGER: "As I have said many times, I have a philosophical problem with players having agents."

OWNER: "That is a point well taken, and I have a personal problem with Slusher. But money should not stand in the way of our making the best possible selection in the draft. I am not one to hide my biases, and I believe in speaking my mind, but just because I know Bruce Bronson well and have been making his car payments, and just because I wouldn't mind getting something back on my investment, and just because Horace has been giving me daily reports about Bruce for four years, and I must admit that I have been impressed by what I've heard, I will defer to the football people, as always. That's why I was wondering what you think, Biff."

COACH: "I like defense."

OWNER: "Who doesn't?"

GENERAL MANAGER: "But Biff is aware of our quarterbacking situation."

COACH: "That's right—it's the best in the league."

OWNER: "I respect a coach who is loyal to his players, even if that loyalty isn't always deserved."

GENERAL MANAGER: "That's why we have a player personnel director. I know this is Sam's first draft, but I have never seen more dedication than Sam and his staff of seven high school coaches from New Jersey have shown in getting ready for this draft. Watching them work has been an inspiration to us all."

OWNER: "All I'm saying is that when we walk out of this meeting, I want us all to be on the same page."

GENERAL MANAGER: "That's something we all want."

COACH: "I want Groin Shot."

GENERAL MANAGER: "I'm sure that no matter whom we take, it will be a great choice because this organization is operating at its usual caliber of efficiency."

COACH (mumbles): "I was afraid of that."

OWNER: "What, Biff? We couldn't hear you."

COACH: "I just want to do what's best for the team."

OWNER: "We all do. So why don't we let Sam continue?"

PLAYER PERSONNEL DIRECTOR: "I suppose we should consider the alternatives."

GENERAL MANAGER: "It's always a wise course."

PLAYER PERSONNEL DIRECTOR: "And we respect all the input we've received at this meeting about Bruce Bronson. He has all kinds of talent, and we might even be able to use some of it in four or five years. But it would be nice if we could bother the opposing quarterback once in a while. It wouldn't hurt if we had another monster on the line, I mean a monster with no teeth who is still mean enough to chew up bones."

SEVEN HIGH SCHOOL COACHES FROM NEW JERSEY (chanting): "Groin Shot, Groin Shot, Groin Shot."

PLAYER PERSONNEL DIRECTOR: "If there is a problem with Groin Shot, we also like Dinosaur Duke, who played on the same State U team with Bruce Bronson. The Dinosaur is 800 pounds, runs the 40-yard dash in 3.9 seconds, and has a 4.0 grade point average. He not only was a first-team All-American, the Dinosaur was also an academic All-American."

SEVEN HIGH SCHOOL COACHES FROM NEW JERSEY (chanting): "Dinosaur, Dinosaur, Dinosaur."

OWNER: "May I interject something?"

GENERAL MANAGER: "Of course. We value your opinion." (Coach thinks, What we value is our jobs.)

OWNER: "Gentlemen, there is a matter of public relations and ticket sales. As you know, we've had the lowest attendance in the league, and I keep thinking that with this fine, young Heisman Trophy winner at quarterback, a boy who has already been on the cover of *Sports Illustrated* and lived to talk about it, will bring certain special chips to the table. Now, you know that I am a hardnosed business man, not someone who is swayed by public opinion . . ."

GENERAL MANAGER: "That much I know for sure."

OWNER: "But we should consider what the public thinks. This young man has glamor. He can be another Joe Namath."

(The coach is thinking, This phenom piled up most of those statistics against Mississippi Valley Teacher's College.)

(The general manager is thinking, When is Sam going to just give it up and take Bronson?)

(Sam is thinking, This is my first draft—do I want it to be my last?)

PLAYER PERSONNEL DIRECTOR: "During the draft, you always should take the best athlete available."

HORACE: "I have never seen a better Ping-Pong player than Bruce."

GENERAL MANAGER: "Bronson is the finest quarterback ever to come out of Van Wert, Ohio."

OWNER: "After we get Bruce, Van Wert will become known as the cradle of quarterbacks."

HORACE: "I once saw Bruce spin a football and then balance it on his nose."

COACH: "Just like a seal."

PLAYER PERSONNEL DIRECTOR: "It does sound like Bronson has a variety of athletic skills."

OWNER: "I want to take the guy that my football staff recommends."

PLAYER PERSONNEL DIRECTOR: "When we pick, if Bronson is there . . ."

SEVEN HIGH SCHOOL COACHES FROM NEW JERSEY (chanting): "Bruce, Bruce, Bruce."

OWNER: "I think we have made the correct decision, one that will change the course of the franchise. I'm glad we're all in agreement on this, and I say let's all dismiss for lunch. Guys, the pastrami is on me."

SEVEN HIGH SCHOOL COACHES FROM NEW JERSEY (chanting): "Pastrami, Pastrami, Pastrami."

This is not an unusual scenario. Wrong picks are made for the wrong reasons. When you sit back and see a team do something stupid and you think, where were those guys' brains? Just read this little play and you'll know.

The player personnel guy would like to make the pick. In the early stages of the draft, he even thinks he will make the pick, but he seldom is in charge of the first round. The general manager doesn't want to make the pick because he doesn't want the blame if the pick bombs. By staying out of it, the general manager can finger the player personnel director for a crummy draft and fire him, thereby saving his own job. As for the coach, he'd like to make the pick, but he doesn't want to get too far into the middle of the mess between the owner, the GM, and the player personnel director. Pushing too hard is a good way to end up looking for another job next year. So in these meetings, the football people try to figure out what the owner wants, and then they give it to him. That is the best method of keeping the checks coming. So first-round picks are made because the guy went to the right college, or because the owner knows the player's father, or because the kid isn't represented by Howard Slusher.

Teams also take the public into consideration. They do want to sell tickets, and the fans like it when their team drafts a Heisman Trophy winner, even though few Heisman Trophy winners end up being worth more than an old sweat sock. Fans like offensive players because they have heard of offensive players, so teams draft offensive players higher than they should.

My draft report is highly regarded and is published in various publications around the country. I compile it not by talking to head coaches or guys in the sports information departments, but by speaking to some pro scouts I trust and by talking to assistant college coaches. Assistants are candid as hell. They know their own players and the players in their conference better than anyone because that is their job. Since they aren't being quoted by me, they don't have to worry about public relations. They can speak straight from their hearts, and they do.

So I don't talk to flacks, to other sportswriters, or to self-proclaimed draft experts. Those guys get their information from head coaches, who don't want to say anything bad about their kids because it would look terrible for their programs. I take the novel approach of speaking to the guys who work directly with the players, the assistant coaches.

The key to drafting is the key to football—defense. And the key to defense is finding disturbed characters. A number of you probably thought I spent too much time discussing backbreakers and spine-snappers when I revealed how football works. But if you want to win in football, you need mean bastards. That's a fact of life in the trenches. The best pick for our football team at the start of this chapter would have been Groin Shot. Dinosaur would have been number two, although I have to admit to being somewhat suspicious of defensive linemen who can read without moving their lips, even if they do weigh 800 pounds and are consensus All-Americans.

I like guys such as Rulon Jones, who was passed over by the Browns one year. Jones liked to smash up hotel room furniture, and he was into eating end tables or something like that. Now *there* is a player with the correct mental outlook on the game.

Another of my favorites was Dexter Manley, who is another quarterback killer. I got the Browns' player personnel man to watch 90 minutes of film of Manley with me before the draft. The Browns' brass just didn't like him. They heard he was deranged, and that's why I liked him. I heard the same things. I want lunatics on the field. Do you think Jack Lambert was a sane person when he wore a football helmet? Football is a game of incredible physical contact. You have to play it with complete disregard for your own body and go out and try to hurt others if you want to play the game well. There is no place in the trenches for anyone with common sense or a rational thought process.

Football people can talk about drafting guys with character all they want, but the best defensive player currently in the NFL is Lawrence Taylor, who has done some time in the druggie joint. Any man who has done a stint in the druggie joint is not a guy with tremendous character—I don't care what anyone says. I don't want to hear about how a football player brings his mother flowers and how he never missed a homework assignment. I want to hear what he can do on the field.

You know the commercial where Bubba Smith smashes beer cans in his hand? That's the mentality I want, even if the scouts don't.

Sometimes I wonder what the pros are doing.

After every draft, they tell us that they "had a good draft." Sometimes, they say "We had a great draft."

Be very careful when they say "We won't know about this draft until a few years down the line." That means they took a bunch of stiffs and they are praying for a miracle.

Another line they always throw out is "When it came our turn to pick, we couldn't believe that our guy was still on the board."

Well, I've seen a lot of those guys play, and I can believe it.

If I were drafting, my picks would probably be booed every year because I would be taking the Groin Shots of the world. The fans and the media all want the glory-boy runners and the pretty-boy quarterbacks, but football still comes down to blocking and tackling.

This is a boring subject for the fans and writers—all this talk about blocking and tackling. But who said they know anything about the draft? Certainly Pete Franklin never did.

# 16
# THE STATE OF BROADCASTING

Brent Musberger is rated the best sports announcer we have. He is a professional, and he works hard, which is a helluva lot more than I can say about a lot of people in the sports broadcasting business.

It appears that personality is gone. Ex-jocks like John Madden are in. What does Madden do? The guy was a great football coach with the Raiders, but now what?

Okay, he's fat.

Okay, he doesn't like to fly, so he rides trains.

Okay, he does a good beer commercial and knows how to yell "Hey, wait a minute."

Okay, he makes noises—doink . . . oink . . . whatever.

But this is talent? This is a great broadcaster? Hell, Porky Pig made better noises than John Madden. What is so special about a beer-drinking fat guy who likes trains and yells "doink?"

In the world of broadcasting, that's charisma. That's what they want.

But is John Madden anything more than a one-joke guy? I sort of doubt it.

In the past, the solid pros such as Mel Allen, Red Barber, and Curt Gowdy were the stars. They deserved to be on top because not only were they competent announcers, but they had personality. They were more than pretty-boy clones or setup men for the fat clowns or the ex-jocks.

But Madison Avenue has ruined sports broadcasting. The network boys have decided that they want Mr. Vanilla Ice Cream doing the play-by-play, and they want the famous ex-jock as the "analyst." Jim Palmer looks great in his underwear, so let's put him on the game of the week. Earl Weaver just quit—put him on the tube. Sparky Anderson isn't in the World Series. Well, let's give him a national forum in which to butcher the English language. Bill Russell mumbles, as does O. J. Simpson, but the network puts them on the tube.

Mickey Mantle is on television.

My God, poor Mick just can't talk. It's not his fault. He wasn't put on this earth to talk up a storm. He was brought here to hit, and he did that very well. Just don't ask him what he hit because it isn't easy for the Mick to explain much of anything. To him, English is a second language, and I don't know what is the first.

But Madison Avenue likes names. So, if the latest name can put together three words without saying "you know" twice, then they deem the ex-jock articulate, and they put him behind the microphone.

Radio is still where you find the best, most legitimate broadcasters. I'm talking about guys such as Jack Buck in St. Louis, Ernie Harwell in Detroit, and Joe Tait doing the Cleveland Cavaliers. The fans hear their radio broadcasters day after day, year after year. After a while, they become part of the family. The fans know them on a first-name basis even though they have never met them. As a fan, you get used to your favorite broadcaster's style, his pace, even his quirks. He tells you who won and how they did it. He gives the scores and a little insight into the players. It is almost like your father or your big brother telling you about the game. It is that familiarity that the network boys now lack.

I realize that there is something special about radio and

how we come to feel about the announcers who do our favorite teams.

But there are some guys on the national level, even on television, who have that magic. Dick Enberg usually does, and Vince Skully sometimes does when he's working a game out of Los Angeles. I respect Enberg because he not only is professional and polished but has wit. He can work with Al McGuire and feed him enough straight lines to make McGuire sound colorful, even if Al really is more tiresome than anything else.

Here is a breakdown of the major broadcasters in each sport:

## BASEBALL

Some ex-jocks are okay.

On the surface, it would seem that Bob Uecker is a one-joke guy. He's the schmuck who always gets the worst seat. In commercial after commercial, he gets stuck in peanut heaven, and we can identify with that. The fan is always getting screwed when he buys his ticket, because the best tickets are being given or sold to the millionaires.

Uecker does have more going for him. He has a sharp, quick sense of humor, and he knows baseball. I will say the same for Joe Garagiola. Like Uecker, he was a terrible catcher. But Joe can speak English, and he doesn't put me to sleep. That is why I basically like Garagiola and Vince Skully as a team.

Also, just because a guy has been on the radio for a long time doesn't make him good. Phil Rizzuto is walking proof of that. Holy cow, holy cow! How can anyone think this guy is a great announcer? I get the feeling that he has done the Yankees for too long and that he doesn't even like his job anymore. He has a hard time staying for the whole game, but who can blame him? If I worked for George Steinbrenner, I'd want to go home early, too.

I'll also give thumbs up to Bob Costas and Tony Kubek, who are the backup baseball broadcasting team on NBC.

Costas will never be a giant in the industry, at least by my standards. But Bob is a nice, clean-cut-looking guy, and he knows how to interview. Costas broke into the big time doing pro football with Bob Trumpy, who is very good and very off-the-wall. That early training with Trumpy helped Costas deal with Kubek. Having worked with one ex-jock in Trumpy, Costas then had the experience needed to get the best out of Kubek.

The nice thing about Costas and Kubek is their enthusiasm for baseball. They both just love the game. You can tell, and it's something that can't be faked by yelling "Holy cow." Got that, Phil Rizzuto? Kubek is outspoken, opinionated, and sometimes gets very intense. He believes strongly in everything he says, and there isn't a phony bone in his body. He'll never be a great play-by-play man, but that's not his role. Kubek is there to analyze, and he does it well. He is perhaps the most candid guy doing baseball on the national level, because he speaks from such a tremendous knowledge of the game. He also has virtually no ego, so you know what he says is not self-serving. It's what he believes.

ABC has a team of Al Michaels with Jim Palmer or Tim McCarver. McCarver has become the latest rising star, mostly because he works in New York and does the Mets. Remember, anyone who stays on the air for more than five minutes in New York is supposed to be great. New York even thinks Ralph Kiner is magnificent, which has to make you wonder. The ABC guys aren't an embarrassment, but I see nothing special here. They certainly are well behind both of NBC's crews.

What happens to be really scary is what the Yankees are doing with their broadcasters. We are getting 50,000 guys in the booth, anyone from Fran Healy to Billy Martin to Bobby Murcer. If you lose your job but still are paid by George Steinbrenner, they put you behind the microphone. This really is bad news for the sports fans, who are denied the chance to hear the next generation of Jack Bucks and Red Barbers. Instead, they give us poor Mickey Mantle fighting his way through a simple sentence. It is very discouraging.

## BASKETBALL

At the moment, Dick Stockton and Tom Heinsohn rule the NBA airwaves. Stockton is okay. But if he should quit tomorrow, would anyone care? For years, Bill Russell was the analyst. Now, it's Heinsohn, about whom Stockton correctly said, "Sounds just like Fred Flintstone." These guys do nothing for me. I don't hate them, but that's about all I can say.

After he got the boot from the network, Bill Russell got to mumble for Ted Turner on WTBS. Thank God Sacramento hired Russell as coach so we don't have to hear him anymore.

Rick Barry also has done a lot of NBA, and this guy has the sense of humor of a door-stopper. When he played, Barry was an unhappy man, and being an announcer has not changed him for the better.

Dick Vitale is the new broadcasting star in basketball. He is supposed to be the next John Madden. Why not? After all, Vitale:

- is ugly
- is cockeyed
- is bald
- sweats a lot
- is from New Jersey
- has the endless capacity to scream about the most trivial things.

Vitale is a character and a phenomenon. He also is a legitimate personality, much more into basketball than Al McGuire. In the next few years, watch Vitale rise and McGuire fall because Vitale works harder.

Another college basketball commentator is Billy Packer, who is like Tony Kubek in baseball. Packer cares about his sport and can talk about it for days without stopping to take a breath. He tells no jokes and has no shtick. I respect him.

The best basketball play-by-play man is Dick Enberg, who can make about any bozo he is stuck with sound pretty good.

## FOOTBALL

John Madden rules pro football, but has anyone noticed that he is a parody of himself? When we were all infants, we made noises. Eventually, we grew up and learned to talk. I keep waiting for Madden to hit that next stage.

Pat Summerall is another media star, which is fine. Instead of taking a sleeping pill, I turn on Pat. He's nice, but so what? The man's goal in life seems to be to be even more boring today than he was yesterday.

My favorite team is Dick Enberg and Merlin Olsen. I've already pointed out why Enberg is so good. The man is the consummate pro, no matter whom he works with or what sport he does. Olsen offers sharp, incisive commentary, and then he gets out. He doesn't overtalk, which is the plague of even some of the best announcers. Olsen is a talented guy, and I don't just mean he does flower commercials. He's not a bad actor; he's educated and nicely understated. He doesn't try to be Madden or Vitale, and that's to his credit. That's also why he'll last a long time. Guys like Madden wear on you while Olsen grows on you.

"Monday Night Football" on ABC was one of the most interesting broadcasting teams ever when it had Frank Gifford, Don Meredith, and Howard Cosell.

Gifford is a very dull man who personifies the ex-jock who got a big break. He really has no business in front of a microphone, but he can tell us that it's second down and eight yards to go. He was a fine football player who is at his best as a broadcaster when he is reading a hardware store commercial. He is a nice guy who has gone a long way being a nice guy. I give him credit for surviving. I don't know how, but he does.

Meredith did a lot of singing and had that nice Texas drawl. He was terrific when he insulted Howard Cosell, because insulting Howard Cosell was something we all wanted to do. In show business, you need the protagonist and the antagonist, and that was Meredith and Cosell. In between, Gifford said it was second down and eight yards to go, and Frank would also give us the score. Then it was back to Howard and Don hammering away.

Nothing was better on those broadcasts than Dandy Don telling Howard to buzz off. But did you notice what happened when Cosell quit? Dandy Don got boring. He had no one to play off, and eventually the network dumped him. Since then, it's been O. J. Simpson, also known as Mr. Mumbles. He's best when he does those Hertz commercials running through airports because we don't have to hear him talk. Then there was Joe Namath . . . yuck.

The reason "Monday Night Football" went downhill after Cosell left was because Howard Cosell *was* "Monday Night Football." He had an opinion about everything. He was obnoxious, provocative, and sometimes downright galling. But the man was never boring. All the listeners said they hated him, but everyone was listening to him. Cosell had that staccato delivery, much like Walter Winchell. It often sounded as if he were patronizing the audience, which he was, or as if he were addressing a jury. He sounded like some Jewish guy from New York, and every anti-Semite in America had a field day ripping him. But he was usually well prepared, and people cared about what he said. That is crucial.

Howard Cosell is an egomaniac, but he is right when he says look what happened to "Monday Night Football" after he left—it became just another game. In broadcasting, that is the deadliest sin of all.

# 17
# WHY I LOVE SPORTS

Throughout this book I have been telling you that I know more about sports than anyone. That's true. Pete Franklin does know more about sports than anyone. But that doesn't mean I am any different from the guys who call my show or who show up at the stadium for baseball games. I have the same interest and the same background as most sports fans, and that's why I enjoy talking to them and why they put up with me screaming "idiot" into their ears. We have a common passion—sports. And we have a common dream—that our favorite teams will win a championship.

I grew up in western Massachusetts, and I had a room like most kids' rooms—the walls were covered with pennants and pictures. I had pennants of the Boston Bruins, which was my favorite hockey team, and the Washington Redskins, my favorite football team. Of course, the Redskins were the Boston Redskins until 1937, when they moved. I liked the Brooklyn Dodgers and hated the Yankees and the New York Giants.

I can still see the pictures of Joe Medwick, Jimmy Foxx,

Lefty Grove, and Lou Gehrig on my walls. I worshiped at the shrine of Sammy Baugh.

You think you were a maniac sports fan as a kid?

Well, so was I.

Along with a million other kids, I invented my own baseball game with dice, and a group of guys would get together to pick teams and play the games. We kept stats, made trades, and did everything they now do in the Rotisserie Leagues. I suppose our equipment was a little more primitive, but the idea was the same. We wanted to have our own league with players who were currently in the majors. Fifty years from now, kids will be doing the same thing. The rules of the game will change, but the principles will be identical. It is a way of bringing pro sports into your own bedroom.

But the biggest thrill wasn't winning a baseball game with dice, but seeing the real thing. My father was a prominent attorney. He was not much of a sports fan, and he died when I was quite young. So during the summers, my family would farm me out to uncles and aunts in Philadelphia, New York, and Boston. I tried to play the sports I loved, but I couldn't hit a volleyball, much less a baseball. Some guys can hit, and some guys just can't. Believe me, I know all about it. I also couldn't catch the ball. Again, that is something either you can do or you can't, and I couldn't. I could throw a baseball pretty well, and that did help me out later in life. But I was not a great or a natural athlete. I loved hockey, but I couldn't skate, so the other kids always stuck me in the net as the goalie. They probably hoped someone would shoot a puck into my mouth to shut me up. The big thing to do was to skate near the goal and try to beat the crap out of Franklin with a hockey stick.

So I played sports like most kids in the neighborhood. It was something to do, but more than playing, I loved watching the games. I'd do about anything to get into the baseball game. When I stayed with my uncle in Boston, I went to Braves Field to watch the old Boston Braves. Or I'd talk him into taking me to Fenway Park to see the Red Sox. When I was with my relatives in New York, I saw games at Ebbets

Field, the Polo Grounds, and Yankee Stadium. I would have gone to a game every day if it were possible. I used to get goose bumps before a baseball game, which is the same feeling of excitement with a touch of tension that I get now before I go on the air.

As a kid, my biggest moment was the day I met Lou Gehrig. I was about nine or ten when it happened. I considered my uncle from Boston to be the smartest and greatest guy I have ever met because he was the man who took me to my first baseball game, but my uncle really became a legend when he took me to a game the day Lou Gehrig spoke to me. It was the first time I ever sat in the box seats. We always called them the "rich seats," because we never could afford to sit there. Of course, back then I figured that anyone who could afford to buy an ice cream cone was rich. One day my uncle either bought or got some box seat tickets, and I couldn't believe how different the game looked from the boxes as compared to the bleachers. I mean, we were so close to the field it seemed like you could reach out and touch these guys. I was so excited that I was shaking. Anyway, it was a few hours before the game, and Lou Gehrig was walking by. My uncle yelled something at Lou, and he came over to the stands by us.

My uncle didn't know Lou Gehrig, but he acted like he did. He introduced me to Lou, and Lou said something like, "How ya doin' kid?" and tousled my hair. That was it. Lou then said good-bye and walked away. After Lou left, I was still trembling. I wanted to say something to Lou Gehrig, but no words came out of my mouth. I bet you find it hard to believe that Pete Franklin was speechless. All I know is I just kept thinking that my uncle had to be someone important since Lou Gehrig stopped to talk to him. My uncle was in the real estate business. He had just a little office, but I was impressed by the fact that he had his own desk and chair. You had to be successful to have your own desk, chair, and office. Besides, he talked to Lou Gehrig.

So I was no different from most of you reading this book. Meeting a star was a thrill of thrills. I stood outside the ballpark after games and collected autographs. As much as I loved sports, I also loved performing. When I was in the service, I was a pretty good pitcher—as I said, the one thing I could do was throw a baseball hard. Just don't ask me to hit or catch it. But I also acted in shows, doing comedy sketches. Sometimes I played the drums.

When I got out of the service, I took my scholarship from the Veterans Administration and went to Columbia University in New York, where they had a special broadcasting course for veterans. We worked at the NBC studios in Rockefeller Plaza. I went to school at night and worked for the BVD underwear company during the day. I was sales clerk in an underwear company in the Empire State Building—what that means, I'm not sure. All I'm saying is that Jim Palmer modeled shorts, but I sold them.

After Columbia, I got my first broadcasting job in 1952 in Oakdale, Louisiana. For those of you who care, that's between Alexandria and Lake Charles. And those of you who know something about Louisiana know that there is nothing between Lake Charles and Alexandria. So, I worked in Nowhere, Louisiana, which was in Cajun swamp country. I worked about 70 hours a week, and my main job was to get to the station early in the morning and kill the snakes. I'm not talking about guys who acted like snakes. I met them later on. But real, honest-to-goodness, crawl-on-their-bellies-with-their-tongues-sticking-out snakes. My wife and I lived in this crappy town, and I was making $45 a week, working day and night beating the snakes off with baseball bats, and reading the farm news. Ah, the glamor of show business.

The first sports event I ever covered was when I moved from Oakdale to McComb, Mississippi. Some promotion, huh? I was in McComb for only three weeks, and I discovered that the reason I was hired was my experience in killing snakes. McComb had even more snakes than Oakdale. But one day when the snakes decided to sleep in, the station manager asked, "Pete, did you ever broadcast baseball before?"

"No," I said.

"Well, that's fine. Right fine, indeed," he said. "You see, we sold us some commercial time on this here Millsapps College baseball game, and you're going to broadcast it for us."

An engineer from the station and I went to Jackson, Mississippi, for the game, and we found out that there was nowhere to sit. No stands, nothing. I ended up climbing a tree and sitting on a branch, talking into the microphone. I always wondered if Red Barber started that way. Well, I never had any real ambition to do play-by-play, and this did nothing to change that opinion.

After my three glorious weeks in McComb, I really hit the radio road. There were stops in Ahoskie, North Carolina; Sylvania, Georgia; Savannah; Freeport, Texas; Houston; Trenton; Bakersfield; Las Vegas; Los Angeles; and San Francisco. Finally, I made it to Cleveland and started the "Sportsline" show in 1967.

So what is the point of all this?

I'm not sure.

Certainly, it shows that I have been around. It shows that I know how to kill a snake and I know how to climb a tree and broadcast a baseball game. I know how to survive in some of the worst cities this country has ever seen.

But most of all, it shows that I love sports. My ambition was to get somewhere and take the talk-show format and make it into strictly a sports talk show. For years, I did straight talk shows—interviewing celebrities, politicians, and authors. But my love was always sports and performing, and the sports talk show was the marriage of both of those passions.

Now, I admit to being different from that little kid who was tongue-tied because Lou Gehrig spoke to him. I don't ask athletes for autographs, and I am no longer star-struck when I meet them. At times, I am appalled by the stupid things they do.

But I still love sports.

I have the feeling that if I were not in the media and I were living in New York or Cleveland, and there was a ball game in town, I'd probably be at that game and acting like the people I insult—the fans. I would buy my ticket, yell at the umpire, bitch about the manager, and argue with the bozo sitting next to me. For me, sports always has been an excellent release, and working in sports has provided me with a lifetime of escape from all the rotten, miserable people and things that inhabit the earth.

There is no question that I still have the same passionate interest in sports that I did as a kid. Of course, it has been tempered by reality because I have been exposed to the business side of athletics. You can't help becoming jaded to some degree when you spend so much time with the people in pro sports. Then you learn that the music business, the movie business, or about any other business is as bad or worse. But they still write great songs and make great movies—not as often as they should, but it still happens. I look at sports in the same context, and I look forward to those great moments of beauty. There was nothing more artistic than watching Sammy Baugh play quarterback or watching Magic Johnson run a basketball team. There are athletes in every sport and in every era that bring out the same feelings in me.

Want to know something else?

I still get psyched up to go to games. In most games, there is someone or something worth seeing. There is a lot of crap behind sports, but the games themselves and the athletes playing them are as wonderful as they ever have been. It is the pleasure you get from watching a superior person perform, and that's why I can still watch a losing team and enjoy it. Of course, it's a lot more fun when your team is winning, but the losing does not ruin sports for me.

The bottom line is that sports are fun. We remember the games we played as kids and the games we've seen as adults. When we go to a game, we are really going back to the playing fields of our childhood. As long as I am in sports, I'm still the little kid who got to meet Lou Gehrig for the first time, only now I get paid for interviewing the Lou Gehrigs of the sports world. Believe me, that's not bad work if you can get it.